To STEPH

A START TO GREAT ADVEN[TURES]
IN AFRICA.

LOVE x CHRIS

DAVID BRISTOW'S

BEST HIKES

IN SOUTH AFRICA

DAVID BRISTOW'S

BEST HIKES

IN SOUTH AFRICA

STRUIK

Photographic credits

All photographs appearing in this book were taken by David Bristow
with the exception of the following:

Shaen Adey pages 69 top, 69 bottom (Natal Parks Board)
Duncan Butchart/African Images page 111 right
Gerald Cubitt pages 28, 42, 46, 47, 98/99, 102, 111 left, 122
Roger de la Harpe pages 66 (Natal Parks Board), 71 (Natal Parks Board),
72 (Natal Parks Board), 77 (Natal Parks Board), 81 top, 93 top
(Natal Parks Board), 107
Walter Knirr pages 96, 114
John McKinnell half title page, pages 52/53, 89, 90
Colin Paterson-Jones pages 19 top left, 88, 99 right, 133 right
Brendan Ryan/African Images pages 84, 118 top
David Steele/Photo Access page 136
Alan Weaving page 139
Zelda Wahl pages 19 top right, 25 left, 27, 33 above, 33 left, 45, 54 left, 75, 117

Copyright for the above photographs rest with the
photographers and/or their appointed agents.

About the maps

The wire-mesh terrain models were computer generated with elevation data digitized from
1 : 50 000 base maps. Each mesh cell represents 250 metres square. The vertical exaggeration is
either three or four times in order to convey the size of the landscape to the viewer. The views
are isometric and so positioned to make the whole trail visible; where the path runs toward or
away from the viewer, the distances are foreshortened.

Map Symbols		Hut	🏠
Beginning	/B\	Cave	◠
End	/E\	Campsite	◬
Forest / Forest Station	🌲🌲	Shelter	∧

Struik Publishers (a member of The Struik Group (Pty) Ltd)
Cornelis Struik House
80 McKenzie Street
Cape Town 8001

Reg No. : 63/00203/07

First published 1992

Copyright © text: David Bristow 1992
Copyright © maps: Pam Eloff, Technodraft, Cape Town (page 9);
Digital Images, Cape Town (computer-generated hiking maps) 1992

Edited by Susan Matthews, Cape Town
Designed by René Greeff, Cape Town
DTP conversion by BellSet, Cape Town
Reproduction by Unifoto (Pty) Ltd, Cape Town
Printed and bound by Tien Wah Press (Pte) Ltd, Singapore

ISBN 1 86825 232 9

PREVIOUS SPREAD: Approaching the Elandsbos River on the Otter Trail.

CONTENTS

INTRODUCTION

My mountaineering activities began in earnest sometime in the early 1970s, at about the same time that the National Hiking Way System was being conceived and the first trails were developed. I thought then that these trails would be the ruin of South Africa's mountains and, eventually, all the wild natural areas left in the country. Even then it was not realized just how extensive this hiking system would become – or how popular. As a purist wilderness lover, I was disdainful of marked paths and huts, and as a form of personal protest I first walked the Fanie Botha Trail illegally, in the wrong direction. A few years later it was only the persuasive powers of a novice hiking friend that prompted me to walk the then brand-new Blyderivierspoort Hiking Trail. Since setting off from God's Window on that glorious summer's day, this trail has remained one of my favourites, and I have subsequently become one of the hiking way system's most enthusiastic supporters.

The first official hiking trail in South Africa was the Otter Trail, opened in the Tsitsikamma Coastal National Park in 1968, but at first few people took much notice of it. Then, in 1973, the Fanie Botha Hiking Trail was opened by its namesake (the Minister of Forestry at the time) as the first section of what was planned to become a continuous hiking system around the country. The 1 000th km mark of the system was reached midway along the Prospector's Trail, and still it keeps on marching. Quite early on it was realized that most hikers preferred trails to be distinct, of limited and varied length and, where possible, circular rather than linear: this greatly altered the original trail system concept. Nevertheless, to date more than 300 hiking trails and one-day nature trails comprise the system. There are also trails in most game parks and nature reserves not under the control of the regional hiking way authorities.

Whatever image is painted of the *status quo*, future generations of South Africans will thank the National Hiking Way Board for bequeathing its hiking system to the nation. This is largely because hiking is the least elitist, most educational, and one of the cheapest of all outdoor recreational pursuits. For these reasons it is the pastime likely to have the widest social appeal and to cross the most diverse cultural barriers.

But given the vast scope of the country's hiking way system, the task of selecting the 20 best trails is fraught with problems. Why, for instance, has the Tsitsikamma Trail been included but the Outeniqua Trail left out; and why the less popular Prospector's Trail instead of the Fanie Botha Trail? While the process of selection was not according to any scientific method, it was not done on a purely subjective basis either. Initially the author compiled a list of the 40 most outstanding trails, relying heavily on the advice of other hiking authorities.

It was then felt that if anyone were given the task of choosing their favourite hikes, these would be grouped into a few areas, namely the Western Cape, the Garden Route, the Drakensberg and the Eastern Transvaal. And yet every one of the existing hiking trails has its own unique attractions and dynamic natural environment. Given South Africa's broad diversity of ecosystems, it was decided to spread the trails as widely throughout the country's natural regions as possible. Therefore I included trails falling within a true desert region (Klipspringer), in fynbos (Cedarberg, Boland and Swellendam) and forest (Tsitsikamma, Amatola and Magoebaskloof), on the Highveld (Suikerbosrand) and in the Bushveld (Umfolozi), in the high Afro-alpine mountain region (Cathedral) and along the rugged coast (Otter and Wild Coast). The Rustenburg Trail was included partly because it exists as a kind of wilderness area within the PWV industrial complex, but mainly for its location within the enchanting Magaliesberg, a fascinating floristic ecotone between the Highveld and Bushveld ecosystems.

But coming back to the issue of why the Outeniqua and Fanie Botha Trails were omitted (when many hikers would choose them among their favourite trails), let me elaborate. So many fine trails are to be found in the Southern Cape and Eastern Transvaal that they could each justify separate hiking guides. Looking at the Southern Cape, my first choice was the outstanding Otter Trail, and here I am sure most hikers will agree with me. After that I had to choose between the Outeniqua and Tsitsikamma trails, with the Swartberg coming in with an outside chance. Selecting more than one of these trails would create too great an overlap of fynbos and forest. An informal survey of hikers revealed the Tsitsikamma Trail to be the general favourite, which finally decided that issue.

The Fanie Botha Trail was also highly regarded by the hikers questioned, but the splendour of the Blyde River Canyon and the tranquillity of the Treur River valley were judged to have greater scenic appeal. The historical theme of the Prospector's Trail, its great variety of habitats, and the added attraction of Pilgrim's Rest village, making it one of the most interesting and unusual of the existing trails, resulted in it being the second choice of the Eastern Transvaal trails.

A final, but not absolute, selection criterion was that each trail chosen should be a recognized hiking trail, falling within the National Hiking Way System (including those falling within various conservation areas but not under control of the regional hiking way offices). There are three exceptions to this rule, namely the Cedarberg and Mlambonja (Cathedral Peak) wilderness areas, and the Umfolozi Wilderness Trail. Reasons for their inclusion should be obvious, since any book that claimed to represent the best of hiking in South Africa and yet overlooked these areas would be blatantly incomplete. While the final selection presented in this publication may not satisfy all active and armchair hikers equally, I am satisfied that it represents the very best of the country's hiking opportunities.

This book is my tribute to the splendour of the country's hiking trails.

BEST HIKES IN SOUTH AFRICA

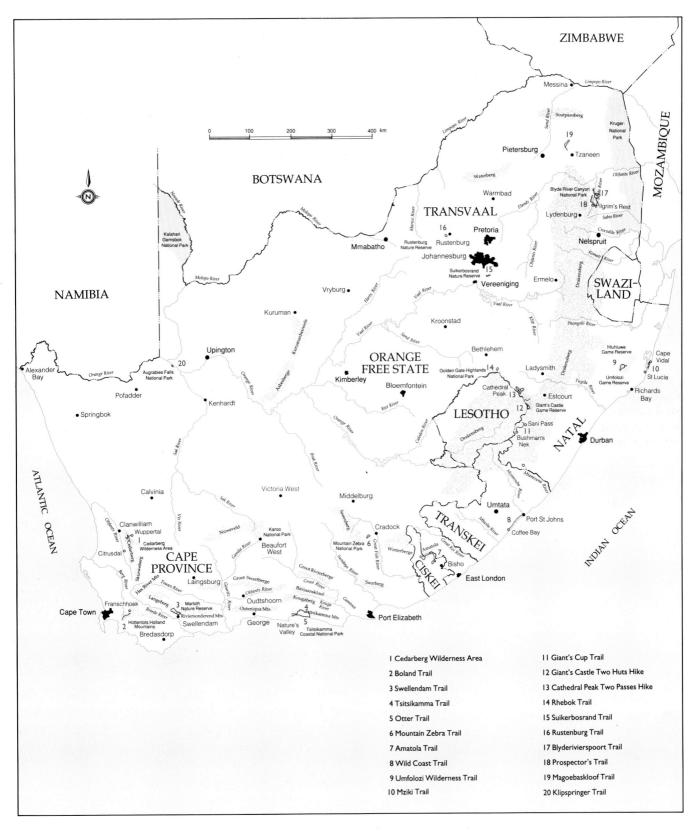

1 Cedarberg Wilderness Area
2 Boland Trail
3 Swellendam Trail
4 Tsitsikamma Trail
5 Otter Trail
6 Mountain Zebra Trail
7 Amatola Trail
8 Wild Coast Trail
9 Umfolozi Wilderness Trail
10 Mziki Trail

11 Giant's Cup Trail
12 Giant's Castle Two Huts Hike
13 Cathedral Peak Two Passes Hike
14 Rhebok Trail
15 Suikerbosrand Trail
16 Rustenburg Trail
17 Blyderivierspoort Trail
18 Prospector's Trail
19 Magoebaskloof Trail
20 Klipspringer Trail

CEDARBERG WILDERNESS AREA

This is one of only two wilderness areas to be included in the book, which is otherwise confined to recognized hiking trails. The Cedarberg Wilderness Area, with its high peaks and rugged ridges, pristine natural vegetation, as well as its system of paths and basic shelters, is a hiker's paradise. After the Drakensberg it is, I believe, the finest mountaineering area in the country.

On this hike the distances are fairly short and seldom strenuous. Each day's walk is designed to finish at a shelter and since only 12 people a day are allowed in each of three wilderness sectors, you should easily find accommodation. The hike can be extended by a day, or shorter sections can be doubled up, taking you back to Algeria to complete a circular hike.

Summers here are very hot, but there is permanent water in the mountains. Winters can be severe, with heavy snowfalls on high ground. For the well-equipped hiker this is a wonderful time to be in the Cedarberg, particularly for those who wish to see the rare snow protea (*Protea cryophila*). An added bonus is that anyone with a mountaineering urge can climb the second and third highest peaks in the range *en route*.

A special treat of the area are the few remaining groves of Clanwilliam cedar and the stark forms of lone trees growing among the weird weather-sculptured rocks. The entire Cedarberg range has recently been declared a leopard sanctuary, with animals captured elsewhere in the south-western Cape being relocated here. These shy nocturnal animals frequently use the footpaths, so look out for spoor. Although you are unlikely ever to see the animal itself, just knowing they are out there is reward enough. The most recent research suggests that about 12 leopards currently use the wilderness area as part of their range.

DAY I *ALGERIA TO MIDDELBERG HUT: 3,5 KM*

Since Algeria Forest Station is a two and a half hour drive from Cape Town, it is feasible to leave town in the afternoon and sleep in the Middelberg hut that night. It is, however, necessary to book and arrange to collect a permit from the overnight box at the guard hut. To find the beginning of the trail, cross the causeway over the Rondegat River and proceed to the far right-hand (south-eastern) side of the campsite to take the path up the valley of a tributary. This path goes all the way up the mountain wall that sweeps skywards from Algeria campsite.

After gaining 200 m the path veers slowly away from the stream gully, then ascends steeply over a broken scree slope for another 100 m before easing off into a series of long but easier zigzag gradients.

Snow-dusted Tafelberg, second highest peak in the Cedarberg, looms above a tarn in the Driehoek River valley. The shale band known as 'Die Trap' can be seen in the middle foreground.

Having climbed about 200 m by zigzagging, the path takes a more direct route to the summit of Boshoek ridge.

On re-entering the upper Waterval stream valley, the vegetation becomes lush and dense, with tall heath bushes (Erica caffra), fountain bushes (Psoralea pinnata), water blossom peas (Podalyria calyptrata) and other riverine species. A short distance before Middelberg the path enters one of the most substantial remaining groves of small to medium-size cedars (Widdringtonia cedarbergensis), creating a stark contrast to the low scrub of the open slopes and valleys. The two Middelberg huts are set in an idyllic vale of the Middelberg vlakte; nearby a stream meanders between large oaks.

DAY 2 MIDDELBERG HUT TO CRYSTAL POOL HUT: 10 KM

From the Middelberg hut the path ascends gently, except for one short steep section between Middelberg West and Pyramid peaks. It then levels off on a wide sandy plain, between the more dominant Protea Peak and Middelberg Central Peaks (a side path leads to the former). Next it passes through a small cedar grove, with the Cathedral Rocks outcrop a little further along and on the right. Passing close to Jurie se Berg, the path curves around to the left to descend gently to Muller se Water stream.

There is a small rock shelter here that can be used when the weather is foul, or as a pleasant tea spot when fair. Some bearded protea bushes (Protea magnifica) can be seen in the area, the heavy flower heads making an impressive display in summertime. The intermittent stream is followed across the Grootlandsvlakte plain, passing a side path to Sleepad on the right, to the Wildehoutdrif River valley. Alongside the river the vegetation is rank and vivid, with Cape bamboo, daisy-like selago blooms in white, mauve and yellow, and the beautiful large painted ladies (Gladiolus carneus), dark pink and splashed with white, hanging coyly on drooping stems.

A well-constructed woodcutters' path leads down the Wildehoutdrif valley to Groot Hartseer ridge, where it begins to climb high above the river and veers away from the valley, to the right. To the left the land falls away into the upper Jan

Dissels River valley, flanked on both sides by impressive peaks and ridges. Here you should prepare yourself for a steep, leg-bracing ascent of some 160 m (in less than 1 km distance), with the path zigzagging up the steepest sections of the Groot Hartseer. After levelling off the path crosses a rocky area for about 3 km, until it comes to an open, flat valley, punctuated with massive boulders. The Crystal Pool is found along a stream at the far end of the valley.

The pool is not large, but a welcome respite on a hot day. This is the last water before the hut, so fill up all your containers here; you will not wish to return later, since it is a very steep 100 m climb to the hut. The hut is situated in a cosy spot at the base of a rocky overhang, shaded by tall gum trees.

The excellent paths in the Cedarberg, many of them paved, were orginally constructed to allow donkeys to drag felled cedar logs out of the mountains. The aromatic timber was destined for Cape Town where it was highly valued by the early colonists. Jan Dunckert was probably the first white man to see these mountains, reaching the Olifants River on a VOC Company expedition in 1661. About 50 years later white farmers began to settle along the fertile valley, while the mountains remained largely inaccessible. The cedars were first mentioned in a report from Willem Adriaan van der Stel to his bosses in Amsterdam in 1700. By the end of the 18th century woodcutters were hard at work in the mountains' cedar forests. By about 1840 alarming reports of decimation of the cedar forests reached Cape Town, but it was only in 1876 that a forest ranger was appointed to Clanwilliam. Today the trees have all but vanished. Buchu and rooibos were also heavily exploited from this area, as was the elephant's foot (Dioscorea elephantipes) – the original source of cortisone.

DAY 3 CRYSTAL POOL HUT TO SLEEPAD HUT: 5 KM

From the hut a badly eroded path descends to a golden-brown, restio-covered valley of the Engelsmanskloof River. While the path to Boontjieskloof veers off left down the valley, the trail path skirts the Klein Hartseer ridge to enter narrow Engelsmanskloof. The kloof is just over

1 km long, making the 200 m vertical ascent to Die Trap none too strenuous. The walk up the kloof is most attractive, alongside the grotesque forms of heavily eroded sandstone, flowering plants such as (Erica caffra), and the stark gnarled limbs of old cedar trees.

Die Trap is a major physical feature of the Cedarberg. It is a level shale band more or less coinciding with the 1 000 m contour and encircling all the major peaks like a running board. Once on Die Trap, hiking in the Cedarberg is a gentle stroll. The path joins Die Trap at the base of Sneeukop (1 930 m), directly below the saddle separating the greater peak on the left and the lesser one. This is the third highest peak in the Cedarberg, and can be climbed via the gully straight ahead, taking a long curve around towards the main peak. The walk up and back should take about four hours.

The walk from here to Sleepad is an easy 3 km stroll, following Die Trap all the way. It is possible to climb Sneeukop and descend to Sleepad hut via a side gully between Twin Rocks and Sneeukop South Peak, eliminating the need to retrace one's steps all the way back to the top of Engelsmanskloof. Sleepad hut is found at the base of Shadow Peak, where it presides over fantastic views of the Central Cedarberg area.

DAY 4 SLEEPAD HUT TO WELBEDACHT CAVE: 6,5 KM

This is a very easy stretch, and can be walked in about two hours. The path is really a 4x4 track that runs along Die Trap, skirting Shadow Peak and the Tafelberg. About midway the path drops down to the Donkergat River, named after the gorge above Die Trap, and after the Sederhoutkop ruins drops yet again, to reach a lower course on Die Trap. Walking this stretch the Tafelberg and Spout come into view, and from this perspective the reason for the Spout's name becomes obvious, for the entire massif resembles a giant teapot.

About 2 km from Donkergat, directly opposite the col between Langberg and Tafelberg, a path down into a shallow rocky gorge crosses the 4x4 track. The Welbedacht cave is found about 200 m down this gorge, directly above and overlooking the stream (the locality of

TOP On a ridge near the Crystal Pool hut the Chisel and Anvil rock formations are silhouetted against the skyline. The ridge can be seen from the banks of the Engelsmanskloof River. LEFT Looking out through one of the awesome Wolfberg Cracks, the greenery of Dwarsriver farm is besieged by burned veld, left by the 'big fire' of the late 1980s. ABOVE The stark limbs of a dead cedar tree seem to grasp at the clouds.

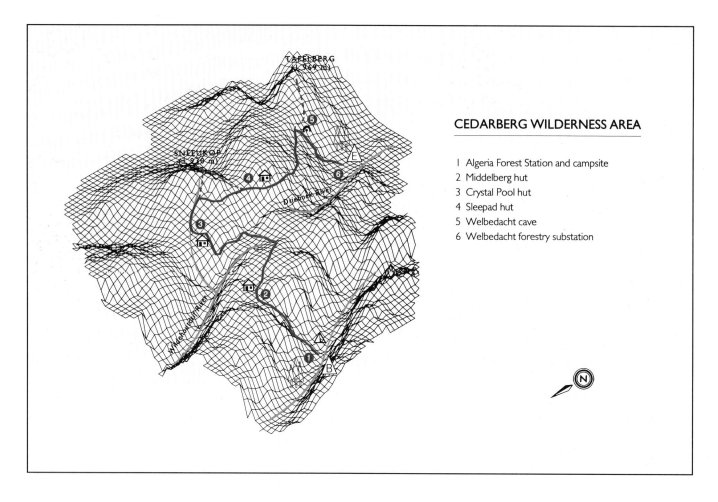

CEDARBERG WILDERNESS AREA

1 Algeria Forest Station and campsite
2 Middelberg hut
3 Crystal Pool hut
4 Sleepad hut
5 Welbedacht cave
6 Welbedacht forestry substation

the cave on most maps is wrong). Because the day's walk is such a short one, you can either carry on down the gorge to Welbedacht forest substation and cross the Driehoek River to the parking area, thus ending your hike, or you can spend the afternoon climbing the Tafelberg and return to the cave for the night.

The Tafelberg (1 969 m) is the second highest peak in the Cedarberg after Sneeuberg (2 027 m). The ascent involves a steady 2 km climb diagonally across the mountain's scree slope. From the gap between Tafelberg and the Spout, carry on around to your left to find the entrance to a water-smoothed corridor that cuts into the Tafelberg. This corridor terminates in a smooth-sided chimney, about 10 m high. This is the crux of the ascent, and should be attempted only by those with a sense of adventure and some gymnastic abilities, as it requires a strong nerve and some skill to surmount (a rope would certainly help). But once at the summit, the whole world seems to be spread out below you. It is certainly worth the effort.

DAY 5 *WELBEDACHT CAVE TO THE PARKING AREA NEAR WELBEDACHT FORESTRY SUBSTATION: 3,5 KM*

Assuming that you have spent the night in the cave, and it is highly recommended that you do, the walk down the gorge and across the Driehoek River to the car park is a steep but not too taxing one. The rock formations here are among the best to be seen in these mountains. Halfway down the gorge the path makes a wide, semicircle detour into a side gully to avoid a rocky outcrop, and then returns to the main gully.

From the substation (an old farmhouse) on the banks of the Driehoek River, follow the 4x4 track to a causeway across the river, then up through a plantation for about 750 m to the parking area. If you do not have a vehicle waiting here, it is a 7 km walk back along the road to Algeria, taking the short cut path down the Old Uitkyk Pass. Being essentially downhill, although steep down the pass, the walk is most enjoyable through lush vegetation. Much of the upper valley is a marsh which becomes alive with colour from spring through summer, while the lower path follows the Rondegat River. A natural pool awaits you at Algeria.

OPPOSITE Middelberg hut is one of the shelters best known to hikers in the Cedarberg. It is an old woodcutter's residence, maintained as a forestry shelter and available to hikers when not in use.

THE TRAIL AT A GLANCE

STARTING POINT : Algeria Forest Station
FINISHING POINT : Welbedacht Forest substation
LENGTH : 37 km, with numerous detours possible
DURATION : Four or five days
GROUP LIMIT : 12 people
ROUTE : The route starts at the Algeria campsite and zigzags steeply up to Middelberg hut. The following day it passes the Cathedral Rocks, Grootlandsvlakte and Wildehoutdrif River to reach Crystal Pools hut. Having ascended the Engelsmanskloof, energetic hikers can climb the Sneeukop, before continuing to Sleepad hut. An easy walk along Die Trap to Welbedacht cave leaves plenty of time to climb the Tafelberg. The final day involves a short descent down Welbedacht gully to the substation and car park.
HOW TO GET THERE : From Cape Town take the N7 past Malmesbury and Citrusdal. About 28 km past the Citrusdal intersection, turn right over the Olifants River to take the Nieuwoudt Pass to Algeria, some 16 km from the turn-off.
BOOKING AUTHORITY : Cedarberg Wilderness, Private Bag X1, Citrusdal, 7340; tel. (02682) 3440.

ACCOMMODATION : Forestry huts, Welbedacht cave and camping; the mountain huts are available only when not used by Forestry personnel.
CLIMATE : This area is situated in the winter rainfall region, where conditions are usually very cold in winter and very hot in summer, although there are sunny and warm winter days just as there can be cold fronts in late summer. Between December and May though, the chances of anything but light precipitation are slight. Most rain falls between May and September, varying from 250 mm on the dry eastern side, to around 1 000 mm on the higher peaks. Desiccating south-east winds are prevalent in summer.
BEST TIME TO HIKE : Since there is plenty of water in summer, and spectacular snow in winter, hiking here is rewarding all year round. For moderate conditions, however, the months from March to May and October to November are probably best.
REFERENCES : Cedarberg 1 : 50 000 map, Dept of Forestry; Camp and Climb/Peter Slingsby 1 : 150 000 Cedarberg flowerland map (1981).
TERRAIN : Although set among a particularly rugged part of the Cape Folded Mountains, a system of old woodcutters' paths makes the going far easier than would otherwise be possible. The mountains are covered almost

exclusively by pristine fynbos, with a few poor cedar and Afro-montane relic patches in sheltered areas. Some rare fynbos endemics found here are the snow protea, rocket pincushion, and of course the Clanwilliam cedar.
WHAT TO TAKE : From January to May only a windbreaker should be necessary for warmth, but always use a warm sleeping bag (I have been cold here in December). The paths are mostly good so, if your pack is not heavy, you can walk in light boots or running shoes for much of the year, unless heavy snows have fallen. Check beforehand if caves and huts are available, so that you won't need to carry a tent.
SPECIAL PRECAUTIONS : Carry your wilderness permit while hiking. No fires are allowed in the the wilderness area.
TRAIL OPTIONS : Being a wilderness area, you are free to hike and sleep where you wish, providing you have the necessary permit. A particularly rewarding walk from Algeria is the one via Crystal Pool to the Shangri-la mission village of Wuppertal. You can camp on the village common or hire a cottage here through the church, but transport back to Algeria or Clanwilliam is a problem, being a 100 km trip by gravel road. For other hikes in the area consult *Western Cape Walks.*

BOLAND TRAIL

The proximity of this trail to all the major towns in the Western Cape, the high number of people allowed on it at once, its exceptional natural beauty and its numerous alternatives, make this an extremely popular trail. The trail is located entirely within the Hottentots-Holland Nature Reserve, which protects what is probably the most species-rich floral area in the world. To get an idea of the diversity of flowering plants found here, the reserve has more than double the species of flowering plants found on the British Isles. At almost any time of the year the floral display of proteas, erica heaths, irises and other bulbous plants here is breathtaking. It certainly impressed early collectors like Thunberg, Le Vaillant and Kew Gardens' Francis Masson, as well as the great taxonomist Carl Linne, who called it 'this paradise on earth'.

Although of only two or three days' duration, the various routes on this trail are all strenuous. Also, in mid- to late summer water can be scarce and the gusting winds desiccating. Alternatively, the south-easter more often than not brings heavy cloud to the higher ridges; fierce and often gale-force, blustering winds, rain and even snow can then be expected. Every year deaths are recorded on this trail, usually those of ill-equipped hikers who have succumbed to hypothermia along the first, demanding section of the trail. The highest average rainfall in the country is recorded on Nuweberg Peak (1 500 mm), which is certainly something to consider when packing.

Among the floral rarities found in the area are the endangered marsh rose (*Orothamnus zeyheri*) and blushing bride (*Serruria florida*). Something to look out for are the numerous lesser genera of proteaceae, such as *Diastella*, *Aulax*, *Sorrocephalus*, *Mimetes* and *Spatalla*. Birdlife is unexpectedly abundant for a mountain fynbos area, ranging from sunbirds and seedeaters to kestrels, harriers and black eagles. Keep your eyes peeled for orangebreasted sunbirds, Cape buntings, siskins, neddickies, Victorin's warbler, grassbirds, and greybacked and Levaillant's cisticolas. Medium-size and small antelope are found in the reserve, as well as leopards and other cats – although chances of seeing them are remote.

DAY 1 *SIR LOWRY'S PASS TO LANDDROSKOP : 23 KM*

The trail begins at the security car park at the top of the pass, on what will prove a tough but rewarding day's hiking. Unpredictable weather along the spine of the Boland Mountains means that any climatic conditions should be expected on any day. To attest to the hazardous nature of this section, there is an emergency shelter halfway along.

At first the path follows a 4x4 track up to the Gantouw Pass, a national monument that marks what was the original

The view from Pofadder Nek, looking down the Enkelbreek pass to Boesmanskloof and Aloe Ridge, with the Franschhoek Mountains to the left.

game track, then horse track and finally wagon track over what Jan van Riebeeck called the 'Mountains of Africa'. The pass is marked by two mounted cannon, just off the trail, which were part of a series of cannon used to announce the arrival of ships in False Bay. The ruts made by wagon wheels can still be seen, carved into the rock. Where a powerline crosses the trail, the path takes a sharp turn to the right away from the 4x4 track.

Plants likely to be seen along this stretch include various types of everlastings in red, white and yellow, as well as numerous species of heath, most conspicuous being the fire heath (*Erica cerinthoides*), red and yellow-tipped Masson's heath (*E. massonii*), and bunches of brown-bearded (*E. plukenetii*) and white heath (*E. imbricata*). The fynbos veld is littered with the red bowls of king proteas (*Protea cynaroides*) and the yellow-green cup-shaped ground rose (*P. acaulis*); in springtime the intricate violet flowerheads of the three petalled iris (*Moraea tripetala*) appear.

The trail hugs the mountain spine, passing behind the prominent peaks of Hans se Kop (with its communications mast), the Langkloofberg, Valleiberg and, highest of all Hottentots-Holland peaks, the Somerset Sneeukop (1 590 m). On rounding Hans se Kop the path meets up with Buys se Pad, which leads back to the summit ridge at Groot Waainek. This is a most demanding part of the hike, for with each loop executed around the base of consecutive peaks, the path gains hard-won altitude, loses it and regains it each time. At the nek, on a clear and calm day, there are spectacular views over False Bay with nought but ocean between here and the Antarctic. From Groot Waainek the trail once again weaves its way behind the jagged peaks, making wide loops as it goes. Where the path encounters Moordenaarskop it zigzags its way up the steepest sections, the dark chasm of Wesselsgat gaping approximately 500 m below.

At the far side of Moordenaarskop the path curves back to the axis ridge, where Klein Waainek is reached. After this it winds in and out, up and down, as it negotiates five major spurs (passing the emergency shelter at the 13,5 km mark). Several waterfalls tumble down into the funnel at the head of Wesselsgat. In this vicinity some fine specimens of the silver

flamebush (*Mimetes argentea*), the trail emblem, are to be seen. This is the largest of the flamebushes, its brilliant red and yellow-tipped inflorescences between silvery leaves making it one of the most attractive plants of all the fynbos.

A few kilometres before the hut, where the path negotiates the back (southern slope) of Landdroskop, a seepage area is covered by a dense carpet of restios of the genus *Chondropetalum*. From here there is a long but gentle descent to the twin Landdroskop and Shamrock huts. The Eikenhof junction is passed on the left 2 km from the huts, and 1 km further on the Jonkershoek junction is passed on the right. Along this section, from mid- to late summer, the fair faces of large painted ladies (*Gladiolus carneus*) line the path, blushing bright pink for the hikers who pass. The Landdroskop hut is a large stone structure that accommodates 40 people; the smaller, wooden chalet of Shamrock Lodge is much cosier and sleeps 30 in two rooms.

DAY 2 *LANDDROSKOP HUT TO BOESMANSKLOOF : 17,5 KM*

Pofadder and Stony neks notwithstanding, this is a most pleasant route in the heart of the Boland mountains, where several subsidiary ranges create a swirling vortex of peaks, ridges and valleys. The path hugs the foot of the Franschhoek range, below the domineering peaks of Nuweberg, Victoria Peak, Emerald Dome, Noordekloof and the Bushman's Castle. Along this section six rivers are crossed, some by way of suspension bridge, with waterfalls and rock pools aplenty. Following winter snowfalls the higher peaks of the range are dusted with snow for weeks at a time, while during summer the pools are sprinkled with a confetti of tiny white orchids (*Disa tripetaloides*) and dainty, small painted ladies (*Gladiolus debilis*).

From Landdroskop the trail to Boesmanskloof takes the service road downhill into a wide bowl-like valley at Eensbedrogen. The text in *Western Cape Walks* says of this section : 'the hiker is completely enclosed by a diorama of sunwashed ridges and peaks, one behind the next, creating a wonderful sense of isolation'. The Riviersonderend Canyon is crossed by a suspension bridge over the

Eensbedrogen Pool. In summer the canyon, known ominously by the locals as Suicide Gorge, makes for a sensational one-day kloofing trip.

A little further on another suspension bridge is encountered, the Red Hat Crossing over the Boegoekloof River. Boegoekloof is another popular one-day hiking trip in the nature reserve. After crossing the bridge there is a steady zig-zag climb up to Stony Nek; when I tackled it, the veld had been recently burnt, and new shoots, fire-germinated plants and flowering annuals were bravely poking out of the charred ground. The path then follows the contours around to Pootjiesglypoel (slippery-feet pool). At the second of two further streams, hikers should fill their water bottles before tackling Die Krulle (the curls) to Pofadder Nek. The next water is found at the hut, a demanding 6,5 km away.

From the nek the path can be seen making its very steep and long zigzagging way down the loose slope until it disappears around the base of the ridge to the right. It passes Tandseer and Bobbejaankloof, finally rounding The Spindles and Die Ridder (the knight), Die Perd and The Lance before crossing the suspension bridge over Boesmanskloof River to the two huts perched on Aloe Ridge. Directly above and behind the huts Bushman's Castle, the Bushman's Teeth and Franschhoek Peak rear up into the sky. A fine bathing pool is found a short distance upstream of the huts. The plant which lends its name to the ridge here, for those interested in things taxonomic, is the fan aloe (*Aloe plicatilis*).

DAY 3 *BOESMANSKLOOF HUT TO FRANSCHHOEK PASS : 13 KM*

The third and final day begins on a gentle note, the path taking an easy line along the base of the Franschhoek range for about 6 km. First it breasts a low rise to a flat stony area called Klipspringerkloof. Then a series of spurs are bypassed and rivers crossed, the path making a succession of wide loops while climbing and falling through each one. The last watering place on the hike is reached at a spot most appropriately named Rusboskloof. A number of small, round pools in the stream bed are fringed by riverine

TOP LEFT Retzia capensis is in a family all of its own, and is one of the more unusual endemic fynbos plants. It was photographed on Nuweberg Peak near Landdroskop hut.
TOP RIGHT A greater doublecollared sunbird, with its dazzling metallic sheen.
BOTTOM Assegaaiboskloof valley, source of the Berg River and possibly the loveliest valley in the Western Cape, from the head of the Jonkershoek valley on the Panorama Walk.

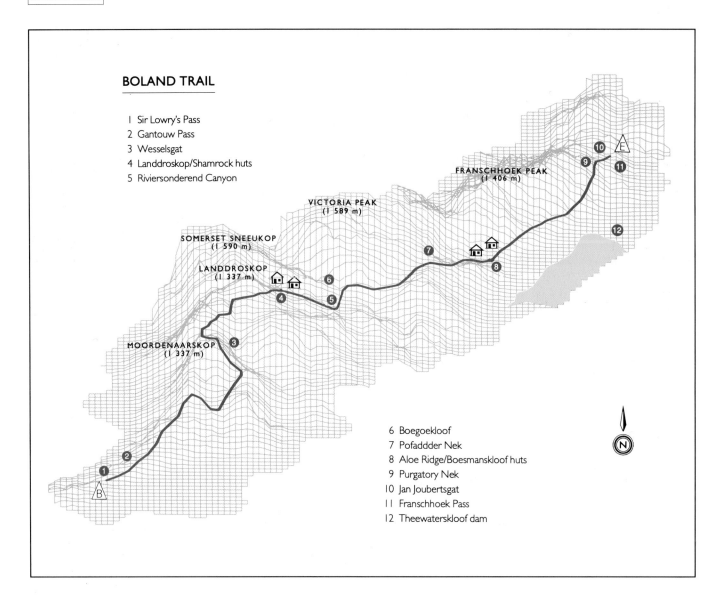

BOLAND TRAIL

1 Sir Lowry's Pass
2 Gantouw Pass
3 Wesselsgat
4 Landdroskop/Shamrock huts
5 Riviersonderend Canyon

SOMERSET SNEEUKOP
(1 590 m)

LANDDROSKOP
(1 337 m)

VICTORIA PEAK
(1 589 m)

FRANSCHHOEK PEAK
(1 406 m)

MOORDENAARSKOP
(1 337 m)

6 Boegoekloof
7 Pofaddder Nek
8 Aloe Ridge/Boesmanskloof huts
9 Purgatory Nek
10 Jan Joubertsgat
11 Franschhoek Pass
12 Theewaterskloof dam

thicket, mainly the water witels (*Brachylaena neriifolia*) and 'skilpadbos' (*Grubbia rosmarinifolia*).

Directly after cossing the stream, the climb up ominously named Purgatory Nek begins. In all, the ascent involves gaining 450 m in altitude over a distance of some 2 km, which is a wholly manageable task if taken slowly. The climb is made all the more enjoyable if one cares to stop to admire the many flowering plants along the way: everlastings, yellow heliopteris daisies, clusters of tiny white corymbiums, bright watsonia trumpets and the metre-high spikes of royal blue aristeas.

From the nek the Laaste Vlakte forms a wide open expanse, a field of golden restios imitating a montane wheatfield. But

the path doesn't go that way (even if the map says it does). Since a new landowner blocked off the original route, the trail has had to be rerouted steeply down into Jan Joubertsgat, to the bridge of the same name. The main problem with the new route is that, besides the 3 km, snaking, ankle-twisting descent, there is no secure parking place available at the end of this linear hike. This means hikers have to leave a vehicle in Franschhoek, hitch-hike or get someone to meet them at the bridge.

While sorting out that logistical problem, contemplate the bridge's attractions: the original elephant path over the Middagkransberg from Olifantshoek (the Franschhoek valley) was improved by a farmer named S.J. Cats in 1819 and was

known as the Cats Pad. But Cats was not much of a road maker and his track was a danger to laden wagons. In 1823 the Royal Engineers and Royal Africa Corps, who were languishing at the Cape after a tour of duty in India, undertook to upgrade the road. The bridge over Jan Joubertsgat was opened in 1825, making it the oldest constructed pass in the country and the oldest bridge still in use.

OPPOSITE Looking east from Landdroskop, morning light over the Boland mountains casts golden hues over the restios and the clouds between the Groenlandsberge and the distant Langeberg.

THE TRAIL AT A GLANCE

STARTING POINT : Sir Lowry's Pass
FINISHING POINT : Jan Joubertsgat Bridge (Franschhoek Pass)
LENGTH : 53 km
DURATION : Three days
GROUP LIMIT : 30 people
ROUTE : Beginning at the top of Sir Lowry's Pass, this linear trail follows close to the summit ridge of the Hottentots-Holland range, and continues on to Landdroskop and Shamrock huts at the centre of this mountain stronghold. From Landdroskop it follows the back (eastern) slope of the Franschhoek Mountains to overnight at Boesmanskloof, and then continues on to Franschhoek Pass.
HOW TO GET THERE : From Cape Town take the N2 past the Strand to the top of Sir Lowry's Pass. A secure parking area is provided at the start of the hike, on the left-hand side of the long curve, just before the road begins its descent to Grabouw.
BOOKING AUTHORITY : Nuweberg Nature Conservation, Private Bag X27, Elgin, 7180; tel. (0225) 4301.
ACCOMMODATION : Stone hut and wooden chalets with bunk beds and mattresses.
CLIMATE : Although situated in what could be called the middle of the winter rainfall area, the fact that these mountains intercept the full force of the summer south-easter wind means that cloud, mist and rain can occur on any day of the year. Alternatively, summer days can be scorchingly hot with desiccating winds. In other words, you have to be prepared at all times for extreme conditions. This is the only hike I have been forced off by appalling weather, and on a summer's day at that.
BEST TIME TO HIKE : For the flowers alone, spring to midsummer is ideal, and this is also the best time for water availability and mild weather, although snow can fall right up to the end of the year.
REFERENCES : The 1 : 50 000 National Hiking Way map has excellent information about the vegetation and floral communities, and can be supplemented by the Botanical Society's guide to the flowers of the Boland Mountains.
TERRAIN : Very rugged and demanding, but with a marked footpath. Footwear can be light or heavy, depending on the weight of your pack and the weather. Every route on the trail, converging on or radiating out from central Landdroskop, includes long ups and downs that should be taken slowly if they are to be enjoyed. The paths generally allow for safe walking.
WHAT TO TAKE : Take warm and additional dry clothing at all times (deaths occur every year on this trail as a result of trailists not being equipped for the severe conditions that often prevail).
SPECIAL PRECAUTIONS : This area experiences the highest precipitation in the country, in the form of rain, hail, sleet and snow. The trail should, therefore, be tackled only with reliable rain gear. In summer water can be scarce in the mountains, so be sure to carry enough – especially when a strong, dry south-easter is blowing and you can easily dehydrate without realizing it.
TRAIL OPTIONS : The Boland Trail (Hottentots-Holland section) is not one linear trail, but made up of numerous routes that resemble a spoked wheel, with Landdroskop at the hub. There are five two-day and two three-day options, with various legs being seasonally closed. There are also several day walks within the reserve, such as Suicide Gorge, Boegoekloof and the very popular but strenuous Jonkershoek Panorama Walk. The three highest peaks in the Boland mountains, namely Somerset Sneeukop, Victoria Peak and Emerald Dome, as well as the Banhoek and Three Ridge Peaks, snow-covered a few times each winter, are accessible.

SWELLENDAM TRAIL

Most of this strenuous trail lies within the Marloth Nature Reserve, directly above Swellendam and named after the scientist, naturalist and mountaineer Rudolph Marloth, who was instrumental in founding the Mountain Club of South Africa a hundred years ago. In total it is a six-day, 81 km trail, but few people complete the full route. Also, the variation described here can be done in either four or five days, as many people choose to double up the two 10 km sections from Boskloof to Protea Valley, skipping Goedgeloof hut.

The trail was pioneered by the indefatigable Jaynee Levy in a monumental three-day push over New Year 1979/1980. It was the first circular route to be incorporated into the National Hiking Way System, and has since been expanded to offer four circular routes of varying duration. The trail crisscrosses the rugged twin ridges of the Langeberg range, encircling some of its loftiest peaks. I have hiked all variations, in rain and shine, in snow and sweltering heat and it is, without doubt, one of my favourite trails.

The Langeberg is not endowed with quite as rich a fynbos cover as the Boland Mountains, certainly with fewer rare and endangered species, but I have found the vegetation here to be even more exquisite and showy. Rather than finding isolated rarities and floral gems (although there is no shortage of them), these mountains become a riot of colour in springtime and summer. One rare species that flourishes along the stream banks at Nooitgedacht is the delicate scarlet orchid (*Disa cardinalis*), distributionally confined and only recently described.

DAY I *SWELLENDAM FOREST STATION TO BOSKLOOF HUT: 16 KM*

The Koloniebos hut, 4,3 km from the forest station, is used only by people who arrive on the evening before the hike begins or who otherwise like to start a hike with a party. Most people just pass it by, although it does have the last flush toilet you'll encounter for the next few days. The easy route to Koloniebos follows forestry roads through plantations. From the hut the route climbs a steep gravel road for just short of a kilometre, and then turns sharp right at the top of the hill to leave the plantation and enter Wamakersbos (wagon makers' forest). Unfortunately all that 'wamaking' has denuded the forest of its best trees; nevertheless, after the ordered, ranked trees of the pine plantation, this small copse of natural forest provides the apt doorway into the magical world of the Swellendam trail.

The walk through the verdant embrace of this Afro-montane forest relict is an easy stroll, crossing streams at either end. This is the last water before encountering one of the steepest and longest climbs of the hike, so fill your water bottles here. While still in the woods the path begins the first climb in a long series of steps that crest the main ridge of the range; there is a short but very steep and slippery chute leading to the forest margin.

The view from Drosterspas over Boskloof, one of the more remote regions of the trail. In the foreground is a king protea (*Protea cynaroides*).

On leaving the woods a fringe of keurbooms (*Virgilia oroboides*) and water blossom peas (*Podalyria calyptrata*), both of which burst forth in sweet-smelling pink blossoms during spring and early summer, protects the delicate microclimate of the forest.

Immediately beyond is a zone of damp, rank mountain fynbos, dominated by the conebush *Leucadendron eucalyptifolium* and various cottonwool-tipped brunia bushes. The smaller, bright yellow conebush is *L. salignum* that in spring glazes the mountain slopes in a syrupy sheen. Among the restio reeds, which are the least showy but most diagnostic element of the fynbos, the pretty caps of Caledon bluebells (*Gladiolus rogersii*) peek out between September and December. For the next 7 km the trail ascends through successive, natural terraces that comprise the Langeberg's southern aspect. The path then executes a long series of zigzags, through 800 m, to reach a high point at Hoekrus. From here the geometrically arranged wheatfields of the southern Cape can be seen stretching out towards Cape Agulhas.

And yet this is still not the end of the ascent, for the path climbs further to round the shoulder of the spur before beginning its descent along the very stony path to the Tierkloof River, an ankle-twisting 2,5 km away. The river forms a deep gorge here which is forded by a sturdy footbridge. The final climb out of the valley to Boskloof hut through the russet restio veld is sprinkled with colourful heaths (*Erica daphniflora* and *E. versicolor*), brilliant white and strawberry red everlastings, and tiny blue and white orchids (*Disa cornuta*). On all four occasions I have walked this stretch at dusk, so that I have only an image of its beauty.

On reaching Boskloof one gains a lofty perspective of the Langeberg's physical form, which consists of two major and numerous lesser parallel ridges and valleys. The hut is found in a secluded corner, and a large bathing pool can be reached a little way up the Boskloof.

The commanding view from the hut takes in a wide panorama of peaks and valleys. Directly in front one sees the ground down the teeth of Ten, Eleven, Twelve and One o' Clock peaks forming the upper demarcation of Boskloof. Down, and to the left, the kloof steepens as it descends to the Buffelskloof.

DAY 2 *BOSKLOOF HUT TO GOEDGELOOF HUT: 10 KM*

From Boskloof the path climbs diagonally across the ridge north of the hut, called the Drosterspas (deserter's pass). Only Stokoe's Pass on the Boland Trail matches this short stretch for floral brilliance: ground disas and gladiolii, king proteas (*Protea cynaroides*) and brown-bearded sugarbushes (*P. speciosa*), a variety of blushing brides and one of the magnificent silver flamebushes (*Mimetes splendidus*) among the fynbos bouquet. The pass levels out at Vulture Rocks, on the very crest of the main ridge, where it executes a tight about-turn: from here one can look along the mountain axis, over dark Grootkloof, past Buffelsjag and towards Ashton. Walking westwards along the ridge to Knuckle Rocks a smaller, somewhat less brilliant species of flamebush, *M. cucullata*, is encountered.

The path winds around two spurs of the second major ridge, before dropping down into the idyllic Zuurplaats valley, through which the Langkuile stream meanders back and forth. In early to midsummer the confined valley gets a dusting by nature's finest make-up artist, leaving it all ablush with flowering heaths (*Erica pulchella*, *E. versicolor* and *E. vestita*) in white, fire-red and soft pink. Downstream of the path are a few pools, their banks in summer strung with necklaces of white and an unusual yellow variety of *Disa tripetaloides* and the small mauve blooms of *Chironia jasminoides*.

Climbing out of the valley the path plays a hide-and-seek game through a labyrinth of rock formations, until cresting the final ridge at Het Goedgeloof, to descend to the Karoo floor at Goedgeloof hut. This northern slope is loose and very stony, steep and long. Above you looms Hermitage Peak and the massive Misty Point (1 710 m). The ridge may be enshrouded in a shading awning of cloud, bringing a welcome respite from the blistering heat in summer. Despite having done this long descent four times, I can remember very little except the feeling of great relief when the hut finally comes into view.

There are two stone huts with cold showers, and a wooden cooking shelter. The nearest farm dam is available for swimming – should the weather permit.

DAY 3 *GOEDGELOOF HUT TO PROTEA VALLEY HUT: 10 KM*

Since I do not care to linger so close to the nearby Little Karoo farms, I prefer to have my lunch here and recover from the morning's strenuous four-hour walk before setting off once more for the next hut. However, those hikers that do overnight at Goedgeloof hut will have the benefit of cool morning shade for their climb up to Protea Valley. For the first few kilometres the going is easy, following a disused 4x4 track along the base of the ridge, dominated by yellow conebushes (*Leucadendron salignum*). The path crosses two streams, where ground woodpeckers can often be seen hopping among the boulders. The stream banks are covered in thickets of fountain bushes (*Psoralea pinnata*) and blue sugarbushes (*Protea neriifolia*). On reaching the second stream drink deeply and, should you wish to make tea at the wonderful gateway to the high valley yonder, then this is the last place you will encounter water until reaching the hut.

The climb up to Warmwaternek is unremitting, and something of an endurance test; only the rich vegetation provides a diversion to keep the spirits up. There are some magnificent specimens of the bearded protea (*P. magnifica*), as well as the pincushion (*Leucospermum calligerum*), which gets its name from the protruding styles of the flowerheads. The delicate cream blooms appear in July, and as they age they begin to darken, turning first pink and finally a deep carmine by summertime. Having tired of nature study, your legs begin to rebel at the seemingly endless succession of horizons that must be overcome. After a while your mind will (by necessity) enter a trance-like acceptance of this uphill treadmill, but suddenly the path emerges on the rounded saddle of Warmwaternek. So abrupt is the transition that the vista has an element of fantasy for, rolling out before you and enfolded by two mountain ridges, lies one of the most beautiful valleys imaginable.

On a clear day the hut, nestling 4 km away at the far end of the valley, is just visible from the nek. The valley itself is a botanical extravaganza, with a cast of at least six species of protea (*Protea neriifolia, P. cynaroides, P. speciosa, P. eximia, P. longiflora* and *P. grandiceps*), conebushes,

LEFT A typical forested gorge in the Marloth Nature Reserve. The small relict forest patches here are the remnants of evergreen forests that once graced all the mountains between here and Uitenhage – until the 'Great Fire' of 1869 swept most of them away. *ABOVE Disa cardinalis*, one of the rarest and showiest plants in the area, is endemic to the Langeberg near Nooitgedacht hut.

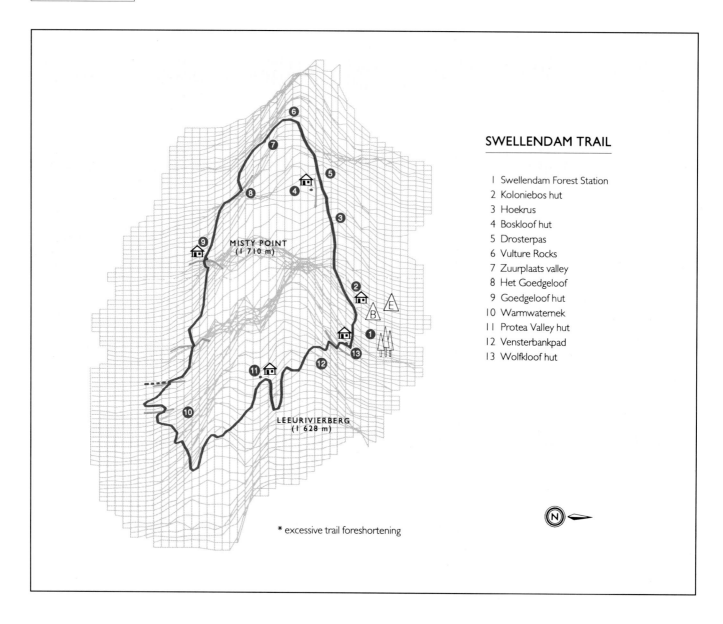

SWELLENDAM TRAIL

MISTY POINT
(1 710 m)

LEEURIVIERBERG
(1 628 m)

* excessive trail foreshortening

1 Swellendam Forest Station
2 Koloniebos hut
3 Hoekrus
4 Boskloof hut
5 Drosterpas
6 Vulture Rocks
7 Zuurplaats valley
8 Het Goedgeloof
9 Goedgeloof hut
10 Warmwaternek
11 Protea Valley hut
12 Vensterbankpad
13 Wolfkloof hut

flamebushes, and many species of heath and everlastings. The hut looks out over the sweep of this long valley, with the cloud-capped summit of the Misty Point standing sentinel at the far end.

DAY 4 PROTEA VALLEY HUT TO WOLFKLOOF HUT VIA VENSTERBANK: 12 KM

This short cut variation begins by following the Nooitgedacht path up a long but gentle ascent to Dwariganek. If a fire hasn't burnt it yet, the trail cuts a path through one of the finest stands of mature fynbos to be seen anywhere: it is dominated by *Protea eximia* bushes and

towering *Leucadendron spissifolium* conebushes. Sugarbirds and sunbirds dart among the flowers, enjoying the copious supply of nectar. On reaching the nek one gazes down into the gnarled Twisniet Valley, thankful that the route branches off here to the left to make its way upwards to the very edge of the awesome Vensterbank chasm.

Standing here and looking down into the deep gash of Leeukloof, one sees Kleinboshoog looming up on the left, while the ground to the right sweeps up to the summit of the Leeurivierberg (1 628 m), second highest peak in the range. Peering through the portals of Vensterbank the view opens out across the Breede River valley, beyond the dark

recess of the kloof far below. The Vensterbankpad takes a high route over the ridge to the right, before beginning its tortuous, 4 km descent to the main trail between Nooitgedacht and Wolfkloof. This path is very steep and often wet and icy in winter, so that it is very much a case of slip-sliding your way down through the seemingly endless zigzags. It is not a route for the faint of heart or weak of knee, but it is a most spectacular one and thus highly recommended.

The path winds its way into cavernous Klein Houtbos, with its giant witels trees, past the top of the Leeurivier waterfall and then across open veld to make a final short, but rather steep, descent to the Wolfkloof hut.

DAY 5 *WOLFKLOOF HUT TO FOREST STATION : 10,7 KM*

I have always maintained that, for an otherwise outstanding trail, the last section is disappointing. Unfortunately the private land hereabouts sneaks far up the mountain slopes so that the trail has to climb steeply up and down several times to circumvent it. It appears that it could just as easily have contoured around at a lower level. The only interesting feature on this section is Hermitage Kloof, with its quaint picnic area beneath tall forest trees. The final stretch, including yet a few more ups and downs, is along logging tracks within pine plantation.

Wolfberg hut is situated at the mouth of an enchanting gorge, worth spending an entire morning exploring. This is the only hut on the main section of the trail where fires are allowed.

THE TRAIL AT A GLANCE

STARTING POINT : Swellendam Forest Station
FINISHING POINT : Swellendam Forest Station
LENGTH : 59 km
DURATION : Four or five days
GROUP LIMIT : 16 people
ROUTE : The trail encircles the Langeberg range directly above Swellendam, proceeding in an anti-clockwise direction around the Marloth Nature Reserve. This route takes in the Koloniebos, Boskloof, Goedgeloof, Protea Valley and Wolfkloof huts, before returning to the forest station.
HOW TO GET THERE : Take the N2 from Cape Town and turn off into Swellendam. From the main street follow the forestry signs up Andrew Whyte Street to the forest station.
BOOKING AUTHORITY : Swellendam Nature Conservation, P.O. Box 28, Swellendam, 6740; tel : (0291) 4-1410.
ACCOMMODATION : Wooden chalets with only bunk beds and mattresses.

CLIMATE : The trail falls within the winter rainfall area, with cold fronts lashing the region about once a week in winter. But, being a mountain environment, daily weather can vary considerably and rain can fall throughout the year. The summer south-easter often covers the high ridges in swirling cloud and mist.
BEST TIME TO HIKE : Spring to early summer is best, for the flowers, daily weather and the availability of water. On any day of the year one should expect a variety of weather conditions, alternating between rain and shine. When it is warm it is hot, and when it is cold it is freezing.
REFERENCES : 1 : 50 000 National Hiking Way map (1989 edition)
TERRAIN : The Langeberg mountains are very rugged and remote in places. Although there is a marked path, it sometimes becomes stony and very steep. Although situated about midway along the Cape Folded Mountains' east-west axis, this trail marks the eastern limit of what is generally referred to as the Western Cape.

WHAT TO TAKE : At all times of the year warm and waterproof clothing, as well as a good quality sleeping bag, are essential. In winter heavy boots are preferable, while light boots will suffice in summer. Running shoes or takkies are not recommended, especially for the Vensterbankpad descent. The trail map provided is a good one, offering all manner of information about human and natural history, as well as species indicators all along the trail.
SPECIAL PRECAUTIONS : Check for approaching cold fronts before you set off, and pack the appropriate kit. Also carry water along the sections where it is otherwise unavailable.
TRAIL OPTIONS : For weekenders, there is a two-day option sleeping over at Boskloof and returning over Tienuurkop. From Protea Valley hut it is possible to avoid the very exposed Vensterbank route by taking an easy descent to Wolfkloof along the shorter Kruispad. The full trail goes from Protea Valley to lonely Nooitgedacht, followed by a hard haul past Middelrivier to Wolfkloof.

TSITSIKAMMA TRAIL

Many hikers I questioned while compiling this book listed this as their favourite trail. Whatever one's personal preference, this is certainly one of the grandest sections of the National Hiking Way System, lorded over by the massive bulk of Formosa Peak (1 675 m), the Witberg, Spitskop, Camelpile and Storm's River Peak. The trail offers an enticing combination of primeval forest and flowering montane fynbos, in one of the most scenic parts of South Africa.

In my opinion it is the availability of water, especially for swimming in, that is the hallmark of a good hike, and in this respect it is hard to beat the Tsitsikamma Trail. Many of the rivers that are crossed at their wide mouths on the Otter Trail are encountered here as youthful mountain streams, playing and laughing on their way to the sea. Although many of the best rivers and pools are not marked as swimming spots, I imagine it would be hard to stop hikers from plunging into the wonderful pool at Waterwitelsgat, for instance, on a hot day. The name Tsitsikamma can be loosely translated from Khoi to mean 'where clear waters rise'.

At the time when white explorers first reached the dense, temperate forests of the Southern Cape, they found herds of elephant and buffalo, as well as other large game inhabiting the area. It took less than a hundred years for them to be shot out (although a few lonely elephants survive in the Outeniqua Mountains), but some forest antelope, grey rhebok, bushpig, baboons and leopards do still occur within the trail environment. The fynbos here is not as species-rich as in the mountains of the Western Cape, but the more varied habitats here support a far richer birdlife than that found further west.

DAY I *KALANDER HUT TO BLAAUWKRANTZ HUT: 16,6 KM*

Hikers should spend the night before commencing the trail in the Kalander hut, beneath tall forest trees on the shores of the tranquil Groot River estuary. For the first 2 km the trail makes its way around the river, crossing it via the R102 bridge, and then re-entering the forest. This next section gives an excellent glimpse of the temperate southern forest type, with some magnificent examples of the 'kalander' or Outeniqua yellowwood tree (*Podocarpus falcatus*). Keep a lookout here for small forest songbirds: I was lucky to see a second chorister robin here within a month, as well as my first clear sighting of that ubiquitous bush species, the bleating warbler, whose persistent call sounds like two marbles being knocked together. You may also see sombre bulbuls (listen for the call 'Willie, won't you come out and pla-aaay') and Cape batises.

Once on the far (eastern) side of the Groot River, the path takes a steep and somewhat sustained turn up the Douwurmpad (dew worm path). None of my

From the wave-cut terrace above Nature's Valley, the rollercoaster Tsitsikamma Mountains reflect the massive folding processes that formed them.

RIGHT About half of the trail is through temperate evergreen forests. Moss- and lichen-encrusted boughs, tall tree ferns and the soft floor litter, together with the cool microclimate, create a delicate fantasy world. *BELOW* Staircase Falls are found in a secret corner of the Klip River gorge. The falls plummet into a large pool, its shaded banks making for an excellent lunch spot.

Afrikaans-speaking companions on the trail knew what a 'douwurm' is, but we did come up with two possibilities: the first is the millipede, which is very common in the damp forest areas, but more probably it refers to those hikers who like to make an early start, and so clear the path of dew for the late-starters.

For 2 km the path traverses Douwurm-kop and the level Covie Commonage, part of a narrow, deeply incised plateau that runs between the sea and the mountains all the way along the Garden Route. This level area represents an ancient sea bed, and it has long been used as a convenient platform across which to travel, whether by foot, hoof or wheel. The fynbos along this stretch is very dense, exceeding 2 m in height. The most visible plants are the white sugarbush (*Protea mundii*), the blue sugarbush (*P. neriifolia*), the tall conebush (*Leucadendron eucalyptifolium*), as well as *Brunia* and *Berzelia* species with their conspicuous white pom-pon flowers. Also conspicuous in the fynbos is a nasty infestation of black wattle (*Acacia mearnsii*); hikers should take it upon themselves to pull out at least one acacia, pine or other alien sapling as they go, to help control their spread. Cutting a diagonal swath across the horizon the Tsitsikamma Mountains fade into a distant blue haze – and that is where the trail is headed.

At the 5 km mark the path enters a keurboom grove and then slips into the Grootkloof forest itself, where it dips to cross a pleasant stream. The most common large trees seen here are white-trunked Cape holly (*Ilex mitis*), white, red and hard pear species, a few large Cape chestnuts and Cape ash specimens, and of course the giant yellowwoods of both *Podocarpus latifolius* and *P. falcatus* varieties. But to those people who take an interest in seeing how the species composition of forests changes from the south-west to north-east of the country, most impressive will be the number of large forest saffronwoods (*Cassine papillosa*). These trees can be identified by the deep saffron colour of the bark, often heavily interspersed with dark green moss and white lichen.

Colourful fungal forms grow to impressive proportions on dead tree trunks, and among the damp forest litter. Most evident are the stink horns (*Phallus rubicundus*); the common name refers to their repulsive odour of rotting flesh to attract flies which disperse the spores, while the reason for the suggestive genus name will become apparent as soon as you see one. A loud cackling high up in the forest canopy should alert you to the presence of redbilled woodhoopoes, which probe much in the way of woodpeckers. The forest is also the habitat of Knysna and olive woodpeckers.

Most hikers here and in other evergreen forests thrill to see the bright flashing colours of Knysna or purplecrested louries, which are in fact quite common residents. Far more difficult to spot, however, is the equally colourful narina trogon. This bird, metallic green and gold with a bright red chest, is slightly smaller than the louries, and is said to have been named by traveller Francois le Vaillant after a Hottentot maid who had caught his fancy. The trogons may perch motionless for long periods, but our party was lucky to see a few of them close up, one of which honoured us with a display flight only a few metres above our heads.

After a while you will notice the growing abundance of a tree that resembles a rough barked yellowwood. This is *Acacia melanoxylon*, the Australian blackwood that was planted during the last century in areas where the natural forest had been depleted through excessive lumbering. You will now be on the Blackwood Path, where the trees are beginning to be harvested for their quality hard timber. The path takes you past the Covie settlement, then onto a 4x4 track that crosses the R102 and 1 km further on goes under the N2 toll road into the Platbos forest. For 2 km the path leads evenly uphill, and then curves sharply around to the left, to reach Staircase Falls and a large pool in the Klip River gorge. The pool is overhung by large witels trees (*Platylophus trifoliatus*), identified by their lanceolate, toothed, pale green leaves. As its name suggests, the falls do not so much plummet as step down the tiered cascade. This is a good lunch spot, being 11,5 km from the start of the trail.

Leaving the pool the path climbs steeply to reach a lush tree fern forest on the banks of a tributary of the Klip River. The path then emerges in pine and gum plantation, where it levels off, and for the last 4,5 km to the hut the going is decidedly easier. But here is a question you can ponder: why does one species of small-leaved, light green fern grow so profusely under the pines, but not under the gums? We could find no satisfactory explanation, but there has to be one.

The hut at Blaauwkrantz is perched on the edge of the Bloukrans River gorge, with the high peaks of the Tsitsikamma mountains crowding the view. Below it the Tolbos River, a tributary of the Bloukrans, plunges down its own side gorge, through a series of pools and waterfalls that are easily reached from the hut. The tributary is named after the attractive yellow and lime-green conebushes (*Leucodendron spissifolium*) that grow in the area.

Its spectacular setting places Blaauwkrantz in a very special class of hiking accommodation alongside the likes of Protea Valley hut on the Swellendam Trail, Scott, Oakhurst and André huts on the Otter Trail, Dontsa hut on the Amatola Trail, and the Giant's Castle hut. Sitting on the front stoep, surrounded by flowering watsonias and fynbos, we marvelled at the view and watched dainty swee waxbills and various sunbirds foraging on grass stems on the slopes below.

DAY 2 BLAAUWKRANTZ HUT TO KEURBOS HUT: 13,4 KM

The day begins with a short, steep descent to the Tolbos River, followed by a steep but longer climb up a ridge called the Ouveldrug (Old Veld Ridge). When I walked it only the veld to the right could be called old, while that to the left was newly burned and bursting with the pale fountains of watsonia blooms. After gaining about 200 m in altitude, the path hugs a hillslope to descend into Buffelsbos. A stream is crossed close to the forest margin, and a little further on a larger one looks inviting for a dip.

The path stays within the enchanting Buffelsbos forest for about 2 km. This and other similar forest patches, such as Benebos further on, are relics of tropical forests that in a past age covered much of the country's eastern extent. With the onset of an arid climatic cycle several thousand years ago these forests retreated towards the equator, as well as up mountain slopes and down into river gorges where they have managed to hold out against the drying environment. In recent times the 'Great Fire' of 1869, sweeping before a gusting south-easterly wind, decimated the Southern Cape's forests from Uitenhage to Swellendam. With current trends, accelerated by man's interference, the temperate evergreen forests in South Africa are earmarked for eventual extinction.

Leaving the forest the path descends gently to the Bloukrans River, 6 km upstream of the hut. Here the river executes a hairpin bend, forming one of the largest mountain pools I have seen. Once again the pool bank is shaded by large witels trees and similar but smaller water witels trees (*Brachylaena neriifolia*). Plan to spend a long time here, for it is a lovely spot, and a long haul awaits you.

The path climbs sharply away from the pool to reach a shoulder above the river gorge, and for the next 3 km it continues to climb, albeit not steeply, along the base of Klein Benekop (939 m). In the heat of late summer the climb seems much longer and harder than it would in cool conditions, for there is no shade or water. But your exertion will be rewarded by some flowering beauties: I saw three showy specimens of the blue, white and yellow orchid *Herschelia graminifolia*, another small white ground orchid (possibly (*Disa sagittalis*), and in a small damp gully a bunch of brilliant scarlet Knysna lilies (*Cyrtanthus pupurens*). Unfortunately the natural floral splendour is marred by the amount of alien hakea, a slender tree with sharp, pale green-grey needle leaves and woody pods. The most common shrub along the path is the iron martin (*Laurophyllus capensis*), easily identified by the female flowers which form dense, spiky, woody structures which many people mistake for parasitic deformities.

A second relict forest patch is reached at Benebos, where the trail seems to be suddenly enveloped by the moist coolness of the murky forest. Just within the forest there is a mounted glass case, displaying some old elephant bones, and therein lies the key to the name, Benebos (bone forest). Legend has it that this area was an old elephant graveyard but only recently did forestry workers come across the pachyderm remains. Early European explorers like the Frenchman Le Vaillant wrote in their diaries of the large elephant herds encountered, and of the immense difficulties in travelling through the rugged forest terrain.

Near the far end of the forest, at about the 10 km mark, a delightful stream lined with tree ferns makes for a good tea spot. Once the path emerges from the forest it climbs 100 m to Ongeluksnek. A stony 4x4 track is then followed down to Keurbos hut, named after the keurbooms (*Virgilia oroboides*) that grow in profusion around the hut. The veld alongside the path, especially at a large seepage area, is aflush with bright pink orchids (*Disa racemosa*). The hut is located on the far side of a small patch of forest, but it has been poorly sited, in an attempt to prevent hikers from abluting in the Lottering River, 1,25 km away.

DAY 3 KEURBOS HUT TO HEUNINGBOS HUT: 13,4 KM

The brisk run-up to the Lottering River is flanked by iron martins, tall conebushes and (somewhat less pleasantly) hakea plants. Luckily, with the help of scientists at the CSIR's Plant Protection Research Institute, various forms of biological control have been introduced to help control, arrest and eventually, it is hoped, eradicate this dangerous invader which would otherwise completely choke the fynbos.

High up to the left stands Formosa Peak, the highest peak along the Tsitsikamma range. The mountain was first climbed from this, the difficult side, by one of the Mountain Club of South Africa's founders, George Amphlett, his wife and a friend over three days from Clearstream, just after the turn of the century. (It had previously been scaled by a surveyor some years before from the easier Little Karoo side.)

Having crossed the Lottering River, the trail ascends the Rushes Pass, a 2 km slog that even in summer is shaded by tall restios (rushes) and other hydrophyllic vegetation for most of the way up. In winter one probably longs for the sun to make its delayed appearance over the mountains and tall rushes. On reaching the nek between Klipbokkop and Elandskop, the view back towards Formosa Peak and the Bene River valley is grand. This vantage point yields views of virtually the entire Tsitsikamma range, with the valleys of the Lottering and Elandsbos dropping away on either side.

The loose, 320 m descent to the Elandsbos River is one where hikers wearing running shoes will probably wish they had chosen to walk in boots instead. Although the map does not show forest on the river bank, the path stumbles unexpectedly into a steep but interesting tangle of riverine bush. The river itself is wide and shallow, its bed a mass of rounded boulders of varying sizes. It is a pleasant spot for a tea break and a dip, although you will not be able to actually swim here. Anyone who has walked the Otter Trail will juxtapose this scene, and those of the Lottering and Bloukrans rivers, with that encountered while crossing their wide mouths.

From the river the path climbs to reach Mangold's Road, an undulating 4x4 track that is followed for the next 4 km, except for one short section of path, around a rocky spur of Fynbos Peak (911 m) and then through a pine plantation. Just before the 11 km mark the path enters Heuningbos, a narrow stretch of forest that encloses the Heuningkloof and its small stream. This forest is much more open than the others encountered, and has a lower species' diversity, suggesting heavy exploitation in the past. After another short section through plantation the path climbs, falls and climbs again to pass through a second small forest patch and to cross the Kleinbos River. The hut stands on a level promontory where the Tweedebos Stream makes a tight cutback. After the non-existent view at Keurbos, the panoramic vista here is a most welcome treat.

The hut has lots of pots and pans, but no table in the fire shelter, while other huts have tables but no utensils. The toilets here (as well as those at Keurbos) were inadequate for humans, although a metre-long puffadder found them to its liking. We also came across a large brown water snake in the river below, but it was harmless and quite sociable.

DAY 4 HEUNINGBOS HUT TO SLEEPKLOOF HUT: 14,2 KM

This is the most strenuous day's hiking on the trail, climbing over two saddles, each one involving a gain in altitude of about 400 m. The path sets off down to the Tweedebos Stream, and almost immediately after crossing it begins the ascent of Splendid Pass to reach the nek at Mostertshoogte.

The pass is named after a beautiful member of the large Proteaceae family, *Mimetes splendidus*. It is one of four very showy 'silver flamebushes', so called for the silvery hairs which cover their leaves, and has the easternmost distribution of all. There are only about 400 known plants, most occurring in small communities of about five plants each. The tall, silvery shrubs are confined to the steepest, south-facing slopes from Swellendam to Storm's River, where conditions are always moist and cool, and the plants receive very little direct sunlight.

They are also unusual in that they are the only silver mimetes occurring wholly east of Swellendam, and the only species which flowers in the second half of the year, mainly from July to September. In about June the top leaves of the plant turn deep red but, approaching flowering time, they change to pale orange and finally yellow.

While the Heuningbos hut is located at an altitude of just over 350 m, Mostertshoogte is at nearly 700 m, wedged between Lloyd se Kop and Witteklipkop. Up ahead the summit of Storm's River Peak (1 019 m) rises into the crisp mountain air. This is one of the most rugged parts of the range, and certainly one where the hiker will feel most isolated and insignificant. From the saddle the path finds its way across to the right onto a spur, which is followed on the long (1,5 km) descent to Mostertsbos and the Witteklip River, where a drink and a dip are a most welcome respite. After crossing the river the path reaches a turn-off, where Mostertsbos' Road leads off down to the N2, Stormsrivier Forest Station and the Tsitsikamma Forest Inn.

The path continues upward, all the way to Nademaalnek 3 km away. At 740 m this is the trail's highest point, squeezed between Storm's River Peak and Heidekop. From the nek the path, as before, makes its way onto a sharp-ridged spur. This is the Teebosrug, named after the small shrub *Cyclopia subternata*, the leaves of which are fermented and then dried to produce the aromatic and delicious honeybush tea. This most refreshing beverage first saw duty as a traditional medicine, being used as a tonic to treat stomach ailments.

The descent of Teebosrug is arduous, losing the same altitude that was climbed from the Witteklip River, but in only half

ABOVE The forested gorges offer the most exquisite interplay of form and texture: the delicate tracery of fern fronds, concentric plumes on a stream, and the pale rounded surfaces of river pebbles are memorable images. LEFT Colourful bracket fungi create an attractive contrast to the greenery of the forest. But they also play a vital biological role: fungi and other decomposers, both plant and animal, help return to the ground nutrients locked in the tall trees.

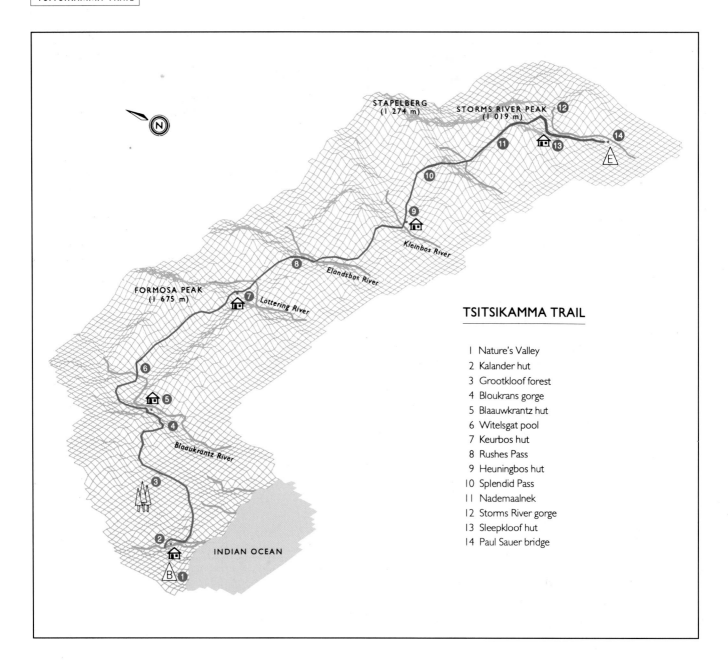

TSITSIKAMMA TRAIL

1 Nature's Valley
2 Kalander hut
3 Grootkloof forest
4 Bloukrans gorge
5 Blaauwkrantz hut
6 Witelsgat pool
7 Keurbos hut
8 Rushes Pass
9 Heuningbos hut
10 Splendid Pass
11 Nademaalnek
12 Storms River gorge
13 Sleepkloof hut
14 Paul Sauer bridge

the distance. During the descent Sleepkloof hut can be seen perched on the edge of a headland between the Sleepkloof and Storm's River gorges, much in the same manner as the Blaauwkrantz hut before. Near the bottom of Teebosrug the path enters forest, where the Bushpig Trail levels out and then climbs gently to the hut. The hut is situated on the edge of the forest, facing the gorge. Forested Sleepkloof is a feeder gorge of the Storm's River gorge, its name implying that it was a place where large timber trees were felled and dragged across to the Skuinsbospad.

DAY 5 *SLEEPKLOOF HUT TO THE PAUL SAUER BRIDGE AND STORM'S RIVER REST AREA: 3,2 KM*

This gentle downhill walk along the Bushpig Trail follows the edge of the Storm's River Gorge, passing through the small Môresonbos relict forest patch *en route*. With colonial expansion from Cape Town, and the discovery of gold first around Knysna and then on the Highveld, the Southern Cape forests came under intense pressure with growing demand for the hard timber trees. The overexploitation of the forests soon became

obvious, and in 1874 a forest conservator was based in Knysna to control this wanton destruction. In the more remote eastern forests around Storm's River, it went on for some time unfettered.

In 1880 the Count M. de Vasselot was appointed superintendent responsible for all forestry in the Cape. With this came systematically controlled woodcutting and silviculture and, finally, some form of protection for the remaining natural forests. At the Storm's River rest area there is a small museum showing the history of the area, and its forestry heritage, and it is well worth a visit.

THE TRAIL AT A GLANCE

STARTING POINT : Nature's Valley, De Vasselot National Parks Board campsite (Kalander hut)

FINISHING POINT : Storm's River rest area, N2 Paul Sauer Bridge

LENGTH : 57 km

DURATION : Five days

GROUP LIMIT : 30 people

ROUTE : From Nature's Valley the trail climbs into the Tsitsikamma Mountain foothills, and traces the length of the range to the Blaauwkrantz, Keurbos, Heuningbos and Sleepkloof huts, before ending at the Paul Sauer Bridge.

HOW TO GET THERE : From Plettenberg Bay, or Storm's River, follow the N2 towards the toll road, turning off to Nature's Valley on the R102, Coldstream road. The parks board campsite and Kalander hut are found on the west bank of the Groot River estuary, about 500 m east of the Nature's Valley turn-off.

BOOKING AUTHORITY : National Hiking Way Board, Tsitsikamma Forestry Region, Private Bag X537, Humansdorp, 6300; tel. (0423) 5-1180.

ACCOMMODATION : Typically spartan wooden chalets of the Cape National Hiking Way trails, with bunk beds and mattresses, firewood, pots and pans at some huts and not others, longdrop toilets – and an entrepreneurial caretaker at one hut who may have cold beers and softdrinks to sell to weary hikers.

CLIMATE : Although this area is in the year-round rainfall region, there is still a wet and dry weather cycle in which the dry periods can be very dry and hot indeed, and the wet periods can be decidedly so, and cold. The two high rainfall peaks are in March and October (111 and 97 mm respectively), with a trough in June/July (54 mm). The hottest month is February, with a daily average maximum temperature of 24.3 °C, and corresponding high humidity, while the coldest month is July with an average minimum temperature of 7 °C. Being essentially a mountain hike, however, the weather can vary considerably from day to day, and even from hour to hour.

BEST TIME TO HIKE : With the exception of a few hill climbs, this is not at all a strenuous trail. Hiking in summer is not normally a problem, although I would avoid the hottest months of January and February if possible. However, since there is an abundance of swimming opportunities I would prefer the heat to what can be very cold midwinter months, from June to August inclusive. The two months on either side of the hottest ones are generally the best.

REFERENCES : National Hiking Way Board 1 : 50 000 hiking map of the Tsitsikamma National Park, showing both Otter and Tsitsikamma trails; the Botanical Society's Outeniqua, Tsitsikamma and Eastern Little Karoo wildflower guide, and two National Parks Board guides.

TERRAIN : The trail is situated near the eastern extreme of the Garden Route, the year-round rainfall area of the Southern Cape, in the foothills of one of the most picturesque ranges of the Cape Folded Mountains. The rock encountered is almost exclusively Table Mountain Sandstone, which weathers to a sandy soil favouring tall mountain fynbos. Forest occurs where the shale horizons weather to form more nutritious, clayey soils, especially in the river gorges. The trail takes a fairly easy route through the foothills, but with the usual ups and downs to be expected.

WHAT TO TAKE : Since the vegetation here is so impressive, you should carry a good flower and tree guide: the best are the Botanical Society/Moriarty wildflower guide for the area and *Trees of the Cape Peninsula* by Eugene Moll and Lindsay Scott.

SPECIAL PRECAUTIONS : The only real dangers on this trail are the possible extremes of weather: in the hotter months you will have to drink often to beat the heat and cloying humidity (hiking in early January I regularly had to wring out my shirt), while in winter snow often falls on the higher peaks, and temperatures plummet. A high quality sleeping bag is essential under such conditions. The paths are mostly in good condition and seldom steep, allowing hikers to choose between boots and lighter footwear. Ticks may be prevalent in summer, so check your legs regularly for the nasty little red pepper ticks. Hikers are requested not to swim in the Lottering or Kleinbos rivers, as they provide drinking water downstream. If you have to, though, refrain from putting any kind of pollutant into the water. Since this is a linear hike, transport from the Paul Sauer Bridge back to Nature's Valley must be arranged beforehand.

TRAIL OPTIONS : It is possible to do shorter two, three- or four-day hikes by using various access and exit routes from the forestry stations at Bloukrans and Lottering, or from the Boskor plant at Kleinbos. There are numerous nature walks located around both the starting and end points, ranging from under an hour to a full day.

Blaauwkrantz hut, the first stopover on the trail, perches precariously above a side kloof of the spectacular Bloukrans River gorge. In the distance can be seen the jagged summit of Formosa Peak (1 675 m), the highest peak in the range.

OTTER TRAIL

T he Otter Trail is probably the best known hiking trail in the country. This is hardly surprising, since in 1968 it was the first official trail to be opened, and it traverses some of the most dramatic, unspoilt natural terrain in southern Africa. During the first decade it was used only sparingly, to the delight of trailists. With the advent of the National Hiking Way System in the late 1970s, however, demands to walk this and other trails swelled from a trickle to a flood. Facilities were upgraded and the number of hikers allowed on the trail increased from 10 to 12 per day. Some people believe the trail is over-used, but such is the demand that it is booked solidly a year in advance. Unfortunately for those unable to get a booking, at least a third of the people who do book don't show up.

This is a year-round rainfall area where the annual average is 1 200 mm. Rivers often come down in spate and it is not unusual for hikers to be trapped along the trail. Should this happen you are advised to use your initiative and either stay put or, if it is not dangerous, return to the previous hut. No matter how macho you are, don't do anything stupid to make the task of finding you difficult – the park staff will come to your aid.

The trail is a fairly easy one for any reasonably fit person, with short to medium distances covered each day. For the unprepared, however, it can be heavy going with many steep (but not very long) ascents and descents. The topography here consists of rocky shoreline, high coastal cliffs and scree slopes, on top of which the wide terrace of a previous sea level stretches back to the foothills of the coastal mountains. The Tsitsikamma coastline is not only protected as a national park, but as a marine reserve as well. Consequently the intertidal and near-shore zones teem with life, and for those who take along goggles and snorkel the tidal pools provide hours of idle fascination.

DAY 1 *STORM'S RIVER MOUTH TO NGUBU HUT: 4,8 KM*

The trail begins at a cairn at the extreme western end of the rest camp. Since the first day is a very short one, you have enough time to explore the area around the Storm's River Mouth, report in at reception and watch a video on the trail before setting off. You might also use this time to organize transport back from Nature's Valley.

For the first 1 km the trail passes through the edge of the dry coastal forest, the sea a fleeting image through the foliage. In only a few places along this trail does the path encounter mature forest, where the dominant species is the white milkwood (*Sideroxylon inerme*), along with candlewood (also called cherrywood), red currant, red saffron and camphor bush. On reaching the rocky shoreline, you should follow the orange otter symbols, painted on obvious rocks along the way.

Oakhurst hut at the mouth of the Lottering River – one of the most breathtaking hut locations of the hiking way system.

The animal for which this trail is named is the Cape clawless otter, although the spotted necked otter also occurs here. The main difference between the species is that while the clawless otter frequents estuaries and coastal waters, the spotted necked otter is found only in open, freshwater habitats. The Tsitsikamma coastline is thus the perfect habitat for the clawless otter, with the result that there is one otter per kilometre of coastline here, the highest concentration in southern Africa.

These animals are as much at home on land as they are in the water, and I once saw one scampering across the open grasslands of Moremi Game Reserve at midday, although they are most active in the early morning and evening. Along the Tsitsikamma coastline, however, they are mainly crepuscular, and few hikers are lucky enough to see them.

Clawless otters can reach a length of 1,5 m and weigh as much as 18 kg. Depending on their habitat, their diet consists mainly of crabs, frogs and fish (making up about 90 per cent of the diet). Few wild animals are as endearing as these creatures: they love to chase each other around in the water, mock fighting and splashing, and will often play with small stones and sticks for long periods and with great dexterity.

After passing the mouth of Guano Cave (where the ammonia stench of bat excrement pervades the cave) the path winds upwards to follow the forest edge for a way, and then returns to the rocky shore where the waves have carved many interesting formations in the soft sandstone. At the halfway mark you reach the waterfall, where only foul weather could possibly deter hikers from a plunge into the cola-coloured waters of a large pool, fed by the tumbling falls. The pool is elevated above the waves, which you can watch crashing onto the rocks below. In the dry season you will need to carry water from here as the stream near Ngubu may have dried up.

To reach the hut the path climbs through forest, before dropping down to a clearing near the shore. Rednecked francolin that inhabit the forest margin here have become quite tame and will scout around looking for food – don't give them any! The hut is named after a park ranger who died tragically some years after the trail was established.

DAY 2 NGUBU HUT TO SCOTT HUT: 7,9 KM

From Ngubu the trail veers inland, climbing steeply within the forest to Olienboomkop, named after the large forest olive tree.

At the time I walked the trail, I remember the second day as being the most enjoyable section, especially where the path crosses numerous fern-frilled streams within the high canopy. At Skilderkrans the view opens out on top of high cliffs, to give vistas of the trail in both directions. For about 1,5 km the path follows the level terrace top, at an altitude of about 120 m, and then descends inland to cross the picturesque Kleinbos River deep within the most established part of the forest.

In his booklet *The Otter Trail and the Tsitsikamma Coastal National Park*, Patrick Wagner writes: 'This river is one of those rivers on the Otter Trail which contains an inexplicable magic… The cold brutality of the steep rock creates an incredible contrast with the clear sheen of the water. Away from the muffled sound of the sea, the quiet natural beauty is stunning.' If you venture a few hundred metres upstream on a side path you will find an enchanting pool that lures you in for a dip. From the river the path begins a steep, 1 km climb to the terrace, and then passes high above the secluded cove of Bloubaai. It is possible to take an indistinct track, from a point where the path begins to climb again, down to the fabulous swimming beach here. For hikers who have made a late start from Ngubu hut, this makes an ideal lunch break.

Ascending back up to the summit of the headland the path reaches one of the highest points on the trail, affording views over the bay and across to Skilderkrans. The path remains more or less level for about 1 km, before falling sharply down into the Geelhoutbos River valley. On the way down, during summer, the delicate powder blue bobbles of 'blue lilies' or agapanthus flowers can be seen. The path emerges on a beach at a river mouth to find Scott hut, the jewel of the trail, tucked into the trees at the forest edge.

The small beaches here are a likely place to spy otters, and the beach in front of the hut offers the best, safest swimming to be found on the trail. In addition, the diving is excellent: the rock pools near the rocky point teem with life.

DAY 3 SCOTT HUT TO OAKHURST HUT: 7,7 KM

After a short forest detour from Scott hut the path follows the rocky shoreline around Flip se Baai, with many opportunities for snorkelling in the deep gullies when conditions are calm. A small climb over a rocky promontory leads around the deeply incut Elandsbos River mouth. The approach to the river crossing is over a wide sandbank, on which large flocks of seagulls and terns often settle. The river twists through its funnel-shaped, sand-choked mouth, overhung by sweeping branches and looping vines. An atmosphere of tranquillity pervades this place, and it is with a wistful longing that one rounds the opposite headland and leaves its perfect calm behind.

From here the going becomes mostly rough and rugged, hugging the lichen-encrusted rocky shore for the next 3 km, with a few detours inland to overcome various obstacles at Blousloep and Jan Swarts. At 5,5 km, after numerous false starts, the path begins a serious ascent up to the terrace lip, where it levels off for about 1 km. Rounding the top of the cliffs at Grobbelaar se Bank one senses an imminent, inevitable drama about to descend – and descend it does, back and forth to the bank of the Lottering River far below. But just before the descent begins Oakhurst hut appears, standing its ground on a wave-bashed point at the river mouth's opposite bank. At low tide stepping stones across the river are exposed, but at other times the trail map should be consulted for advice on how best to cross.

Drinking water can be a problem in the dry season, necessitating a swimming-wading-walking trip upstream on the strong tidal bore to fetch fresh water beyond the reach of the tide. But it will be an interesting detour, especially since the resplendent Knysna lilies (*Cyrtanthus purpureus*) splash the verdant banks here with crimson dabs. Once settled at the hut, its wild and wind-tossed location can be appreciated: the sea is almost always seething, and it is here that dolphins are most likely to be seen in the tumbling, translucent breakers.

DAY 4 *OAKHURST HUT TO ANDRÉ HUT: 13,8 KM*

This section, the longest on the trail, aptly explains why the hike – although of modest distances – is unrelenting. The path cuts back and forth, up and down, between boulder beaches and higher forested slopes, seldom giving the hiker time or space in which to pace out the kilometres. Numerous stream crossings require the path to dip and rise consecutively, through forest and open fynbos, but it is possible that many of these streams will be found dry. Therefore water aplenty should be carried on this section, especially since the Bloukrans is a tidal river and does not yield drinking water.

Apart from where the path cuts inland to ford valleys, the forest is low and often sparse, with a dry floor, and hardly deserving of the name forest at all. At one such crossing, even when the stream itself is dry, a pool hangs high above the sea, on the cliff edge. We called this the 'pool with a view' and took the customary dip on a hot and sweaty day. After 10 km the Bloukrans River mouth is reached, guarded on both sides by jagged cliffs. But legend and first appearances are misleading for at low tide the crossing poses no problems at all, and it is possible to wade across the shifting sandbars. At high tide and during floods, however, an adventure awaits, although the trail map does offer advice on how best to make the crossing. The river mouth provides excellent swimming and bodysurfing in the safe, rolling swells. This is also a good lunch or tea spot, with the overnight hut some 4 km away.

Leaving the river behind, the path keeps just within the forest treeline, close to the surging sea, emerging on a pebbled beach for a short stretch before climbing up at Clinton's Bank. Once up on the terrace again, the path levels out and passes through the fynbos veld above Roman's Bank, aflush with orange pincushions, mimetes and proteas, ericas and, if you look closely, various geophytic lilies and orchids. Cisticolas love the restio beds, while any one of five species of sunbird could be seen flitting about the fynbos blooms. This exposed stretch of cliffline offers unrestricted views right across Nature's Valley to Plettenberg Bay.

Finally, the path drops down into the Klip River valley, and what a welcome respite it is. After Scott, I found this to be the most pleasant overnight spot: the hut nestles just inside the forest margin, overlooking a jumble of rocky points and promontories, coves and sandy beaches. The shallow but perennial river provides fresh water and decent bathing pools about 100 m upstream of the mouth. At sunset the high cliffs on the far side of the bay create an ever-changing technicolour backdrop to an already dramatic setting.

ABOVE Seagulls laze on the sandbars at the Elandsbos River mouth, waiting for the sea to deliver food scraps to their feet. The river's lower reaches are the more likely spots to see otters at play.

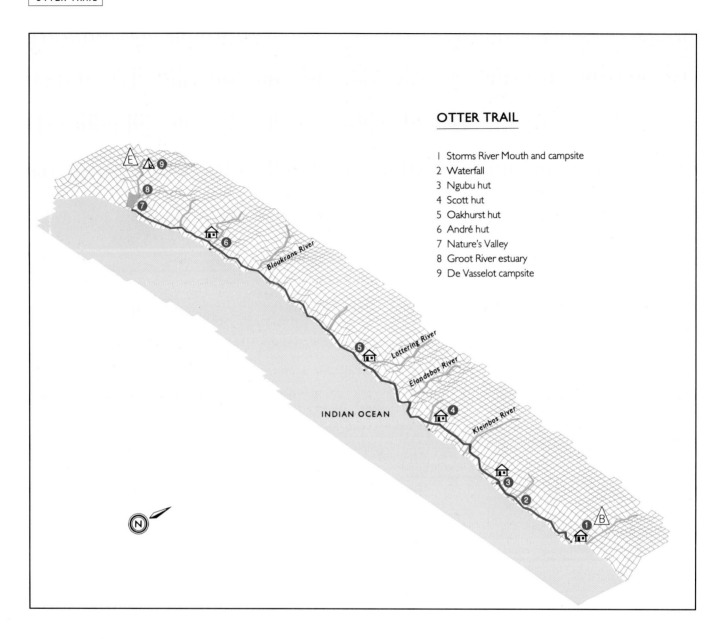

OTTER TRAIL

1 Storms River Mouth and campsite
2 Waterfall
3 Ngubu hut
4 Scott hut
5 Oakhurst hut
6 André hut
7 Nature's Valley
8 Groot River estuary
9 De Vasselot campsite

Bloukrans River

Lottering River

Elandsbos River

Kleinbos River

INDIAN OCEAN

DAY 5 ANDRÉ HUT TO NATURE'S VALLEY: 9 KM

Having watched those cliffs of Martiens se Bank in rich splendour the previous night, hikers now have the daunting task of ascending to the top of them. The route crosses the Klip River's shallow mouth and then climbs very steeply for 120 m to the terrace level. The path follows the cliff edge through open fynbos veld for about 2 km, affording views along the entire trail length. It then skirts the forest edge, executing a wide loop before deciding to commit itself to forest. Within the forest the trail crosses first a tributary and then the Helpmekaar

River, necessitating substantial cutbacks to clear their respective valleys. A deep gorge has to be avoided, the path making yet another cutback before regaining the cliff edge in open fynbos.

Our party named this section the 'misty cliffs' for it seems they are often enshrouded in billowing liquid lace and, here too, the views over Nature's Valley and the entire Tsitsikamma coastline are breathtaking. One gets the feeling that, should the mist clear, one would have a view clear across to New Zealand.

Before long the path reaches the tip of a headland overlooking Nature's Valley; this is the official end of the trail, but it is still another 3 km to the car park. The

path makes its way into a gully and down onto the deserted sandy beach east of the Groot River estuary. It is pleasant to swim on the inside of the headland's cliffs, before setting off once more to round the lagoon, bypass the village and reach the car park on the R102, further up the shore of the estuarine lagoon.

OPPOSITE At Roman's Bank the path hugs the cliffs that form the edge of a coastal plateau; this plateau terrace runs the entire length of the Garden Route between the sea and the coastal mountains. In the distance the outline of Robberg can just be made out.

THE TRAIL AT A GLANCE

STARTING POINT : Storm's River Mouth
FINISHING POINT : Nature's Valley
LENGTH : 41 km, plus 3 km to the car park at Nature's Valley
DURATION : Five days
GROUP LIMIT : 12 people
ROUTE : This is a linear trail which follows the notoriously rugged southern Cape coastline between the mouths of two large and well-known rivers. It falls entirely within the Tsitsikamma National Park.
HOW TO GET THERE : From the N2 a few kilometres west of the Paul Sauer Bridge that spans the Storm's River, a signposted and tarred road leads off to the national park and Storm's River Mouth (not the Storm's River Township).
BOOKING AUTHORITY : National Parks Board. Pretoria : P.O. Box 787, Pretoria, 0001; tel. (012) 343-1991.
Cape Town : P.O. Box 7400, Roggebaai, 8012; tel. (021) 22-2810.
ACCOMMODATION : Wooden chalets, two at each overnight spot, sleeping six each, with bunk beds and mattresses, chemical toilets and firewood.
CLIMATE : The park falls within the year-round rainfall area, with obvious consequences. Winters can be very cold and wet, while summers are mostly warm but also wet. Late summer is the driest season,

when water at the huts can become limited. The climate is classified as temperate, and the weather conditions can vary greatly within each season.
BEST TIME TO HIKE : All year, but October to April is usually best.
REFERENCES : National Hiking Way Board 1 : 50 000 map; colour booklet *The Otter Trail and Tsitsikamma Coastal National Park* by Patrick Wagner; field guides on the regional flora (Botanical Society) and intertidal life (National Parks Board).
TERRAIN : Rugged rocky coastline typical of the southern Cape coast, with high sea-facing cliffs, small coves and beaches, and deeply incised river valleys. The vegetation is mostly dry Afro-montane forest, with fynbos communities on the high-lying wave-cut terrace.
WHAT TO TAKE : Take diving gear, if only a pair of goggles and snorkel, to make the most of the park's abundant intertidal rock pools. Large, preferably collapsible water containers may be necessary in late summer when the huts' tanks run dry. Running shoes or light boots will be the best footwear for tackling this trail.
SPECIAL PRECAUTIONS : Check the water situation at each hut before setting out, especially from midsummer to autumn; you may have to carry water to some huts from the nearest river (remember to collect drinking water above the area of tidal flow).

Some streams indicated on the map as drinking spots may be dry. Since this is a linear trail, you will need to make transport arrangements between start and end points. If weather reports indicate rain, emergency procedures and escape routes should be checked with the park authorities before setting off.
TRAIL OPTIONS : From the rest camp at Storm's River, four shorter walks can be explored. The Mouth Trail is perhaps the most popular, past coves and through dry forest to a Strandloper cave and the suspension bridge over the Storm's River mouth. The 1 km Lourie Trail explores the moist, tall forest close to the campsite; if that small taste of mature temperate forest excites your senses, take the Blue Duiker Trail an extra 2 km into these enchanting woods. The Waterfall Trail gives day visitors an enticing glimpse of the Otter Trail's beauty, leading to a tumbling fall which surges into a deep and inviting pool. For those with aquatic leanings the Scuba Trail offers a unique trail experience: a two-star certificate is needed to explore the pristine sub-tidal wonderland (no scuba or air facilities available).
From De Vasselot (Nature's Valley) there are also a number of nature trails and day walks, or you could hike the first day of the Tsitsikamma trail, overnighting at Blaauwkrantz hut.

MOUNTAIN ZEBRA TRAIL

The Mountain Zebra National Park is situated in the Cape Midlands, in a transition vegetation zone between the Karoo shrublands and eastern grasslands. It was set aside in 1937 to prevent the Cape mountain zebra (*Equus zebra zebra*) from following its brother the quagga down the road to extinction. Only five stallions and one mare lived on the original expropriated farm and after one year a filly was born. By 1945 only two stallions remained, but some neighbouring farms still had small herds and 40 more zebra were driven into the park over the next few years. During this time more land was bought up for the park.

Today the reserve's carrying capacity is about 200 mountain zebras, but scientists believe that to ensure the long-term survival of the species they need to increase the park size to allow for a 500-strong herd. In the meantime, however, zebras have been translocated from here to the Karoo National Park near Beaufort West, Tsolwana Game Park in Ciskei, the Karoo Nature Reserve near Graaff Reinet and the Cape of Good Hope Nature Reserve at Cape Point to establish other breeding herds. Smaller populations also occur in the Gamka and Kammanassie mountain reserves.

Mountain zebra are smaller and stockier than Burchell's zebra, but the key to identifying them is in the pattern of their stripes. Firstly, the stripes over the spine, from the front of the pelvis to the base of the tail, form a characteristic grid-iron pattern, and secondly, the three upper stripes on the rump are very broad and have no shadow stripes between them.

Another animal that has thrived here is the mountain reedbuck, so much so that the species now has to be culled. Springbok, blesbok, black wildebeest, eland, red hartebeest and ostrich have been introduced to the park, while kudu have moved in from the surrounding farms of their own accord. Other small antelope occur naturally, as do numerous species of smaller carnivore. A breeding pair of booted eagle, one of about 40 migrant pairs that breed in the Eastern Cape, are the guests of honour in the park.

DAY 1 *REST CAMP TO OLIEN HUT : 9,2 KM*

From the caravan park follow the black and yellow zebra trail markings along a 4x4 track that ascends the slopes of Grootberg, a lesser prominence of the Bankberg range. Where the 4x4 track comes to an end the path crosses the Grootkloof River: the riverine bush here harbours an unexpectedly high diversity of passerines and other bird species, so hikers can spend some time engaged in the esoteric pursuit of 'twitching'. As intimated, most of the species are small warblers, larks and prinias, but there are also buffstreaked, stone and mountain chats, ground woodpeckers and red-throated wrynecks, bulbuls, Cape and

The Mountain Zebra National Park near Cradock was proclaimed in 1937 to protect some of the last remaining members of the species.

Karoo robins, southern boubous and common waxbills. Unlikely to be seen though is the secretive and rare Cape eagle owl, which rests up during the day in rocky nooks.

Along the river courses grow larger trees such as the karee (*Rhus lancea*) and sweet thorn (*Acacia karroo*), the most widespread tree in the country. The wild olive (*Olea europaea*), another plant ubiquitous in South Africa, is widely used in traditional medicine by indigenous people. Other plants of the river courses are the Karoo bluebush (*Diospyros lycioides*) and sagewood (*Buddleja salviifolia*), with its grey-green, furry lanceolate leaves, and long drooping branches.

Continuing in a south-westerly direction, the path passes a huge boulder, estimated to have a mass of approximately 6 000 tons. In March 1976 it broke loose from the hillside 200 m above and came tumbling down, carving a deep scar in its wake. From here the trail rises steadily up the Grootberg, to reach the ridge separating Grootkloof and Fonteinkloof. This vantage point overlooks Babylons Toren, farmstead of the original property from which the game reserve expanded. I cannot say for sure what other hikers will experience up here, where the view sweeps out across the broken Karoo landscape on all sides. Perhaps the sky will be glowing mother-of-pearl in early morning light, or maybe bleached pale by searing summer sunlight, or even tinged with purple as anvil-head thunder clouds rear up thousands of metres into the sky.

The path descends quite steeply into Fonteinkloof, meeting a 4x4 track and then crossing the river. During the drought years of the 1980s I visited the park twice, but never saw any river flowing in the park. It must be a pleasure to find this one gurgling with chilled mountain water. A steep climb out of the kloof leads onto a plateau, across which the trail follows the 4x4 track off to the right and down into Weltevredekloof.

And indeed it is with satisfaction that you will enjoy the secluded hospitality of Olien hut, named after the wild olives that proliferate in the gorge. On a hot day you might wish to take advantage of the swimming hole, which can be reached by taking the 4x4 track above the Weltevrede homestead that can be seen from the plateau above.

DAY 2 *OLIEN HUT TO KAREE HUT: 9,2 KM*

Almost immediately after setting off on the second day the path begins its longest ascent of the trail, rising about 400 m up the boulder-strewn slopes of the Bakenkop (1 957 m), the park's highest point. On some hikes a similar climb would not be of great consequence but here, in summer, it can be exhausting. These hills owe their existence to sills of dolerite, a type of volcanic intrusion so dense that it has been given the common name of 'iron rock'. Growing among the boulders are tall mountain cabbage trees (*Cussonia paniculata*) and smallish white stinkwoods (*Celtis africana*), known in the Karoo as camdeboo trees. Also found on these rocky slopes is the striped aloe, or blou-aalwyn (*Aloe striata*), a small member of this typically southern African genus.

On reaching the Bankberg plateau, buttressed by large dolerite domes, the vegetation is notably different from that of the valleys and slopes. These sour grasslands are dominated by coarse and bitter species such as lemon grass (*Merxmuellera disticha*) and turpentine grass (*Cymbopogon plurinodis*). The common, scratchy shrub scattered around the grasslands is the renosterbos (*Elytropappus rhinocerotis*), more commonly associated with the Cape fynbos flora. Other shrubs of the plateaux habitat are two types of taaibos (*Rhus* spp.), and the dogwood or blinkblaar bush (*Rhamnus prinoides*).

From the plateau the landscape draws the eye down across the distant Wilgeboom River valley, the park's central topographical feature. On summer days one can usually enjoy the spectacle of cumulo-nimbus thunderheads swelling angrily and bruising the sky. The tension is electric, in anticipation of a thunderstorm and the hope of precious rain. But most often the clouds merely taunt the parched land: thermals rising from the sun-scorched ground can be so strong that rain vaporizes before it hits the ground, only to be taken back up into the clouds whence it came.

On this exposed spot you might wish to make a pact with your god, or protecting spirits, against the force of the storm. But why not take a leaf out of the book of traditional medicine: various parts of the dogwood shrub are used as charms against lightning, a force considered by

many indigenous people to be the most mysterious and malevolent weapon of the spirit world's arsenal.

Winding eastwards across the plateau, the trail curves around to the north before taking a long, steep descent into Berghofkloof. On the descent some massive boulders are passed, one of which conjures up the rude image of gigantic buttocks. Also, attractive large clumps of coarse golden grass grow here;

unfortunately this is the alien and unpalatable nasella tussock grass, a species currently invading the eastern grasslands at an alarming rate.

As you near the hut a 4x4 track is followed for a short distance, before the trail branches off to the hut. The Karee hut is named after the attractive willow karee (*Rhus lancea*) that grows in the valley; it is a popular small garden and roadside tree of the interior of the country.

DAY 3 *KAREE HUT TO REST CAMP: 7,2 KM*

The third day's hike is really a stroll back to the rest camp over gentle, if stony, terrain. This area is a good one for spotting the fleet mountain reedbuck, especially if you make a quiet and early start (most of the larger game is to be found in the distant Rooiplaat area). The path follows a small tributary of the Wilgeboom River,

crosses a circular drive route, and then enters the main Wilgeboom River valley. After a second crossing of the gravel road, it negotiates the Weltevredekloof at about the 2,5 km mark and, 1,5 km further on, Witkruiskloof.

ABOVE Doornhoek farmstead, overlooking the dam of the same name, has been restored as a typical Cape farm home of the 1830s.

45

So far the trail has undulated gently downhill, but from Witkruiskloof it rises to skirt around rocky Rondekop, with Doornhoek Dam lying below and to the left. If you wish to spot waterbirds and large waders, you can meander off down to the dam to see herons, including the goliath species, egrets and reed cormorants, dabchicks and shelducks. If history is more your line of interest, visit the Doornhoek farmstead, a typical home of the 1830s that has been restored as a guest cottage. (This is the area in which the *Story of an African Farm* was set, and the family home of Olive Schreiner is preserved nearby.)

Leaving behind Rondekop the trail re-enters the Wilgeboom River valley to pass through the Fonteinkloof, which was crossed higher up on the first day of the trail. Soon the path veers away from the river, climbing gently for about 1 km before finally dropping down to the welcome greenery of the rest camp gardens.

BELOW The Cape mountain zebra has bred so well here in recent decades that it has now been reintroduced to several protected mountain areas in the province. *OPPOSITE* From Grootberg the rest camp can be seen below, while in the distance the Sneeuberg peaks slice the sky.

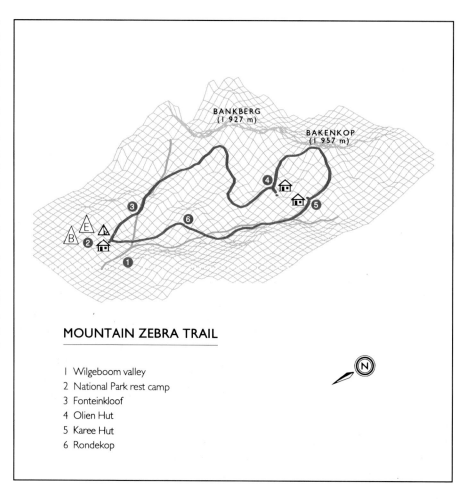

MOUNTAIN ZEBRA TRAIL

1 Wilgeboom valley
2 National Park rest camp
3 Fonteinkloof
4 Olien Hut
5 Karee Hut
6 Rondekop

THE TRAIL AT A GLANCE

STARTING POINT : Mountain Zebra National Park rest camp
FINISHING POINT : Mountain Zebra National Park rest camp
LENGTH : 25 km
DURATION : Three days
GROUP LIMIT : 12 people
ROUTE : The trail plan resembles the letter B in the south-east section of the park. The first day's route climbs steadily to the Olien hut, except for a sharp dip and rise to cross Fonteinkloof. On the second day the trail negotiates the Bankberg summit and then drops down to Karee hut. The last day is an easy and fairly level stroll back to the starting point at the rest camp.
HOW TO GET THERE : From Cradock take the Bethesda Road (R61) towards Middelburg. About 5 km out of Cradock a sign points to the park, 16 km away to the north-west.

BOOKING AUTHORITY : National Parks Board. Pretoria : P.O. Box 787, Pretoria, 0001; tel. (012) 343-1991.
Cape Town : P.O. Box 7400, Roggebaai, 8012; tel. (021) 22-2810.
ACCOMMODATION : Stone huts with bunk beds and firewood, chemical toilets, and showers when water is available. The rest camp has chalets and a camping-caravan park, as well as a small shop and restaurant.
CLIMATE : This area of the Cape Midlands is a true Karoo region, with a low average rainfall of 400 mm. Most rain falls in occasional and often violent summer thunderstorms. In late summer temperatures can reach up to 42 °C, with scorching winds. Winter days are mild to bitterly cold, with snow frequently blanketing the higher peaks and plateaux.
BEST TIME TO HIKE : Spring and autumn
REFERENCES : Sketch map in the trail brochure
TERRAIN : Stony paths over the stepped,

rocky landscape of the Bankberg mountains, through sparse Karoo and sour grassland vegetation. The park is situated on Beaufort Group rocks, the most extensive member of the Karoo Supergroup that covers about two-thirds of South Africa. The higher ground is composed of dolerite, an intrusive volcanic formation, while the low-lying areas are composed of shales.
WHAT TO TAKE : This depends very much on the season, as weather can be extreme. In summer it is essential to avoid sunburn and heat exhaustion. Lightweight boots should be worn but, since distances are short, running shoes are sufficient for the nimble-footed hiker.
SPECIAL PRECAUTIONS : Although the Wilgeboom River flows through the park, it is most common to find no water along the trail itself. Therefore, especially in summer, you should carry about two litres per person between huts.
TRAIL OPTIONS : None.

AMATOLA TRAIL

T his trail is situated in the Amatola range, one of the most magical mountain areas in southern Africa. The Hogsback hamlet (immortalized as the place that fired the imagination of a young J.R.R. Tolkien with visions of hobbits, dwarf lords and elfin kings of the Middle Earth kingdom) is perhaps the best known area of the Amatolas, and its surroundings provide a glimpse of what the trail has to offer.

What it does have to offer is a little bit of everything: whole days are spent in high climax Afro-montane forest; there are rolling mountain plateaux swathed in rich mountain fynbos and littered with wild flowers; countless rivers and streams, waterfalls and pools. There are isolated peaks and dark secretive gorges, open grassy glades and distant views across the Evelyn, Keiskamma, Wolf, Tyume and other lush river basins. If you do only one hiking trail in your life, then this should be the one.

It is not, however, an easy hike, with days as long as 22 km and averaging 17,5 km over the 105 km, six-day trail. But aside from the overwhelming natural environment, an aspect of the trail that makes it even more fascinating is that it was the focus of some decisive battles between British and Xhosa forces in the 100 years of the Frontier Wars. Much of the conflict between 1834 and the ninth and last war in 1878, during which time the military might of the Xhosa nation was broken, took place in and around these mountains. Amatole or Amathole (anglicized as 'Amatola') means 'place of many calves'; the meadows here were used as grazing lands by the Xhosa, and by Hottentots before them, from spring through the summer — and still are. I found that each day of the trail presented a different scenario of landscapes and events and I have named them accordingly.

DAY I THE DAY OF FAIRY FORESTS (MADEN DAM TO EVELYN VALLEY HUT : 15 KM)

The trail begins at the information kiosk just above the picnic site and parking area. After about 1 km the path passes some concrete foundations near the forest margin, all that is left of Howse's Mill. The mill is named after one J.E. Howse who in 1897 was granted the sole concession for lumbering in the Pirie Forest. (The forest itself was named after the Scottish Missionary Dr Alexander Pirie, who established several mission stations in the area when it was known as British Kaffraria.)

Howse built a timber chute and a 4 km-long railway line from Timber Square, in the forest, to the mill. The path climbs alongside the line of this railway, past the ruins of his trestle bridge over Hutchins Stream, to Timber Square. For his railway Howse cut sleepers from the wood of lemonwood (*Xymalos monospora*) and mountain hard pear (*Olinia emarginata*), which are among the most abundant hard woods of the Amatola forests. For his bridge he used coffeebean strychnos

Amatole, or amatola, means 'place of many calves', derived from these mountains' time-old usage by Khoi and Xhosa herders as a summer pasture.

49

(*Strychnos henningsii*), its heartwood heavy and durable, and thus favoured for fence posts and implement handles.

Frontier hunters and pioneers were drawn to the area immediately south of the Amatola range, first by the herds of game that concentrated there, and then by the well-watered valleys with their rich soils. The people who lived in the Keiskammahoek valley, at King William's Town and other frontier settlements made heavy demands on the mountains' forest resources until 1883 when demarcation began. In only seven years around the turn of the century nearly half a million cubic metres were taken from the Pirie Forest alone.

The Rharhabe Xhosa, first under the reign of Ngqika and later his son Sandile, resisted the encroachment of white settlers, and engaged in nine wars between 1779 and 1878. Sandile was born with a withered left leg and so seldom took part in fighting, but he was a shrewd tactician who pricked the British pride. In May 1878, pursued by colonial forces, Sandile hid in a large cave that can be visited on the Sandile Walk. A few days later he was captured by Mfengu mercenaries who, it is said, beheaded him.

But back in Timber Square, a sign points the way to go, which is upwards through indigenous forest for 5,5 km, rising to a height of 1 040 m at the plateau behind McNaughton's Krans. On the steepest parts, encountered after the second crossing of Hutchins Stream, and a little further on where the path finds its way behind McNaughton's Krans, the path executes what seems to be an endless progression of zigzags to gain height. Since a long trail lies ahead, your pack here will be heavy, and this climb will be a strenuous one. But the forest here is nothing short of exquisite and very much like those that are found in the proximity of Hogsback itself. A word of warning: you may not find water in the river during the drier months.

The canopy here is so high (reaching up to 30 m) and dense, that very little light filters down to the forest floor, with the result that there is little understorey growth. The spaciousness gives the woods a feeling that they might be inhabited. The massive, buttressed trunks of forest pears, lemonwoods and yellowwoods, the moss-carpeted floor all sprinkled with tiny, pale mauve *Streptocarpus*

flowers, and the columnar, arching trees must be some of the elements that gave Tolkien (who was born in Bloemfontein and spent his early boyhood holidays at Hogsback) his visions of another, more magical world.

Once on McNaughton's Plateau, at about the 10 km mark, there is a delightful resting spot, with log seats and wooden tables. Soon afterwards the trail meets a forestry track that is followed through pine plantation and natural forest for the last 5 km to the hut. Along this section there is the occasional break in the vegetation allowing views out across the Evelyn Valley. While walking this section we watched the cumulo-nimbus clouds building, swelling and bruising a deep purple in the distant sky, and braced ourselves for a whopping storm.

By the time we reached the hut, a charming old forester's quarters, the tops of the anvilhead clouds were bathed golden in the fading sunlight, and lightning and thunder pulsated in the twilight. However, this display proved to be only a dress rehearsal for what we were to experience later on the hike. Meanwhile, the forest, the two dams and the Evelyn Valley 600 m below slowly slipped into their quilted corduroy bed, the stars appearing like embers of a hunter's fire as dusk drew near. All the signs were right, foretelling of the unique adventure that lay before us.

DAY 2 DAY OF THE LONG WALK (EVELYN TO DONTSA HUT : 22 KM)

Before I proceed with a description of the day's walk let me explain why, perhaps, I was already so charged up with feelings of adventure. I lived in the Eastern Cape for some years, exploring much of this area and still, many years later, I feel a tightening in my stomach when I approach this old frontier land. It has something to do with the pervading sense of history and conflict in which my forebears played a small part. It also has something to do with this area's biological status as a 'tension zone', a meeting place of seven major vegetational ecosystems that advance and retreat around each other, the dance choreographed by an erratic rainfall pattern. At times it looks like English parkland, at others it resembles the desolate Karoo.

Most of all I'm fascinated by the region's enduring Africanness, where modern structures have not destroyed the inherent tribal customs or hastened the pace of time. Pale blue plumbago flourish along dusty roadsides, cattle and white-painted *abakhwetha* youths stroll the countryside: time seems suspended here while the world outside rushes on.

If the previous day was an arduous one, then day two is even more so; although the route on this section is never steep, it is still uphill virtually all the way. Deep in the forest there are no landmarks or views by which to orientate oneself, making the day seem even longer than it actually is.

I started off late and managed to reach the hut just as the last light melted away into the forest's murkiness. About 3 km before reaching the hut, with the last light of day creating fleeting penumbral images in the deep forest, I was startled to see a small group up ahead. Later they told me that they too had been alarmed, since incidents of hikers being accosted on trails were common at the time. The point is that the day is a long one, and even in midsummer it is wise to carry a torch for such eventualities. I certainly would not like to pick my way through the forest in what soon becomes a velvet-black night.

This is the habitat of the legendary, endemic giant earthworm (*Microchaetus* sp.). The largest recorded specimen was said to be a stunning 7 m long and had a girth of 8,5 cm; I have seen one about 1 m long, and that was long enough! Now nothing loves a good earthworm quite as much as a mole, and so it is not surprising to find that the forest also shelters a very special kind of rodent in the giant golden mole (*Chrysospalax trevelyani*), also endemic to the region. This mole is by far the largest of the golden moles found in Africa, reaching up to 23 cm in length. However, the chances of seeing one of these subterranean oddities, or anything other than the casts of the giant worms on which they feed, are slim.

What you will see on the forest floor, however, especially in summertime, are wildflowers such as the delicate *Streptocarpus* trumpets that are found along the damp stream banks in the shady forest, and clustered on the mossy banks alongside waterfalls, as well as white, yellow and blue wild iris (*Dietes iridoides*), whose

flowers last for only a day. Less pleasing, however, is the infestation of wattle (*Acacia mearnsii*). Birds likely to be seen in the tree canopy include the Knysna lourie, the more elusive narina trogon, and the mannequin coloured Cape parrot, a mostly green bird with red flashes on its forehead, chin and shoulders.

Among the many forest trees, most of which are difficult to identify for the simple reason that their leaves are out of range, a few stand out. Most South Africans with even a smattering of outdoor experience should be able to identify a yellowwood tree, since they are the largest as well as the most widespread of the temperate, evergreen species. The Amatola forests have a higher species count than the more southern forests, since they are influenced to some extent by the sub-tropical communities found in Transkei and Natal, as well as those to the south-west in the Knysna region. As one moves east and north from the Cape Peninsula (where the westernmost forests are found), the number of species increases, from about 125 species in the

Knysna forests, to about double that number here, and continues increasing as one approaches the equator.

Two species which are particularly common here, and among the easiest forest trees to identify, are the knobwood (*Zanthoxylum davyi*) and the lemonwood (*Xymalos monospora*) which, together with the coast coral tree, red beech and coffee pear, reaches its southernmost limit here. The lemonwood is often an untidy tree, the flaky bark exposing the yellow wood beneath with its conspicuous geometric patterns and whorls. It often forms extensive coppices and, with its heavy foliage, excludes other species; this is usually a sign of a degraded area, as is evident throughout this hike. The knobwood, with its chunky, knobbled armour, needs no introduction, and in the Dontsa area it appears to be ubiquitous.

After I had passed the Dontsa forest station, another old forester's residence, twilight began to enclose the dense woods. I made a point of travelling quietly, hoping to see some of the elusive inhabitants of the deep forest. My caution

was rewarded when in a small glade on the banks of a stream I came across a fully mature ram and ewe bushbuck, nibbling away at green shoots on the littered floor. We were about 20 m apart when we sensed each other's presence, and by stopping without too much commotion I managed not to startle them. With my heart thumping but my body still, we watched each other for at least a minute before the bushbuck turned to skip off into the darkness.

The Dontsa hut is a fairly rudimentary structure, with timber walls on three sides, a stone fireplace and a sloping roof. This to me is all a hiking shelter need be, but some people on the hike with me preferred the one at Zingcuka, about which we shall read further on. The hut is reached about 100 m over the Dontsa River, and about 300 m upstream of the Dontsa Falls. Directly below the

ABOVE The traditional dung-floored Xhosa huts at Cata glow in the dawn light. Behind them the dolerite Geju Peak sweeps up in a wide amphitheatre.

hut a weir and a pool are found along a stepped path, but take care here. Not long ago a hiker stepped over the weir to inspect the top of the falls – and that was the last thing he ever did. Rather take the path downstream to the bottom of the falls, which offers a short, steep but rewarding detour. I found the water in the rain tank to be fetid, which ruined a full mug of whisky, and thereafter took all my water from the river.

DAY 3 DAY OF THE STORM (DONTSA TO CATA HUTS : 17,5 KM)

Leaving the hut the path heads upriver along a 4x4 track, lined with wildflowers and their attendant butterflies. Soon the path leaves the track to enter the damp forest, but the butterflies are no less plentiful here. After about 2 km the path reaches one of the most regal waterfalls I have ever seen, tripping down the rocky steps in a train of diaphanous lace, surrounded by delicate ferns, glistening with spray, and bouquets of arum and fire lilies.

Only the most noble of butterflies are found here: the forest king charaxes and emperor swallowtails. The latter species is the largest butterfly found in South Africa, and this is the furthest south that it occurs. It can be recognized by its black-brown wings, with yellow dots, red and blue 'false eye' spots, and long tails on the hind wings. Although it likes to fly low down in open glades and along the margins of forest roads, it is usually too swift and skilful to be caught. Its host plants include knobwoods, the Cape chestnut, and cultivated citrus trees.

From the waterfall the path climbs steeply for a short way to reach an alpine meadow, and then dips down to a waterfall. If you pass this way in summer, look out for the fire lilies (*Cyrtanthus angustifolius*) which light up the cliffs on either side of the falls. Although the blooms are not all that large, the flame colour is most striking against the glossy green leaves and stems.

In South Africa only the Drakensberg and Amatola Mountains are distinguished by having an alpine vegetation zone. The Amatola's Afrikaans name – Winterberg – refers to their being snow-bound for part of every winter.

LEFT The Knysna lourie, a common but shy resident of the extensive forests that are encountered on the first, second and last days of the hike. In flight the brilliant crimson underwings easily give it away, but otherwise it is camouflaged as it scampers through the dense upper canopy. *ABOVE* Most of the colourful fungi found on the rotten forest tree trunks are members of the family Polyporaceae. They include the brilliant 'orange polypore', the banded, greyish 'turkey tail', the pinkish 'blushing bracket', and the 'horse's hoof bracket'.

Once again the path ascends to emerge on the level of the alpine meadows, where it remains for much of the rest of the day. The correct biological term for this vegetation zone is indeed 'alpine', being characterized by the fynbos-type heathlands, despite being far outside the actual mountain fynbos region of the Cape Folded Mountains. In reality it is the fynbos area that is the floristic oddity, for this type of vegetation is of tropical origin (as are the forests), existing as montane islands in a sea of grasslands and savanna.

As the climate has fluxed, so the woodlands and heathlands have ebbed and flowed up and down the highlands as rainfall has allowed. In East Africa these heathlands are found only on the highest, wettest places, such as on Kilimanjaro, Mount Kenya and in the Ruwenzoris. As one moves south the heaths are found at lower and lower altitudes, above 2 500 m in the Drakensberg and a little lower than that here. In the Western Cape, the climate is such that these so-called 'alpine' heaths are able to thrive at sea level, as well as on the highest mountains, where they have found environmental conditions just right to flourish.

From October through to March these meadows are aflush with wildflowers, such as delicate harebells, fire lilies, ixias, gladioluses, royal blue aristeas, and many others. But most characteristic of the heathlands perhaps are the everlastings, represented as a number of different species here. The local people call them *ipepa*, and believe them to contain the spirits of dead ancestors which can be consulted in times of crisis or celebration. The power of the everlastings is released by burning them to produce smoke, or by boiling them in water.

The most stunning of the everlastings is the golden guinea (*Helichrysum argyrophyllum*) that grows in dense clusters of up to a metre high and at least that again in diameter. The individual flowers are about the size and colour of a golden guinea, and together they form a dazzlingly bright display.

From these meadows the path begins a long climb up to Doonhill, past a trig beacon on Mount Thomas, and then zigzags steeply down a boulder-strewn, partly wooded slope to a forested basin.

Earlier in the day we had been buzzed a few times by a police helicopter flying low over the mountains, and we wondered what they were up to. Climbing Mount Thomas I pulled away from the rest of the group and then found a lone pine tree under which to lay down and rest. I dozed off, but the flies were incessant about my body and at one stage I sat up to swat at them, when a most amazing sight unfolded before me, as if I were watching a silent western movie.

A herd of cattle swarmed over a hill in the middle distance, chased by agitated herdboys and their dogs. Soon they were followed by three men on horseback who, I later surmised, were mounted police led by a local guide. As they drew close to the fleeing herd a shot was fired, followed by what appeared to be a general mêlée. Then the helicopter returned and, we were later to learn, lifted a wounded cattle rustler back to Queenstown, from where the herd had come. The cattle were rounded up, and all driven back over the hill down which I had first seen them racing.

Once all the excitement was over, I continued on my way. After a short descent into forested Eseka Valley a stream is reached, with a string of shallow pools leading down to a crossing. This is the best spot of the day for lunch and a swim. The path then climbs to join a forestry road, which undulates in and out of alternating patches of forest and plantation. Here I saw samango monkeys in the trees, while a sparrowhawk and a jackal buzzard flew overhead. At one point the road diverges, with the upper track leading through open fynbos to the huts, while the lower one goes by way of a steep forested slope and the Waterfalls Forest. I chose the upper road, but before long huge mushroom clouds, which for some time had been swelling over the Keiskamma valley below and above Geju Peak, began to take on an angry countenance.

I had not progressed more than 500 m when a telltale breeze began to rustle the restios, thunder started rumbling closer and closer, and lightning flashed in the suddenly dark sky. Within minutes a ferocious hail storm was unleashed upon me; the pecan-nut size stones were driving almost horizontally across the slope, and I had nothing but the low reeds to shelter me. With a light raincoat that was

all but useless, and with my pack on my head, I crouched for about 15 minutes, feeling like King Lear's fool lost in the storm, until the first lull.

I then shouldered my pack and made a dash for the huts which, I calculated, should have been about 1 km away at the base of Geju Peak. But I had not gone more than 100 m, with visibility down to about 8 m, when the next squall hit and I had to dive once more for cover in the prickly restios. After about another 15 minutes the large hail stones abated and I made a second attempt to reach the huts, which turned out to be less than 50 m away in a large basin. The huts consist of three rondavels and a thatched cooking boma with a fireplace. I set about in the post-storm rain, trying to rectify some of the damage before the others arrived – which they did over the next hour in various stages of shock and disarray.

The one person who had chosen to take the lower route via Waterfalls Forest very nearly drowned while trying to cross the swollen stream alongside the huts. He rescued his pack but lost some belongings as the river rushed him toward the edge of a waterfall. The rain stopped around sunset, as the huts and embracing hillside were bathed in a deep crimson light. When one hiker lyrically suggested that nature was God's symphony, another quipped that the angels obviously liked to play the cymbals and bass drum.

DAY 4 DAY OF WATERFALLS
(CATA TO MNYAMENI HUT : 14,4 KM)

The first half of the path follows the river upstream, past some inviting pools and then into a most refreshing wooded gorge. Drink deeply here, for beyond the gorge the climb is long and dry. The path emerges from the kloof very near to the uppermost source of the Keiskamma River. Here we were greeted by recently burned veld, bursting with wildflowers: gladiolii in yellow and green, pale blue and creamy brown, yellow-green pineapple flowers, watsonias and everlastings, pink ixias, and brown and yellow ground orchids.

Nearing the top of the climb one path forks off to follow the cliffline around to the left, while another follows a rocky ridge to crest a high shoulder. Just over

the shoulder some boulders and tall erica bushes provide shade that on hot days will be a most welcome respite. Before you stretches a wide, high plain, at the end of which Gaika's Kop stands like a defiant sentinel. Gaika was a chief who, during the early conflicts between Xhosa and British, had sided with the latter. At the Battle of Amalinde in 1818 a combined force under Chief Ndalmbe and the prophet Makana defeated Ndalmbe's nephew Gaika, who fled into the Amatolas and took refuge with his people and their cattle on the mountain that now bears his name.

The path sweeps down across the plain to a river, interrupted with a series of rapids, and continues to a viewsite which looks down into a massive cleft. The veld along this section is mainly tall sour mountain grasses pocked with isolated protea bushes. The path crosses a fence over a stile, and then slips down a steep slope into the gorge. Where the path reaches the river a small glade serves as an ideal lunch spot.

After lunch the path descends steeply to a lovely pool at the base of a waterfall. Standing on the edge of the pool the icy blast from the spray will almost knock you backwards. The path maintains its steep downward course, squeezing through a crack in a cliff so narrow that I had to take off my pack and push it through sideways. A second and third set of falls and pool are encountered, but soon you will stop counting them, as the path passes seven waterfalls in all. It seems incredible that such a gorge can exist in mountains that from above appear to be gently rolling among a few prominent peaks.

Every now and again the Hogsback peaks appear through gaps in the canopy, and eventually the path finds its way to the river bed where the gradient is a little less steep. For the next kilometre the path crisscrosses the river, where massive Cape holly trees (*Ilex mitis*) grow on the banks, their roots bathed in water. When the river is high these crossings become tricky, and without a stick you are likely to get dunked every so often. After dropping 800 m the path emerges onto a grassy knoll above the river, and less than 50 m ahead are the twin Mnyameni huts, built in basic traditional style but connected by a curved interleading passageway.

DAY 5 DAY OF POOLS (MNYAMENI TO ZINGCUKA HUT : 17,7 KM)

Most of the altitude lost in the previous day's spectacular descent must be regained in the first few kilometres of day five, but luckily this is climbed mostly in the cool embrace of a forested gorge behind the hut. Linger in the gorge's lower reaches, where you can enjoy the sensual wonders of the forest, listen to the songbirds, and use the exquisite light to experiment with your camera. Higher up the gorge splits and the path follows the right-hand branch, before making a short exit to pass through the left-hand one.

Here the trail emerges onto a high slope of the Hogsback; these are hills formed by steeply angled caps of iron-hard dolerite, the same rock that forms the characteristic Karoo koppies. The path circles around to the left below the cliffline, eventually finding its way into a shallow, funnel-shaped basin where a river rises. The path drops down to reach the river at a spot where it forms a few deep pools, alongside of which you may find cattle grazing. For the next 5 km the path follows the two main tributaries of the Wolf Valley, first tracing one downstream, then rounding a spur to follow the other upstream for a distance.

The fynbos along here is high and scratchy, and your legs will be frequently ambushed by sharp-thorned briar. The path passes pool after pool, each one seemingly more attractive than the previous one. At various times of the year different proteas will be in flower, most common of which is the 'suikerbossie' (Protea caffra), flowering from October to January. The other widespread protea of the eastern grasslands is (P. simplex), a low, thick-stemmed species with creamy-green to red bracts, that seems to flourish with regular burning.

The best pool for swimming is the last one encountered before the path begins its ascent to the top of a cliffline. After being enclosed in river gorges for most of the past two days the dramatic views over the Schwarze Forest, from which tall yellowwoods emerge all draped with old man's beard lichen, and across the Wolf River valley are most liberating. At the far end of the crag the path makes a sudden turn down to the left, to drop below the forest canopy and immerse itself in the Zingcuka Forest.

I am sure that by now one forest description is much the same as the one before, but in all my hiking days I have not come upon such an enchanting path, flanked by massive yellowwoods and lemonwoods, red and white pear trees, assegaai and ironwood trees, Cape plane and beech, forest bride bushes, qwar and white witch hazel trees. While I have given some clues as to how to identify lemonwoods, the rest of the list might seem daunting, and yet the key to identifying them is only a few steps away at Zingcuka hut.

The luxurious hut is set in a clearing of the high forest, and in the paved garden the various forest trees can be found, each one labelled. Again I was the first to arrive at the hut, and was able to discern among the many sounds the guttural call of louries, the high-pitched squawking of parrots, a woodpecker's creaking, like an unoiled handpump and, most rewarding of all, the melodious piping of a chorister robin which I was lucky to see in the thick undergrowth.

DAY 6 DAY OF RAIN AND CLOUD (ZINGCUKA HUT TO HOGSBACK : 16,5 KM)

After intermittent rain and sun the previous day, and heavy rain during the night, the sixth morning dawned misty and cold. The trail description promised it to be the most exciting section of the trail, through exquisite forest and up past two waterfalls, over the Hogsback peaks to Hogsback village. What impressed me most was a display in the hut showing the Redcoats on the open slopes, facing Xhosa impis high up on the forested cliffs during the Eighth Frontier war of 1850 to 1853. An arrow on an old picture of the battlefield points to where the British cannonfire was concentrated, labelled 'you are here'. The picture is a copy of a Thomas Baines painting, and above the second waterfall you can see the spot where he sat to paint the scene.

As Sandile succeeded his father Ngqika who died in 1829, so Sarhili, also known as Kreli, succeeded his father Hintsa in 1835. Then Harry Smith, as governor of the Cape, deposed Sandile as part of his ill-conceived plan to end the existing treaty system with the Xhosa. In 1878, Sandile and Sarhili combined forces for a last campaign against the British. They

attacked the fort at Kentani but were decimated by concentrated grapeshot fired by the British guns. This finally allowed the colonial government to annex the land of the Xhosa.

On the previous day I had looked out over the green Wolf and Tyume river valleys, thinking what a splendid place it must be for a child to grow up. Tom, who was on the trail at the same time as I, told me that he had grown up in the Tyume River valley that lies directly below the Hogsback. In the late 1960s, when white-owned land here was bought out to create the Ciskei homeland, he had to leave the small but prosperous farm that his father had nurtured, by planting gardens, trees and hedgerows, and always being careful not to overgraze the land.

Ten years later Tom went back to visit the old home, and found only broken-down walls where his bedroom had been. Another 10 years later he took his children to see their roots; this time he found only the pit of what had been a rain storage tank, dug into the bedrock beneath the house. Gone were the tall trees his father had planted, the veld was rudely overgrazed and eroded, and in the rain pit were the rusting remains of an abandoned blue Ford Prefect.

As my feet gobbled up the last few kilometres, I sang to myself as I anticipated tea and scones at Hogsback Inn. I recalled the haunting lines of the old Juluka song African Sky Blue: 'What will the future hold?' The Xhosa have been given back their land, in a manner of speaking; eventually Tom's Ford Prefect will rust away as his memories of it fade, and who knows what fate awaits the 'place of many calves' in the New South Africa? Through the rise and fall of numerous empires these mountains, their skirting forests and high alpine meadows remain, little changed from when mankind set its first tentative step on the African continent. And this primeval endurance is perhaps my most persistent memory of the trail.

OPPOSITE This unnamed waterfall, found about 2 km upstream of Dontsa hut, is one of countless falls to be seen on this most regal of all hiking trails.

AMATOLA TRAIL

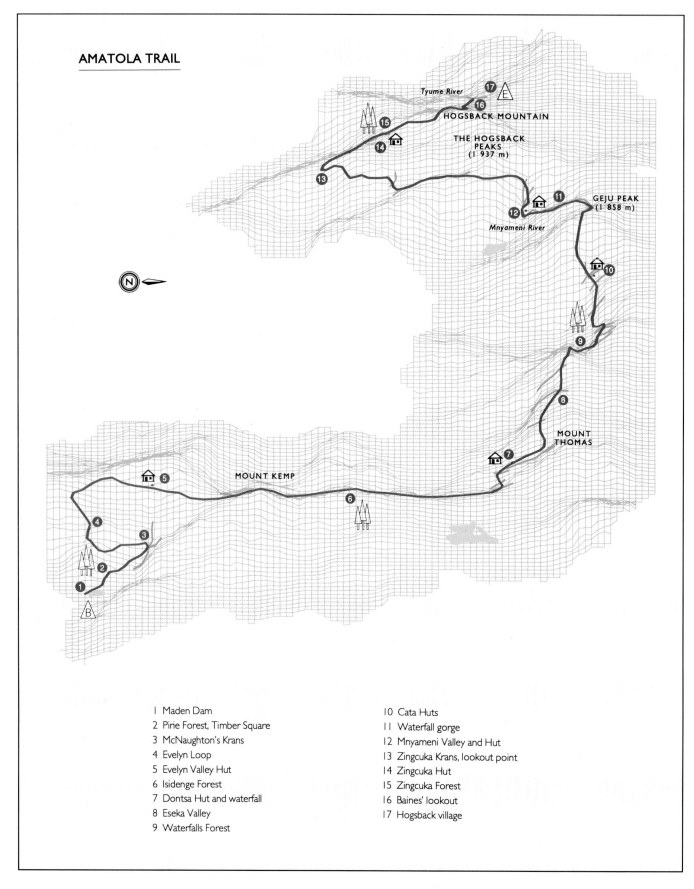

1 Maden Dam
2 Pirie Forest, Timber Square
3 McNaughton's Krans
4 Evelyn Loop
5 Evelyn Valley Hut
6 Isidenge Forest
7 Dontsa Hut and waterfall
8 Eseka Valley
9 Waterfalls Forest

10 Cata Huts
11 Waterfall gorge
12 Mnyameni Valley and Hut
13 Zingcuka Krans, lookout point
14 Zingcuka Hut
15 Zingcuka Forest
16 Baines' lookout
17 Hogsback village

On descending the western slope of Geju Peak, the flat crown of Gaika's Kop dominates the skyline, while the rolling plain is carpeted with heliopteris everlasting flowers.

THE TRAIL AT A GLANCE

STARTING POINT : Maden Dam, past Rooikrans Dam

FINISHING POINT : Hogsback village

LENGTH : 105 km

DURATION : Six days

GROUP LIMIT : 12 people

ROUTE : From Maden Dam, the trail ascends the forested mountain range, and then follows a serpentine, but basically linear route through the moutains, past the Evelyn Valley, Dontsa, Cata, Mnyameni and Zingcuka huts, to Hogsback village.

HOW TO GET THERE : From King William's Town, take the Alexander Road (R30) northwards towards Stutterheim. After 21 km turn left onto a gravel road, past Rooikrans Dam, to the picnic spot at Maden Dam, about 8 km from the turn-off.

BOOKING AUTHORITY : Ciskei Tourist Board, Contour, P.O. Box 186, Bisho, 5608; tel. (0401) 9-2171 or 95-2115.

ACCOMMODATION : Each of the five huts is different, and each one quite special. The first is the spacious old colonial forestry house at Evelyn Valley, while the hut at Dontsa is a rudimentary three-sided cabin. The Cata huts are traditional Xhosa rondavels, complete with dung floors, with those at Mnyameni being a more lavish variation on the traditional theme, but still with dung floor. Finally, the Zingcuka hut is the most extravagant of all hiking huts, with paved courtyard, donkey boiler for hot showers, solar-powered electric lights and flush toilets. Elsewhere toilets are of the chemical or longdrop variety, but very well maintained; firewood is provided at all huts.

CLIMATE : The trail falls within the summer rainfall area, with snowfalls on the high areas common in winter. Between December and early March the average daily maximum temperature is around 22 °C, dipping to 15 °C in June/July. The average daily minimum for the same periods are about 12 and 6 °C respectively. Monthly rainfall recorded at the Evelyn forest station peaks at just over 200 mm in March, and drops to around 50 mm in June/July. Mist and drizzle are common in the rainy season.

BEST TIME TO HIKE : Each season is special, but given the extent of cool forest and the abundance of water in summer, I would choose the period from October to early March, even though some days may be hot and humid. To experience these mountains under a blanket of winter snow and ice is an unrepeatable experience.

REFERENCES : Contour 1 : 50 000 Amatola, Pirie and Sandile Trail hiking map and brochure; *Ciskei Hiking Trails* booklet with fauna and flora checklists.

TERRAIN : Although composed mainly of (Karoo Supergroup) Beaufort Group shales, these mountains have a lot of similarities with the Natal Drakensberg. These two ranges are the only ones in southern Africa that share an Afro-alpine heathland vegetation on the upper peaks, ridges and plateaux, as well as sour grasslands and Afro-montane forests in greater or lesser proportions. The Amatolas are not nearly as rugged as the Drakensberg, but they are grand mountains reaching up to 1 880 m on the Geju Plateau. Paths are all well-constructed and marked, and although they are very steep in some places, for the most part the trail is undulating.

WHAT TO TAKE : The first thing to pack is your own toilet paper. You might wish to consider carrying trout fishing gear, once you have obtained the necessary licence through Contour. This is a long and strenuous trail, so whatever else you carry is up to you, but all year round do not forget a good raincoat, and something warm to wear. Candles or a small gas stove would be useful, as well as firelighters. For the scratchy fynbos, briar bushes and bush ticks, long socks or gaiters are recommended.

SPECIAL PRECAUTIONS : The most serious danger on the trail is fire: on dry winter days when berg winds blow, try not to smoke in the open, and be careful when making fires at the huts or for tea on the trail. There is a problem with poachers (usually with their dogs), so report anyone suspicious to the nearest forester, but do not try to apprehend anyone. After all, you are on traditional tribal land here that has for centuries supported the local people. Be prepared for sudden changes in the weather, and do not hesitate to take any one of the emergency exits if it turns bad, or to ask foresters for help. Despite being in forest all the way, there is very little water on the second day, so carry enough for your needs. In winter you should always carry water, as streams along the way may be dry.

TRAIL OPTIONS : At either end of the trail there are shorter, two-day trails, the circular Sandile, Pirie and Zingcuka walks, while hikers can enter and exit the trail at numerous points along the way. Depending on your available time you can book for any section, but parking is available only at Maden Dam, Dontsa, Cata and Zingcuka forest stations. The trail is linear so transport must be arranged back to the start. Taxis can be taken between most places, quite cheaply, but the road back to Maden Dam is a circuitous one.

WILD COAST TRAIL

hile the trail between the Mtamvuna River at Port Edward and Port St Johns offers some of the most spectacular coastal scenery in the country, the 10-day route is beyond the capacity of most hikers. The section south of Port St Johns is my personal favourite, where short walking days allow for extensive exploration. It also has some outstanding features, not least of which are the mangrove swamp forests at Mngazana, the Hluleka Nature Reserve, the hotels at the start, at Mngazi and at Coffee Bay, and the many secluded beaches along the way. Since routes taken by different parties may vary considerably, exact distances are not given for this trail description. However, they are all relatively short, the daily average being 12 km.

The vegetation of the entire Transkei coast is classified as coastal forest, although long-term habitation by farmers has led to the decimation of the woodlands, and most of the resulting grassland is kept in a cropped, park-like state through continuous burning and grazing. Small relict forest patches remain, the actual species composition varying considerably according to soil type. The three major forest communities are eastern coast-belt forest, dune forest and mangroves. The largest forests to be seen on this hike will be those covering Mount Sullivan, which flanks the mighty Mzimvubu River. All others are small and under threat of extinction.

Most of the wild animals and birds associated with the Wild Coast are confined to the larger forests, such as those at Mbotyi, Port St Johns, Cwebe and Dwesa. Small antelope, monkeys, bush pigs, small cats and tree dassies are the most common of the forest animals, while birds include Knysna lourie, woodhoopoe, southern boubou (shrike) and sombre bulbul. On the forest edges you are more likely to see trumpeter hornbills, fork-tailed drongos, rednecked francolin, blackeyed bulbuls, brownheaded king-fishers, spotted prinias, streakyheaded canaries and, most showy of all, paradise flycatchers. Near rivers there are fish eagles and various kingfishers, dikkops and other waders, while along the sandy beaches black oyster-catchers, cormorants, common terns and small waders are plentiful.

DAY 1 SILAKA BAY TO MNGAZANA

Although Silaka Bay is the official starting point you will first have to get there from Port St Johns. Take the tarred road south from Second Beach, which soon reverts to gravel and crosses a causeway over the Bulolu River. Follow the road up Mount Thesinger to the Silaka Nature Reserve, where you can leave your car. Check in at the ranger's house, and if you intend spending the night at the hut, find out whether it is open. The hut is found in a small wooded gorge in the reserve only about 1 km away.

Hole-in-the-Wall – early sailors called it *Penido das Fontes*, the rock of fountains; in Xhosa it is *esiKhaleni*, the place of sound, or 'Holy-in-hol' to the children.

Once at the hut you can take either the higher inland route, or follow the rocky beach to a small bay guarded by Sugarloaf Rock, a small island inhabited by cormorants. From here the trail climbs the steep grassy hill, studded with aloes which in winter point flaming fingers at the sky. This plant is *Aloe ferox*, the bitter or Cape aloe that is widely used in traditional medicine and as a kraal stockade.

Nearing the Mngazi River the path reaches a grove of river euphorbias (*Euphorbia triangularis*), a large spiky succulent tree that features strongly in local folklore. It is believed that this tree, when planted by the father of twins, will protect them from witchcraft. Throughout their mutual lives, the twins and the tree will influence one another's fate.

The Mngazi River, the 'river of blood', is reached about 6 km from Silaka. A very pleasant resort hotel is situated here, and the staff will be happy to serve you ice-cold beverages. A sandbar often chokes the river mouth, while at other times you will have to make an arrangement at the hotel to be ferried across. Having reached the other side it is another 3 km, either along the soft sandy beach or via an inland route, to Mngazana River, where the finest mangrove community on the Wild Coast is found. There are three mangrove tree species found in southern Africa, and this is one of only three places where white, black and red species are found together.

The trees of these odd forests root themselves into the mud of a river estuary's intertidal area, colonizing new ground as they proliferate. Unfortunately, in recent times southern Africa's mangrove communities have been dwindling, while those at Mngazana River are under threat of giving way to a harbour development; currently ski boats berth on jetties within the forest. Patience is needed to appreciate the complex web of life that occurs within the mangroves: tiny snails, colourful fiddler mud crabs and giant river crabs, mangrove kingfishers and sandpipers, mud skippers and the many fish found in tidal estuaries. The mangrove trees are totally dependent on tidal flow and silt, with bizarre-looking buttressed or aerial root systems adapted to their fluctuating environment. No other plants can tolerate the extremes of saline and fresh water, flood and drought of the constant tidal wash.

At Mngazana River you will need to alert the ferry, which operates by courtesy of the general store here. The hut is situated close to the mangrove community. You should have ample time to sit and meditate on the mangrove's dynamic interconnections, for meditate is what you will have to do to see the shy creatures emerge from their muddy tunnels.

DAY 2 MNGAZANA TO MPANDE BAY

The beach south of Mngazana River is a jumble of dolerite boulders, and hell to cross. Therefore the path to the Brazen Head headland goes by way of an inland route, leading across open grassland, cultivated fields and through small forest patches (although I have known hikers to brave the beach crossing). The wild seascapes to the left and tribal African scenes on the hills to the right are, to me, the very essence of the trail and the entire Wild Coast. It is perhaps one of South Africa's greatest charms that such traditional lifestyles co-exist with the machinations of industrialized cities.

The local name for Brazen Head is *Ndluzula*, derived from the crashing sound of angry waves bashing up against the dolerite cliffs. At Luhlango village the trail joins a 4x4 track bearing left, and follows it for a short way before heading off along a path to the right over the back slopes of Brazen Head. Descending the hill to the Ndluzula River the path enters a fine patch of coastal forest, where the peeling, greenish-grey bark of the forest corkwood or commiphora tree (*Commiphora woodii*) can be seen. After crossing the river you will have to ascend a steep hill, but are rewarded with views over the Sinangwana River and Mpande Bay, still 3 km away. On descending this hill the path follows a stream past a rocky section to the beach at the Sinangwana River mouth.

It is usually possible to wade across the river, after which a walk along the beach or an inland path leads to idyllic Mpande Bay. During my university days in the Eastern Cape I came to know virtually every nook and cranny of this coastline, and few places do I recall with more joy than Mpande, with its holiday cottages and its perfect beach. The hiking huts are a few hundred metres beyond the last cottage and a short way inland.

DAY 3 MPANDE TO HLULEKA NATURE RESERVE

From Mpande the trail heads inland along an old 4x4 track, to cross the Mtonga River. I am not sure whether the inland route has been chosen to avoid a rugged coastline with an impassable river mouth, or for variety, for I have never seen the river mouth. It is, however, interesting to pass villages such as Sikelweni near the Mnenu River which, under most conditions, is easily crossed. The trail continues from this river mouth along a beach for about 1,5 km to the Hluleka Nature Reserve boundary fence.

The trail turns inland here along the fenceline, to enter the reserve's northern gate, and then winds its way seaward to reach the hiking hut. The 'hut' here is actually an old stone building, being part of the manager's house, and far more aesthetic than the stilted wooden A-frame guest chalets. The hut is surrounded by a well-established colonial-style garden, which blends into the encircling forest. Both beach and landward side of the reserve should be explored, especially along the stream. The birdlife is prolific in this 770 ha reserve, which has been stocked with eland, impala, blesbok, wildebeest, red hartebeest and zebra, while bushpig, bushbuck, common duiker and blue duiker occur naturally.

Most interesting here are the forest birds, among which you might see the green coucal and Cape or brownnecked parrot. In their book *The Guide to Hiking Trails* the Oliviers suggest that crowned eagles might frequent the area, and although I have seen them at Mkambathi and Port St Johns, I suspect their presence here is at best tenuous. You might, however, glimpse some other uncommon to rare water-dependent species such as the finfoot, osprey and whitebacked night heron. In the open grazing areas you might see ground hornbills.

DAY 4 HLULEKA NATURE RESERVE TO NGCIBE HUT

From the hut the trail follows the main road to the park entrance and on to Hluleka village, where you might wish to visit the general store to buy soap bars, candles, tinned fish, plastic shoes, rope-like tobacco and stale bread. Leaving the

village the trail heads for the coast to reach Banana Bay, named after the wild banana plants (*Strelitzia nicolai*) that abound in the area. Unfortunately the fruits are inedible, consisting of a lobed, woody capsule, but the tree makes up for this by producing impressive displays of graceful white and blue crane flowers from July to December.

The path follows the coast to Strachan's Bay, apparently named after the first man to be made an honorary Xhosa, who built his dressed stone home in what is now the Hluleka Nature Reserve. Near here is where the British freighter *Forest Bank* caught fire and ran aground in 1958. All that can be seen of that unfortunate vessel is some rusting machinery washed up on the beach. From Strachan's Bay there is a choice of either a path to the left leading up a hill, or a more inland route into the Mtakatye River valley.

This river presents one of the most problematic crossings of the trail, espe-cially after heavy rains and at high tide. It is a deep estuary, where sharks may be a problem; therefore, the more inland route is suggested, to cross at a fordable place between 1,5 and 2 km from the mouth. The trail route returns to the beach and continues along it for some way before veering off into the low hills at the end of the beach. The high vantage point inland of Prelies Bay affords grand views over beach and sea, the river val-ley and its expansive estuary.

About 1,5 km after leaving the beach the path joins a gravel road to the tiny holiday hamlet of Lwandile. Here the river of the same name is easily crossed and, a little way further on, the Lwandi-lane or 'little Lwandile' River also forded. The path then rises steeply, before mak-ing an easy descent into the beautiful Ngcibe River Valley. The two small huts are tucked away on a stream bank, each affording impressive views of the magni-ficent coastline.

DAY 5 NGCIBE HUT TO COFFEE BAY

From the Ngcibe huts the trail runs par-allel to the coastline, keeping as close to the beach as possible, until reaching the Mdumbi River. The river mouth can be tricky to cross, and it is safer to wend one's way a little upstream until a safe crossing is found. The trail then returns to the beach to pass Tshani village, and shortly thereafter, the resort village and Anchorage Hotel – as wild a wind- and wave-whipped, salt-encrusted watering hole as ever there was.

From here it is about 2 km to the Mtata River mouth, site of another mangrove community. The river flows into a ser-pentine estuary, and presents the last major river crossing of the hike.

ABOVE One of the attractions of this region is that despite political and social upheaval, the rural lifestyle has changed little over the centuries.

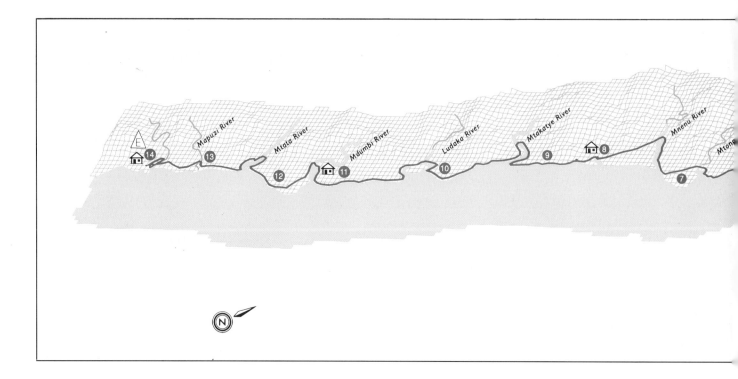

There are various claims as to how the Mtata River got its name, some references referring to the sneezewood (um-Thathi) trees that once grew in abundance near its banks. Others say it is derived from the verb *mthathe*, to take, the theory being that when in flood the river is the taker of life. If transient sand-bars do not provide an easy fording of the mouth, the unreliable ferry will have to be gambled upon, failing which an up-stream adventure is in the offing.

The coast from here to Coffee Bay becomes progressively rockier and more craggy; cliffs drop into the sea which makes the beach route impassable. A fisherman's track is followed for approximately 4 km, to reach the tarred main road to Coffee Bay. Having rounded the golf course on top of the flat headland just north of the resort, the road makes a steep final descent to the bay. In the wet season you should cross the causeway where the road enters 'town' near the general store; otherwise the Nenga River mouth is usually closed to the sea.

There are two hotels at Coffee Bay, plus a forestry campsite where the hikers' huts are situated. The bay was named after the coffee beans that washed ashore from a shipwreck in 1863. Today it is a holiday resort and popular weekend playground of Umtata residents.

While elsewhere the shoreline is exploited by indigenous people for food, the rock pools at Dwesa Nature Reserve remain in a near-natural state.

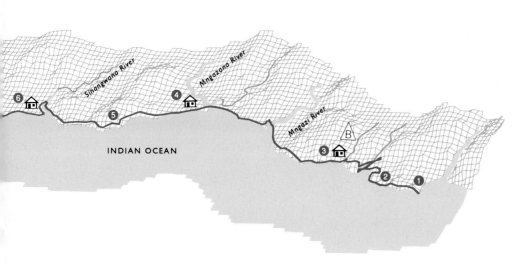

WILD COAST TRAIL

1 Port St Johns
2 Second Beach
3 Silaka Nature Reserve and Hut
4 Mngazana hut
5 Brazen Head
6 Mpande Hut
7 Rame Head
8 Hluleka Nature Reserve and Hut
9 Strachan's Bay
10 Prelies Bay
11 Ngcibe Hut
12 Umtata Mouth settlement
13 Mapuzi Point
14 Coffee Bay

THE TRAIL AT A GLANCE

STARTING POINT : Port St Johns, Silaka Bay
FINISHING POINT : Coffee Bay
LENGTH : 60 km
DURATION : Five days
GROUP LIMIT : 12 people
ROUTE : The route follows the Transkei coastline southwards from Port St Johns, with overnight huts at Mngazana, Mpande, Hluleka, Ngcibe and Coffee Bay.
HOW TO GET THERE : From Umtata take the road via Mlengena Pass to Port St Johns. This route is under construction and probably always will be. Alternatively, take the winding road from Brooks Nek on the Natal Border, through Flagstaff and Lusikisiki.
BOOKING AUTHORITY : Transkei Nature Conservation Section, Dept. of Agriculture and Nature Conservation, Private Bag X5002, Umtata; tel. (0471) 2-4322, or 24-9309.
ACCOMMODATION : Huts with bunk beds, firewood, limited water, refuse bins and toilets.
CLIMATE : The area is a typically sub-tropical, summer rainfall one, warm to hot in summer and cool in winter. Some rain may occur in autumn and spring, while winters are usually mild, unless swept by cold fronts.
BEST TIME TO HIKE : October to April

REFERENCES : 1 : 50 000 trail map available from booking office. A booklet guide to the Transkei coast and nature reserves, including information about the trail, has been written by Duncan Butchart and published by the Wildlife Society.
TERRAIN : From north to south the wild coast becomes progressively less rugged; the section north of Port St Johns rivals the Tsitsikamma coastline for ruggedness. Mostly the trail traverses grassy hillocks and bypasses rocky headlands, crossing some forested river valleys and following sandy beaches across river mouths.
WHAT TO TAKE : Since this is essentially a coastal outing, take your beach gear, including equipment for snorkelling in the gullies along the way. Carry chemicals to purify all the water you drink. This trail can be hiked in just about any footwear, but most popular are good running shoes. Well-padded soles are essential, while ankle support will be appreciated along the rocky stretches.
SPECIAL PRECAUTIONS : Although this is a wonderful trail, bear in mind that you are a guest in a strange land. Above all, respect the privacy and customs of the local people, and pay or barter for all services or purchases. Beware of theft and never leave anything unattended. There are heavy fines for

collecting firewood and camping outside the designated areas, as well as for illegally catching crayfish and possessing dagga. Since it is not advisable to drink from rivers, carry water every day and preferably boil it or chemically purify it before drinking. There are several obligatory river crossings, which should be forded on the low tide. There are ferries at some of the mouths, while others have sandbars or closed mouths which can be easily crossed. Open estuaries host sharks so it is better to cross upstream than to swim through deep water. If you do cross open water, always try to cross on an incoming tide: ideally you should carry a tide table in your pack.
TRAIL OPTIONS : I have chosen the middle of the three trail sections that constitute the incomparable Wild Coast Trail. The northernmost section begins at the Mtamvuna River on the Natal border, and ends in Port St Johns, with ten huts along the 100 km route; this is the most dramatic and remote part of the coast. The southernmost section from Coffee Bay down to the Mbashe River mouth can be hiked in four days. From there you are free to hike all the way to the Kei River and, although no facilities are available along the way, you can stay at the various small hotels or camp under the stars.

UMFOLOZI WILDERNESS TRAIL

No book claiming to cover the best hikes in South Africa would be complete without at least one game trail – even if this type falls outside the strict definition of a hiking trail. At a time when guided trails are becoming popular in South Africa's game reserves, Umfolozi was the natural choice, since it was here that Ian Player pioneered the concept of wilderness trails back in 1958. This is probably the wildest, most natural Bushveld environment in the country, where all the big game is found, yet unlike private parks and even the Kruger National Park, trail fees at all Natal Parks Board reserves are still reasonable and not aimed at the international tourist market. It is also easier to get bookings here.

The Umfolozi Game Reserve is one of the oldest game reserves in the country, and indeed in the world. This area, at the confluence of the White and Black Umfolozi rivers, and nearby Hluhluwe, were part of the royal Zulu hunting grounds, both later preserved by the British Colonial authorities in 1897. It was this region that saw the rise of the Zulu nation, and the concurrent subjugation of the other Nguni clans in northern Natal. The reserve covers nearly 50 000 ha, the southern half of which has been set aside exclusively for wilderness trails. It was predominantly here, as well as in Hluhluwe, that the squarelipped (white) rhino was saved from extinction through an aggressive breeding programme. There is little chance of not seeing both species while on trail.

You should also see buffalo, lion, zebra and giraffe, nyala and kudu, wildebeest, numerous antelope and birds, birds, birds. The vegetation is typically wooded savanna or Bushveld, dominated by tamboti and to a lesser extent acacia trees. All three bush camps are sited along the White Umfolozi River, in riverine bush. In years past the river banks were shaded by massive wild fig and fever trees, but these were ripped out by the devastating floods resulting from Cyclone Demoina in 1984 and the floods in 1987.

DAY I *MNDINDINI TO NGILANDI*

You should enter the reserve not later than 15h30 on the evening before the trail begins, reporting first to the superintendent at Masinda camp, who will direct you to Mndindini. Here dinner will be provided, usually venison or other culled game meat, as you sit around a fire looking out over the Mfolozi Emhlope (White Umfolozi River). Catering on these trails is no meagre affair: a cook and camp attendant take the donkeys between camps, setting up before you arrive. On the first night a three-course meal prepares you for the sumptuous time ahead.

Trailists gaze out over the White Umfolozi River floodplain. The devastating floods that followed Cyclone Demoina in 1984 ripped out the wild fig trees that used to grace the river banks.

The first morning begins with trailists packing their personal effects into duffel bags, which are then loaded onto the pack animals. Water and a picnic lunch are distributed between the hikers, who set off with the trail officer and game guard, following a wide loop that the river makes to the north.

Moving uphill and away from the river, you are likely to enter a thicket of tamboti trees (*Spirostachys africana*). This is one of the 'jumping bean' species, their seed pods often becoming infested with moth larvae, which flex their bodies and cause the pods to spring a few centimetres. The tree's most significant feature is the very poisonous milky sap, which can cause all manner of ailments. It is used as a fish and arrow tip poison by indigenous people, although it does also have medicinal properties. Van Wyk, who produced the definitive tree guide to the Kruger National Park, tells of a ranger there who developed severe toothache while on patrol. An African ranger with him put a drop of tamboti sap into the tooth cavity, and after a moment of intense pain the root was deadened. The wood is extremely hard and virtually indestructible: pieces in good condition were found in the Zimbabwe Ruins and dated at about 1 500 years old. Neither termites nor borers attack the trunks, but porcupines love to strip the bark off saplings to eat the soft wood beneath.

Despite what many foreign tourists expect when they first come to Africa, game is never to be seen on demand. It is possible to walk for days in the bush and see little other than insects and birds. It depends on many things, such as how much noise you make, the clothes you wear, your stealth and tracking abilities, as well as game movements. To avoid disappointment, it is usual on wilderness trails to spend the first day learning to look more closely at the veld, rather than just going after big and furry animals. Examining and discussing the many properties and uses of the tamboti tree will take time, as will identifying the different spoor you come across.

The highlight on my first day was reaching a rocky ledge projecting high above the river, with a wide sweep of the valley before us. We watched a pair of raptors, possibly African goshawks, gliding above the tree tops, and looked down on herds of antelope grazing among the

woodlands. We then descended to the river and waded across a series of sandbars to Ngilandi. The camp's name is a Zulu corruption of the colonial motherland – England – because you have to cross the water to get there. The camp is set in a golden grove of tamboti trees, the large canvas tents placed in a semi-circle around the enchanting fireplace.

DAY 2 *NGILANDI TO ENQABANENI*

On the second day, after a glorious English breakfast well befitting the camp's name, you are more attuned to the bush, so now is a good time to find animals, as we did. First we discovered lion spoor on the river bank, which we followed into a forest dominated by jacket-plum trees (*Pappea capensis*), also called the indaba tree. Beneath these trees is a good place to 'indaba' since the fruits are edible and they make an intoxicating drink. The lions seemed ready for a lazy indaba too: we almost walked right into a sleeping family group, which headed off into the dense woods. We followed, guide Andrew with his rifle cocked... a commotion in the bush next to us and a warthog came within millimetres of becoming our supper. The lion pride, with two subadult males as well as cubs, eventually gave us the slip but left our bodies pumping adrenalin.

A tree, or more often a bush, that you will encounter on this day's outing is the buffalo-thorn, or shiny-leafed wag-'n-bietjie (*Ziziphus mucronata*). This tree is credited with special powers, its various parts being used as a remedy for almost any pain, against boils, lumbago, dysentery and chest complaints. The tree is believed to be immune from lightning and legend has it that if one is cut after the first rains, drought will ensue. Then there is *uGobendlovu* – the tree that even an elephant can't bend. This is the African mangosteen or red ivory tree (*Garcinia livingstonei*), well known for its edible, tart fruit. Parts of the tree are used as an aphrodisiac and its Zulu name reflects its symbolism as one of male virility. The tree is believed to have antibiotic properties, but this use in traditional medicine has not been recorded.

On the way to camp that evening we spotted a herd of white rhino in our path, with the wind luckily in our favour. This

allowed us to approach within less than 70 m before they showed any alarm. One brute had a horn at least a metre long. When we crept closer, they began to shuffle nervously. At about 50 m they made the typical defensive circle, the low light making them all the more nervous. Then they charged with alarming speed and force, many tons of thundering pachyderm coming within metres of us as we cowered behind an insignificant bush, those deadly horns slashing back and forth at the unidentified transgressors. I had in the past been charged by black rhino in the Kruger Park and by elephant in Moremi, when I was a direct target. But in this exciting encounter, in the last golden light of day, I felt safe. It made me reconsider Ian Player's claim that, unlike its hooklipped cousin, it is only confusion resulting from poor eyesight that will drive a white rhino to trample or gore a human.

DAY 3 *ENQABANENI TO DADETHU*

On day three you are likely to leave the river valley for higher ground near the reserve's southern boundary. The veld will be drier as you climb the rounded dolerite hills to find, hopefully, water-filled pans which draw the game out of the surrounding bush. Trees here are less plentiful but also more varied: there are knobwood acacias, bushwillows (*Combretum* sp.) with their familiar winged pods, boer-bean trees (*Schotia* sp.) that flower in a spray of crimson blooms, and wild pear trees (*Dombeya rotundifolia*) with blooms resembling white confetti. Again you will encounter buffalo-thorn trees and the *uGobendlovu* tree.

With the varied soil types of the hills and slopes giving rise to this sprinkling of plant types, birdlife here is abundant. We saw whitebacked vultures, martial eagles, bateleurs and brown- and black-breasted snake eagles in the skies, while yellowbilled apalises, tchagras, wood-hoopoes, whitehelmeted shrikes, blue waxbills and bronze mannikins were some of the more visible birds in the bush. On less stony, open ground grow those trees whose fruits are so highly valued by man and beast – the marula. This is also the furthest south that the tall, flat-flowered *Aloe marlothii* is found, named after the famous Victorian scientist, natu-

LEFT A waterbuck grazes on tall, sweet red grass. As their name suggests, these large antelope are never found far from water, and so hikers are quite likely to spot them. *BELOW* One of Africa's greatest conservation success stories is that of how the white, or squarelipped, rhino was saved from extinction in the Umfolozi and nearby Hluhluwe game reserves.

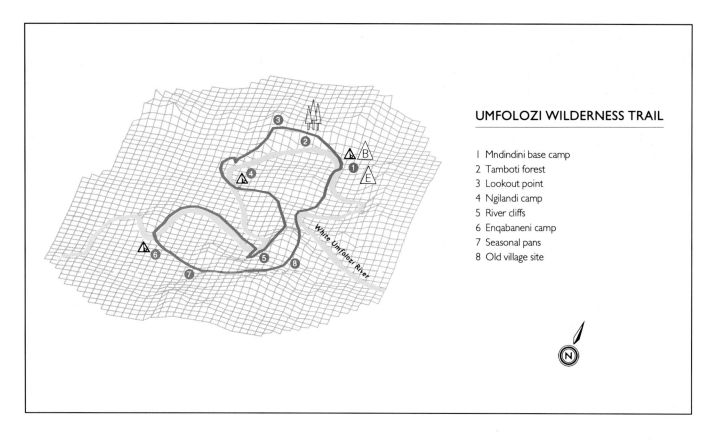

UMFOLOZI WILDERNESS TRAIL

1 Mndindini base camp
2 Tamboti forest
3 Lookout point
4 Ngilandi camp
5 River cliffs
6 Enqabaneni camp
7 Seasonal pans
8 Old village site

ralist and mountaineer Rudolph Marloth.

Depending on which route is chosen, it is likely that at least one river crossing will be undertaken. For most of the year the river is seldom more than knee-deep, since upriver erosion causes this potentially great river to silt up. But even at this depth small crocodiles may be encountered. Despite a fearsome image and a reputation for being man-eaters, crocs are shy creatures that, unless hungry, would rather make a hasty departure than be caught in the open. As you return to camp in the evening, be on the lookout for buffalo, which push their way through the reedbanks to drink at the river. They are, however, skittish creatures and you are unlikely to get close to them.

DAY 4 *ENQABANENI TO MNDINDINI*

This section of the hike is through low-lying thorn bush, habitat of the black or hooklipped rhino. These animals have a reputation for being more aggressive than the squarelipped, grazing species, although their preferred browsing habitat may have something to do with their

behaviour. The trail officer will almost certainly take the party to a group of small pans, in search of rhino and any other game that is in the area.

If game is less than plentiful, you should at least see some of the raptors that inhabit the area. At one pan you may see a squat, thickly branched tree with a rounded canopy and notably light coloured trunk. This is the shepherd's tree (*Boscia albitrunca*). Although widespread in the more fertile eastern woodlands of southern Africa, it is only in the drier west that its reputation as the 'tree of life' is significant. The small, clustered leaves are greatly favoured by browsing game and livestock, while the hollowed trunks of old trees are a source of water in dry times. The roots and leaves are used for a variety of food, medicinal and magical purposes, and some indigenous people hold the tree in such high regard that they forbid its destruction.

You may also visit Dengezi, the 'place of pot shards'. Although you are unlikely to find any of these shards, you may well come across abandoned grindstones, rounded grinding rocks, hollowed out grain pits, the remnants of iron ore smelting ovens and old Zulu graves. Before

Shaka arose as a mighty warlord, there was a peaceful village here. But during his rise to claim sovereignty over all Zululand, his impis fought a decisive battle here in 1819 against another Nguni clan, the Ndwandwe clan of Chief Zwide. The Ndwandwe had earlier defeated Dingaswayo's Mthethwa forces, killing the chief. Shaka, a member of the minor Zulu clan who had risen to become commanding general under Dingaswayo, assumed control of the Mthethwa clan. He then used this powerful base to subjugate the other clans of northern Natal, elevating the Zulus to the royal household. And this, just before crossing the river back to Mndindini, is a fitting conclusion to a king among wilderness trails.

OPPOSITE Trailists carry their shoes across the White Umfolozi River to reach the bush camp at Ngilandi, a Zulu corruption of 'England' since one has to cross the water to get there.

THE TRAIL AT A GLANCE

STARTING POINT : Mndindini base camp
FINISHING POINT : Mndindini base camp
LENGTH : Variable. Distances are not demanding, but you will be far too absorbed to even notice such mundane things – few experiences concentrate the mind more than tracking lion in dense bush or being charged by a herd of rhino.
DURATION : Three or four days
GROUP LIMIT : Eight people
ROUTE : From Mndindini the trails officer will choose a route to Ngilandi, Enqabaneni and Dadethu tented bush camps, and then back to Mndindini, depending on the party and local conditions.
HOW TO GET THERE : Take the N2 northwards from Durban for about 270 km, and 3 km past the turn-off to Mtubatuba (the nearest town) turn left along the signposted road to Nongoma and Umfolozi (R618). Carry on for 24 km, past the Somkele trading post, and take the signposted turn-off to the reserve gate, 5 km further on.
BOOKING AUTHORITY : Natal Parks Board, P.O. Box 662, Pietermaritzburg, 3200; tel. (0331) 47-1981.

ACCOMMODATION : Fixed tents with mattresses, sheets and blankets; bucket showers and 'spade patrol' toilets. All meals are provided, prepared in the best colonial safari fashion so all you need to take are your own personal effects. All equipment is carried between camps by pack donkeys, which frequently fall prey to lions.
CLIMATE : This is tropical Africa, blazingly hot in summer and warm to cool in winter. As wilderness trails are run here only between March and November, the worst of summer is avoided.
BEST TIME TO HIKE : This varies greatly according to recent rainfall and state of the vegetation, but March-April and October-November are usually best.
REFERENCES : There is only a 'wilderness trails' booklet available from the Natal Parks Board, but numerous other general texts can be used (see references).
TERRAIN : The lie of the land here is hilly, wooded savanna, but not too rugged. Mostly the guide will stick to game paths where the going is easy.
WHAT TO TAKE : Light hiking boots should be considered essential, if only for protection against nasties, of which are plenty.

Your clothing should be light, comfortable, and dull coloured, and you should pack a light raincoat or windbreaker. Gaiters are useful for thick grass and bush. Binoculars, camera, and a bird book are virtually compulsory. Fridges are available at base camp, and ice at the overnight camps, so take along whatever drinks you fancy, especially considering you don't have to carry them.
SPECIAL PRECAUTIONS : This is a malaria area so precautions are recommended. However, since trails are suspended in the epidemic months, you can use your discretion here. Pepper ticks are, however, always epidemic and you will need an insect repellent to keep them off your legs. An antiseptic or antihistamine lotion and plasters are recommended for your toiletry kit, as is a sunscreen.
TRAIL OPTIONS : There is a guided primitive trail option here, where trailists carry all their own equipment. Although food is provided, it must be carried and prepared by trailists, who sleep out in the open (party members keeping night watch). There are also guided wilderness trails in the St Lucia and Mkuzi game reserves.

MZIKI TRAIL

*I*n 1977 the Eastern Shores Nature Reserve was established on land previously controlled by Forestry. It now forms part of the St Lucia complex, the core of which was established in 1897, making it the oldest game reserve in Africa, along with Hluhluwe and Umfolozi.

The Mziki Trail is fairly relaxing as hiking trails go, with the individual hikes being easy and the same luxurious base hut used each night (and yet some people still write in the visitor's book that there should be fridges, transport to the hut and so on – they should stay at home and watch TV, or content themselves reading this book). This is a naturalist's outing, rather than a physical challenge, passing as it does through so many intriguing habitats: dune forest, Umdoni parkland, swamp forest, pine plantation, sandy and rocky beaches.

The trail has been given the Zulu name for reedbuck, since the largest population in South Africa is found in the Eastern Shores reserve. Such has been their breeding success here that first cheetah were introduced to control their numbers, and then culling and relocation programmes commenced when the cheetah failed to live up to their job demands. The St Lucia estuary also has the country's largest populations of hippo and crocodiles, and probably sharks as well should anyone care to count them. The complex is the country's southernmost tropical habitat, hosting 367 species of bird, some 120 marine species including stingray, swordfish and four types of shark, and six types of freshwater fish. There are 37 different amphibians, 61 reptile species including the deadly gaboon adder and seasnake, as well as loggerhead and leatherback turtles that breed along the northern Zululand coast.

DAY I NORTH COAST LOOP : 18 KM

From Mount Tabor this trail takes the 4x4 track out to the north, along the dune ridge between the Indian Ocean to the right and Lake St Lucia to the left. The trail is marked with very visible yellow reedbuck hoofprints on a green background, with each consecutive marker visible ahead. Descending the ridge the trail leads down into Bokkie Valley, a grass-covered valley between dune ridges. Originally the dense bush here was cleared by indigenous inhabitants to open up areas for stock grazing and to make charcoal for iron smelting. The valley's name comes from the fact that the reserve's highest concentration of reedbuck is found here.

These medium-size antelope rely on camouflage for protection, so that if you walk quietly you might virtually step on them before they rush off with white tail flags flying. If you have a camera you should keep it at the ready for just such an occasion, especially since the animal is likely to stop about 50 m further on to look back at you. The succession of long grassy valleys here are fringed with

St Lucia, South Africa's largest, richest, and in many ways most threatened estuary. The trail lies to the north of the Umfolozi River's double mouth.

73

bush, making up the 'parkland' component of the Umdoni parkland habitat. Umdoni is the Zulu name for the waterberry tree (*Syzygium cordatum*), a common, medium to large evergreen tree, with edible, black olive-like berries.

The most conspicuous tree here is the common coral tree (*Erythrina lysistemon*), especially when the scarlet flowers appear in spring, attracting insects and the birds that feed on them, such as square-tailed drongos and little bee-eaters, as well as sunbirds and starlings. In the grasslands you are likely to see, or at least hear, the croaking cisticola, Rudd's apalis (a special sighting for the area) and yellowthroated longclaw. Marula trees (*Sclerocarya caffra*) and the mangosteen (*Garcinia livingstonei*) are also common.

From the Umdoni parklands the trail enters the dune forest habitat, which encloses it for the next 4 km. These dune forests, a very endangered habitat, have the distinction of being the tallest and most elevated of such forests in the world. The dominant trees of this habitat are the white milkwood (*Sideroxylon inerme*), water iron-plum (*Drypetes arguta*), wild banana (*Strelitzia* sp.), green-flower tree (*Peddiea africana*), and that heavily spiked climber, the thorny rope (*Dalbergia armata*).

The dune forests are home to one of the deadliest snakes in the world, the gaboon adder (*Bitis gabonica*). Its poison is cytotoxic, like that of the puffadder, but is produced in much larger quantities – five to seven times more than is needed to kill a human. Despite its horrifying reputation it is a most attractive snake, with geometric patterns of pastel purples and browns along its back. This coloration imparts excellent camouflage as the snake lies amongst the leaf litter on the forest floor, waiting in ambush for large rodents, other reptiles or ground birds. It is a protected species in Natal.

This is also the habitat of birds such as crowned hornbills, Knysna and purple-crested louries, as well as fish eagles which use the elevated tree tops of the dune forests for roosting and, one assumes, for nesting. Bushpig, vervet and samango monkeys, leopard, mongoose and red duiker are also found. (The blue duiker is found in similar habitat south of the Umfolozi River, the presence of either species precluding the occurrence of the more widespread common duiker,

while the tiny suni is found in the False Bay part of the complex.)

Where the trail emerges into small open glades you might be surprised to see various plants commonly associated with the Cape fynbos flora: the blombos or *Metalasia*, passerina and lobelia, vygies and the water blossom pea (*Podalyria calyptrata*). At about the 9 km mark the trail descends the steep seaward dune slope to the narrow beach. Hopefully you will have collected a tide table from the trails officer, and consulted it for the best time to do the walk, for trying to negotiate the beach at high tide will provide a tale for you to tell around many a camp fire. Long stretches of alternately sandy and rocky shore offer hours of fossicking and tidal pool gazing. Although the sea here is usually rough and dangerous, there are numerous rock pools and inlets ideal for a quick dip.

The last part of the beach walk is the most interesting, with two craggy headlands standing like book ends at either end of a wide beach. This is a safe place to swim and to watch ghost crabs in the late afternoon. From here the path ascends the steep dune face, within a forest canopy, and then joins a 4x4 track where it emerges from the forest. The track seems to lead ever upward, through forest and plantation, curving in a wide back-to-front 'S' to reach Mount Tabor.

DAY 2 SOUTH COAST LOOP TRAIL: 10 KM

As a personal opinion, I found this to be the least satisfying of the three walks, the trail passing through pine plantation for most of the first half of its length. The trail is marked with occasional numbered spoor plates, these referring to places of interest. Look out for number 7, and weep: the concrete beacon marks a prospecting site. Against the spirit of the reserve, prospecting for minerals has been undertaken by numerous mining concerns. Among the minerals found is titanium oxide, used in paints and strategic weapons.

Mount Tabor and the surrounding forest-cloaked coastal dunes is where the Richard's Bay Mining Company wishes to open its controversial mining operation. The mining of coastal dunes is easy – you simply scoop them away and filter

out the minerals you want. Then you pile the processed sand behind you and move on, gobbling up the dunes. There are arguments for and against the mining, but from a conservation point of view it is no more acceptable than strip-mining the Kruger National Park for coal.

Trail number two heads directly south from Mount Tabor, back towards the outpost and on past it into the plantations beyond. There is a four-way trail junction in the forest on the way to the outpost, but when I was there it required only common sense to see that the direction markers for the second and third hikes had been transposed. It is quite common to come upon reedbuck feeding along the forest and plantation margins, before they vanish into the dense undergrowth. The attractive African dogrose (*Xylotheca kraussiana*) is one of a few plants that can tolerate the unnaturally high acidic soils under the pines.

After crossing the road to Mission Rocks, the path enters a stand of old pine, where the fern *Stenochlaena tenuifolia* creates an unexpectedly lush carpet beneath the columnar trees. After about 4,5 km the path leaves the plantation, where spreading acacia trees provide cover for a now disused picnic spot. It is then a short downhill trot (for the path is steep) to the beach at Rangers Rocks. The beach northwards to Mission Rocks is mostly rocky, with some coves that enclose steep beaches, or pebble and boulder-strewn stretches. Again, ensure that you tackle this section at low tide, for the sea in places comes right up to the densely vegetated, steep dune faces.

The next major outcrop of rocks is encountered at Perriers Rocks, which would make a wonderfully secluded rest spot, but for the fishermen who litter the place with their garbage. Also, the cove beach alongside is littered with flotsam and jetsam. Carrying on towards Mission Rocks, another popular fishing spot, the shoreline consists of a long line of shelf rock, where brightly mottled red, yellow, black and dark green Natal rock crabs, *Grapsus grapsus*, scuttle about in their hundreds. The other common species is the duller mottled green and yellow *Grapsus fourmanoiri*.

At Mission Rocks take the road inland, past the car park and toilets, towards the outpost. Just before reaching the outpost a trail marker points the way through the dune forest back to Mount Tabor.

DAY 3 *MFAZANA PAN LOOP: 10 KM*

As for the previous hike, make your way from the hut down towards the outpost, as far as the trail junction in a bush clearing. Take the trail incorrectly signposted No. 2 (it was when I did it, but is marked hike No. 1 on the Natal Parks Board map) towards Lake St Lucia. The path dips down into the tallest forest stands in the area, often laced with dangling thorny ropes, and then crosses the Cape Vidal road before slipping back into tall forest as it makes for the pans. The dense forest is alive with sounds, most of which are hard to identify, other than those of louries and monkeys which are plentiful. Shortly after meeting a 4x4 track deep in the verdant forest, there is a junction: the left-bearing option goes to a hide off the main path, while the main hide on Mfazana ('small wife') Pan is found along the right-bearing path.

Be absolutely quiet when approaching the hide, although even then the hippos

ABOVE The upper reaches of St Lucia estuary are a principal breeding ground of the white pelican, among the world's largest and most graceful birds.

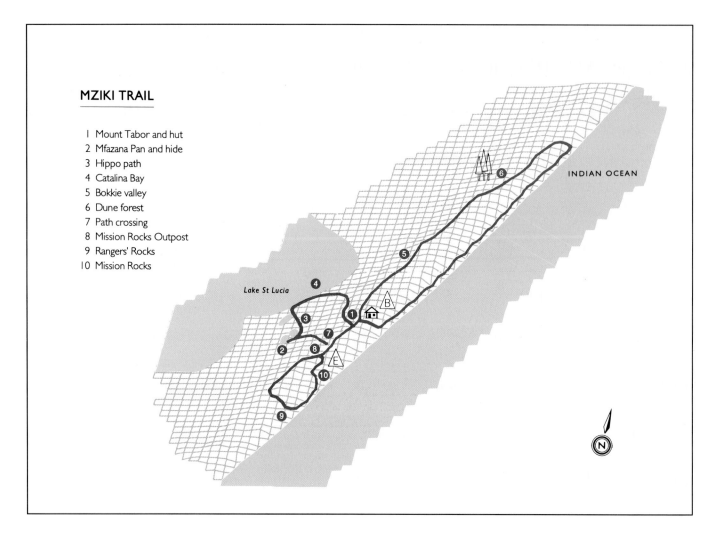

MZIKI TRAIL

1 Mount Tabor and hut
2 Mfazana Pan and hide
3 Hippo path
4 Catalina Bay
5 Bokkie valley
6 Dune forest
7 Path crossing
8 Mission Rocks Outpost
9 Rangers' Rocks
10 Mission Rocks

Lake St Lucia

INDIAN OCEAN

are likely to sense your approach. Scan the sides of the pan for basking crocs and for birds. I saw a pair of roosting fish eagles and what I'm sure was an osprey on the far side, although it was in shade and thus difficult to confirm. In just five minutes at the hide I also saw giant and pied kingfishers, spoonbills, goliath heron, spurwing geese, African jacana, blacksmith plover, Hartlaub's gulls, yellowbilled and little egrets, and some other small sandplover-type waders that were too far away to be identified.

The main trees found in forests here are the rare forest fig (*Ficus craterostoma*) and the Cape ash (*Ekebergia capensis*), with its smallish, glossy green compound leaves. On the forest floor grows mother-in-law's tongue (*Sansevieria aethiopica*), a fibrous shrub with strap-like leaves, used by spectacled weavers for nest building and by indigenous people for making twine. The sweet-scented flowers appear

around November. Along the paths here, rooting and scats of bushpigs are widely in evidence.

Shortly after leaving the hide the path emerges into the Umdoni parklands, where reedbuck like to congregate. Crossing the flat grassland, the path approaches Catalina Bay, base of a World War II flying-boat squadron. With Mount Tabor as the lookout and radar centre, these planes searched the Indian Ocean for German U-boats and acted as escorts to Allied ships.

A sign on the path alerts hikers to the fact that they are now walking along a hippo highway, where the bloated pachyderms definitely have right of way. As the path approaches the thin strip of forest along the edge of the lake, keep alert for the animals, as they like to lie up here in the heat of the day. They use the path at night when grazing in the parklands, and retire to the lake to escape the

attentions of parasites and biting flies. Dung scattered along the path is a hippo's way of marking its territory.

Taking a note from the Natal Parks Board booklet, it is wise to remember that: 'Despite their comical appearance and bulk, hippo can move very fast and can be extremely dangerous. Treat them with respect...' In the event of meeting one, the booklet offers this advice: 'You will have to make an instant decision. Should the hippo seem non-aggressive stand perfectly still and then withdraw quietly. If it appears cross, get out of there fast and don't go back. Alternatively, get up or behind a tree – not a bush or sapling, a tree.'

Having braved hippos, crocs, sharks and pepper ticks along the edge of the lake, the path climbs a sand bank and heads back across the parkland, to re-cross the Cape Vidal road and head diagonally up the dunes to Mount Tabor.

THE TRAIL AT A GLANCE

STARTING POINT : Mission Rocks, Natal Parks Board outpost
FINISHING POINT : Mission Rocks, Natal Parks Board outpost
LENGTH : 38 km
DURATION : Three days
GROUP LIMIT : Eight people
ROUTE : There are three one-day loop routes, all starting and ending at Mount Tabor. The longest, 18 km loop, goes north through dune forest and grassland tracts, and returns along the beach. A 10 km loop goes westwards to two pans and then along the eastern shore of Lake St Lucia's Catalina Bay, while another 10 km loop goes south, mainly through plantation, and then back up along the rocky shore to Mission Rocks and through the dune forest back to Mount Tabor.
HOW TO GET THERE : From Empangeni travel north along the N2 to Mtubatuba, where you turn off right to St Lucia. After crossing the estuary, turn left at the T-junction and pass through the Natal Parks Board gate into the Eastern Shores Nature Reserve. Drive along the bumpy gravel road and take the turn-off to Mission Rocks. Park under the tall pine trees at the outpost and report to the trails officer between 14h00 and 16h00 to get your permit and trail booklet.
BOOKING AUTHORITY : Natal Parks Board, P.O. Box 662, Pietermaritzburg, 3200; tel. (0331) 47-1981.
ACCOMMODATION : Mount Tabor hut is an old World War II radar station, equipped with single beds, tables and bunks, pots, pans, crockery and cutlery, gas stove, kerosene lamps, tanked-in drinking water, a bucket shower and longdrop toilet. Then there is Betty who comes to clean up every morning, for which you should tip her generously (she speaks only Zulu and is quite an institution here). Another institution is sundowners on the hut roof, where you can sleep in good weather.
CLIMATE : This is Zululand, so winters are mild to warm, while summers are hot to very hot. While daytime temperatures seldom rise above 30 °C, it is the saturated humidity that seems to suck the breath out of one's lungs: it also causes one to sweat profusely. The 1 000 mm average annual rains fall mainly in summer frontal squalls, sometimes as cyclones.
BEST TIME TO HIKE : April to October
REFERENCES : Natal Parks Board *Mziki Trail* (free) and *St Lucia* booklets (on sale at main Natal Parks Board office in St Lucia).
TERRAIN : The coastal terrain here is very gentle, apart from the sea-facing slopes of the coastal dunes. The base hut stands at the highest point in the reserve (130 m), and from there all three nature walks go down to sea level and then back up again.
WHAT TO TAKE : Since you won't need to take any catering equipment, a day pack should suffice. Take camera and binoculars, a bird field guide, a hat and sun cream. A veld and spoor guide will also be handy. You can walk the entire trail in running shoes, or even sandals, but some people may prefer ankle-high boots as the dune forests here are the southernmost distribution limit of that awesome reptile – the gaboon adder.
SPECIAL PRECAUTIONS : This is a malaria area, so if you plan to visit in summertime be sure to take the necessary precautions. Take ample supplies of insect repellent, both for mosquitoes and for ticks that infest the veld.

The St Lucia estuary, although no deeper than 2 m at any place, harbours large populations of hippos and crocs, as well as man-eating Zambezi sharks which come in to feed: therefore, resist going in for even a quick dip, even in the hottest weather. For the record, hippos and crocs account for about equal numbers of human deaths in Africa, and more than all other wild creatures combined.

The dune forests are the habitat of the gaboon adder, one of the deadliest snakes in the world. However, you are unlikely to see any of these reptiles, firstly because they are so well camouflaged, and secondly because they have been overexploited by collectors. They are also surprisingly tolerant creatures, preferring to lie still and avoid being detected than launching an attack.

You may come across a seemingly abandoned reedbuck lamb, which you should avoid – its mother is watching you from a nearby hiding place. Carry plenty of water on all the hikes, for you will not find any on the trail.
TRAIL OPTIONS : There are four- and five-day Wilderness Leadership Trails conducted through the Eastern Shores Nature Reserve, while launch trips from St Lucia, Charter's Creek and False Bay offer a chance of seeing something of the lake's remote areas, as well as its abundant birdlife. You should also visit the crocodile research centre and interpretation centre near the reserve's entrance. A primitive trail has recently been opened in the Sodwana State Forest to the north, and it promises to be one of the wildest, most remote hikes in the country (together with a canoeing option). There is also a new trail in the Kosi Bay area, administered by the kwaZulu authorities.

A hiking party descends the coastal dunes to the rocky shore. These dunes may yet be strip-mined for their rich titanium oxide deposits.

GIANT'S CUP TRAIL

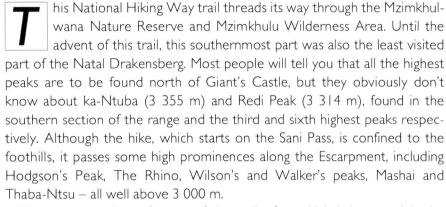

This National Hiking Way trail threads its way through the Mzimkhul-wana Nature Reserve and Mzimkhulu Wilderness Area. Until the advent of this trail, this southernmost part was also the least visited part of the Natal Drakensberg. Most people will tell you that all the highest peaks are to be found north of Giant's Castle, but they obviously don't know about ka-Ntuba (3 355 m) and Redi Peak (3 314 m), found in the southern section of the range and the third and sixth highest peaks respectively. Although the hike, which starts on the Sani Pass, is confined to the foothills, it passes some high prominences along the Escarpment, including Hodgson's Peak, The Rhino, Wilson's and Walker's peaks, Mashai and Thaba-Ntsu – all well above 3 000 m.

The most prominent feature of the trail, after which it is named, is the 'cup', a deeply formed saddle between the twin Hodgson's Peaks just south of the Sani Top. The peaks were named after the unfortunate Thomas Hodgson, member of a commando sent out to track Bushmen cattle rustlers in the area in 1862. On spotting a young Bushman they gave chase, and in the confusion Hodgson was shot in the thigh by one of his comrades. He was in a bad way and so half the party went off to find medical aid. The group looking after the wounded man spent two miserable, rain-washed days in the open, surrounded by Bushmen with their dreaded poisoned arrows. It appears they panicked, and stories at the time hinted at their abandoning the dying man to make good their own escape. This second group split up, and there followed another débâcle of mistiming and misfortune… about which you can read more in Reg Pearse's definitive drama of the Drakensberg, *Barrier of Spears*.

I completed this hike as part of a marathon, three-month traverse of the Drakensberg to produce *Drakensberg Walks*. Prior to this my mountaineering exploits in the 'Berg had been confined to the northernmost regions. There I was always on the lookout for bearded vultures, which I was occasionally thrilled to see in the distance. On this trip I saw plenty of the birds, both adults and juveniles, and presumed the endangered species must be on the increase. My assumption has now been confirmed, and it appears that 'vulture restaurants' are the cause of this. On one occasion I saw at least 50 Cape vultures and 10 bearded vultures circling above what I guessed must be a carcass. This is the first of three Drakensberg hikes described in this book, each one encapsulating the best of the southern, central and northern 'Berg respectively.

The Little 'Berg foothills below Thaba-Ntsu ('mountain of the bearded vulture'), near trail's end at Bushman's Nek.

79

DAY 1 SANI PASS TO PHOLELA HUT: 13,3 KM

The path starts off along an easy 2,5 km flat section, strewn with boulders, and then climbs about 120 m to cross the ridge between the Mkomazana and Gxalingenwa rivers, round a headland and then descend to the very large Ngenwa Pool. A log footbridge leads across the river just upstream of the pool. If you require privacy, stroll upstream through the rock corridors to any of the smaller pools you will find. This is a most beautiful and tranquil spot, situated in a deep and steep valley. The approach slope to the river hosts a large community of silver protea (*Protea roupelliae*). The large, rusty-red flowers appear in winter, although in some areas they will bloom as early as March.

If the weather is less than pleasant, then climb up out of the valley and make for a small cave at the top of the opposite slope, which serves as an alternative lunch spot. The next 4 km are spent rounding the buttress of the Ndlovini hill, over fairly flat ground. At the 9 km mark the landscape opens out over the Trout Beck valley, a small but very appealing tributary of the Pholela River. For 2,5 km the path follows the river, crisscrossing it at intervals. If the river is flooded, you will have to follow the left-hand bank downstream as best you can, to reach a suspension bridge opposite the Cobham Forest Station.

On the other hand, if you have collected your licence at the Himeville Hotel, you could make your way upstream where trout rise to the fly. The hut is the original converted Cobham farmhouse and is fairly civilized (in contrast to the campsite which has only one long-drop toilet). Many hikers miss this first day to begin at Cobham, which is a foolish decision since it is the most pleasant section of the trail.

DAY 2 PHOLELA HUT TO MZIMKHULWANA HUT: 9 KM

This short section allows you to explore the fascinating surrounding area, or laze around the pool near the hut at Mzimkhulwana. The trail leads off behind Pholela hut to climb for 2,5 km out of the Pholela River valley. The next 3 km is an easy stroll past the Tortoise Rocks and Bathplug Cave, where a small stream flows in through a hole in the cave roof and disappears down a 'plughole'. There used to be paintings in this cave, but I couldn't find them. (Someone on the trail said she had found some in a cave above that indicated on the map, but I have not managed to verify this.)

Having rounded the south-eastern spur of eSiphongweni hill (2 258 m), the path makes an easy descent to the hut on the far bank of the Mzimkhulwana (little Mzimkhulu) River. You should reach the hut by mid- to late morning, leaving ample time to explore the wonders of Siphongweni. Although the paths are sometimes indistinct, you can easily use your common sense to follow the river upstream and then ascend to the back of the hill, reaching a long plateau arm below the summit. To find the Siphongweni shelter and the cave, make for where the steep slope of the upper conical peak meets the northern edge of the plateau: if you find this spot you will be looking down into the Pholela River valley, with eSiphongweni Hill behind you and to your right.

The shelter is a roomy gap underneath one of the largest of a group of massive boulders lying scattered on the plateau. The cave, with its unique paintings, is reached up the constructed path which, in the other direction, leads down into the valley.

DAY 3 MZIMKHULWANA HUT TO WINTERHOEK HUT: 12,2 KM

The trail crosses the suspension bridge below the hut, and then climbs steadily for nearly 4 km up to the plateau level of the Little Bamboo Mountain, named after the rank grass (*Arundinaria tesselata*) that grows here. On the plateau is Crane Tarn, frequented in season by blue cranes and, on occasion, known to have hosted one of the region's most endangered species, the wattled crane.

Where the path begins its descent towards the Killiecrankie Stream, the remnants of a petrified forest have been exposed on the surface. Unfortunately, so many hikers have carried off bits of this geological phenomenon that not much remains to be seen. The path follows the left-hand stream bank for about 1 km, when it comes to a large boulder damming the stream to form a deep bathing pool. The tall but sparsely branched (*Protea subvestita*), with pale creamy-yellow flowers, grows abundantly along the descent to the river.

After this the route becomes less interesting, following the Garden Castle road across the Mzimkhulu River and then veering off to top a small hill, past some kraals on the way to Winterhoek hut. At first glance the hut appears less than inviting, in its exposed position. In fact it is most pleasant here, with a swimming hole found at a weir nearby. Sundowners or tea under the mature oak trees that surround the rondavels is jolly civilized.

DAY 4 WINTERHOEK HUT TO SWIMAN HUT: 12,8 KM

Behind the hut the path begins its 2 km climb up Black Eagle Pass, the hardest part of the trail, but a jaunt compared to some paths described in this book. True to form, I saw both black eagles and bearded vultures while negotiating the pass. Above and to the left loom the cliffs and stacks of the massive Garden Castle formation, named by some historic Scot for its resemblance to Edinburgh Castle, so the story goes.

The rest of this section is pretty, but fairly monotonous, traversing typical 'Berg montane grassland. The path meanders and undulates across a grassy ridge that protrudes above the Mzimkhulu and Mlambonja rivers, with views over the Navarone Dam. The veld here is typical of the southern Drakensberg, punctuated by *Protea caffra* sugarbushes, and studded in spring and summer with orange and crimson watsonias, yellow and mauve daisies, and variously hued everlastings. In the distance the Escarpment wall stretches in both directions, crowding the skyline.

As the path approaches the turreted Swiman outcrop, a high outlier of the Escarpment, the famous Rhino formation can be seen thrusting its horned peak out from the high mountain wall. The final stretch to the hut involves an undulating 3 km run-up. Upstream of the hut the Mlambonja River (not to be confused with the larger river of the same name in the Cathedral area) yields trout to those with the necessary licence.

RIGHT AND BELOW One of many caves in the trail area that house an impressive outdoor gallery of San rock art. These images were painted by artist-shamans when they were in deep trances, and depict visions of the supernatural realm.

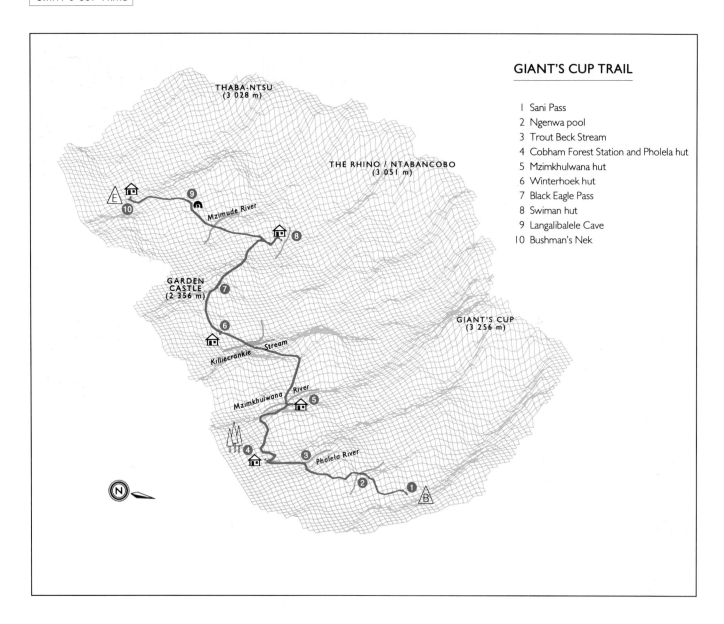

THABA-NTSU
(3 028 m)

THE RHINO / NTABANCOBO
(3 051 m)

Mzimude River

GARDEN
CASTLE
(2 356 m)

GIANT'S CUP
(3 256 m)

Killiecrankie   Stream

Mzimkhulwana   River

Pholela River

N

GIANT'S CUP TRAIL

1 Sani Pass
2 Ngenwa pool
3 Trout Beck Stream
4 Cobham Forest Station and Pholela hut
5 Mzimkhulwana hut
6 Winterhoek hut
7 Black Eagle Pass
8 Swiman hut
9 Langalibalele Cave
10 Bushman's Nek

DAY 5 *SWIMAN HUT TO BUSHMAN'S NEK : 13 KM*

From the sandstone castellations of Swiman the trail's final section begins with a gentle climb for about 3,5 km to Bucquay Nek, near the end of a long spur. It then descends gently for 2 km to the wide Mzimude River valley where a suspension bridge is crossed. The path winds none too steeply up towards a wide saddle on Langalibalele hill (2 270 m), which can be identified by the lookout tower on the summit. The famous Langalibalele Cave is found on the far side of the hill. It is named after the rebellious Zulu chief who gave the colonial authorities quite a run-around in these

hills and mountains – about which you can read more on page 86.

The last 4 km is, thankfully, all downhill from the watershed, crossing numerous other paths on the way down. This section is a twisting, turning one, as the path negotiates its way over the crinkled, stream-dissected hillsides. The Bushman's Nek hut has been built on a spur some way off the main descent path to the guard post and car park; most people choose to bypass this last hut and head for home. If you have an extra day to spend in the area, then you should consider exploring the Little 'Berg valleys above Bushman's Nek police post, an area that has the highest concentration of caves and rock art in the Drakensberg.

OPPOSITE Midway between Sani Pass and Cobham, the path reaches Ngenwa Pool, where a halved log provides a makeshift bridge across the Gxalingenwa River.

THE TRAIL AT A GLANCE

STARTING POINT : Hiking Way car park on Sani Pass
FINISHING POINT : Hiking Way car park at Bushman's Nek forestry guard post
LENGTH : 60 km
DURATION : Five days
GROUP LIMIT : 30 people
ROUTE : This is a linear trail through the Little 'Berg, traversing plateaux and valleys, and running parallel to the main escarpment wall.
HOW TO GET THERE : On the gravel road between Underberg and Nottingham Road, the turn-off to Sani Pass is about 15 km north of Himeville. Pass Mokhotlong Motor Transport and the Sani Pass Hotel, and proceed up the pass for about 5 km to the Hiking Way car park.
BOOKING AUTHORITY : Natal Parks Board, P. O. Box 662, Pietermaritzburg, 3200; tel. (0331) 47-1981.
ACCOMMODATION : The first overnight stop at Pholela (Cobham) is in a converted farmhouse, with bunks and mattresses, flush toilets, a boiler-heated shower, fireplaces

and braai places. Swiman hut at Garden Castle also has flush toilets and a cold shower, but otherwise the huts are typical National Hiking Way fare, with only rudimentary facilities – a roof and a bed.
CLIMATE : Thunder showers through the otherwise hot summers, snow in winter, and mist and drizzle in autumn and spring is what you can expect in the wet southern part of the 'Berg. This does not mean that fine days do not prevail, because they do – just be prepared for the worst of each season. Since you are not in the high mountains, however, conditions are never extreme.
BEST TIME TO HIKE : Depending on whether your preference is for snow or shine, mist or mild, any season is pleasant here. For wild flowers spring is always best, right up to midsummer.
REFERENCES : National Hiking Way 1 : 50 000 map, Forestry/Peter Slingsby 1 : 50 000 South Drakensberg map, *Drakensberg Walks*, and a field guide to the Natal Drakensberg published by the Wildlife Society.
TERRAIN : Despite being situated in the foothills of the sub-continent's highest

mountains, this is a surprisingly easy hike with no demanding gradients and only moderate distances to cover each day.
WHAT TO TAKE : Since the going here is relatively easy, your footwear should depend on the season and the weight of your pack. I would recommend taking along the Wildlife Society's excellent field guide by the Irwins and Ackhurst. For those with an interest in the subject, some of the very best San rock paintings are to be found in the trail vicinity, but require exploring to locate. Water is plentiful on the trail and, since I hiked after good rains, I didn't bother to carry any.
SPECIAL PRECAUTIONS : Cave paintings are one of the richest treasures of our national heritage; they are all national monuments and are irreplaceable. If you encounter any, enjoy them but do not touch or do *anything* to disturb them. This is a linear hike, necessitating transport arrangements between end and starting points.
TRAIL OPTIONS : There are short nature walks as well as multi-day hikes leading out from the forestry stations at Cobham, Garden Castle and Bushman's Nek, details of which can be found in *Drakensberg Walks*.

GIANT'S CASTLE
TWO HUTS HIKE

This Drakensberg hike lies in the shadow of the country's fifth highest peak, Giant's Castle, which forms a sharp, 3 314 m-high prominence on a ridge extending from the main Escarpment. The trail makes use of two traditional mountaineers' huts, similar to those that have now been removed from the wilderness areas beyond the reserve's borders. In a region drenched with the blood and tears of history, Giant's Castle has seen more action than most. It was here that rebellious Zulu Chief Langalibalele made his last stand against the colonial forces. It was here too that the last known 'wild' Bushman in South Africa was shot.

In 1903 the Giant's Castle Game Reserve was declared to protect some of the few remaining eland in Natal, which migrated annually between the sour montane grasslands of the Little 'Berg and the sweet grazing lands of the Thornveld around Estcourt. What a tragedy it seems today, that only a few years previously Bushmen were exterminated from the area, for here they might have found a sanctuary. Compounding the tragedy is the fact that the last, lonely individual had a leather belt around his waist, onto which were attached small antelope horns filled with pigment – indicating that he was also the last in a very long lineage of rock artists. A guided tour of the Main Caves Museum, with part authentic and part reconstructed Bushman scenes, is virtually obligatory for all visitors to the reserve.

You are sure to see herds of eland grazing the plateaux grasslands or browsing on the sagewood bushes along the streams. Baboons and grey rhebok are also common, while duiker, mountain reedbuck and bushbuck are common in their respective habitats, but a little harder to see. Other game in the reserve includes blesbok and oribi, hartebeest and baboons. But it is the mountain raptors, attracted largely by the hide 'restaurant', that most visitors now come to see. At the weekly summer feedings Cape vultures, black eagles and jackal buzzards swoop in to feed on the carcasses, followed by lanners, ravens and crows. But most impressive are the bearded vultures, those magnificent gold and black birds that dominate the hide, the park, and indeed all the mountain skies of southern Africa.

From the main Giant's Castle camp
a path weaves its way diagonally up
through the Little 'Berg, to meet the
Contour Path at a point near to where
The Thumb protrudes from the
Escarpment wall.

DAY 1 DAY VISITORS' CAR PARK TO GIANT'S CASTLE HUT: 10,5 KM

Before setting off up the Little 'Berg, it is recommended that you join a guided tour to the Main Caves Museum, enjoy the forest and pools of the lower Two Dassie Stream valley, and meditate on events past at Durnford's Camp – all within a short distance of the rest camp. Here hikers should drink heartily before starting the trail, for the awaiting climb is long and sustained, with neither water nor shade for comfort.

From the car park the trail follows the path behind the workshops and warden's residence, marked 'Giant's and Meander huts'. It then climbs the slope above and to the east of the rest camp, bearing right to pass the Meander hut turn-off. Below and to the right spurs and valleys of the Little 'Berg converge to form the upper Bushman's River catchment, the steep-sided gorges fringed with sandstone cliffs. This is oribi and mountain reedbuck terrain, and you might well flush some of these medium-sized antelopes from the shortish grass where they lie up.

The veld here, tawny in winter and green in summer, is studded with protea trees, mainly *Protea caffra*, the common sugarbush, and *P. roupelliae*, the silver protea. These trees might be more widespread were it not for the fact that this is a fire-climax community, maintained through regular burning of the veld. Centuries of this regime has ensured that the trees are found mainly on the steeper, rocky slopes, and along the rock-paved edges of the Little 'Berg gorges. On the higher slopes the smaller *P. dracomontana* and the tall but sparse *P. subvestita* are more common.

After passing three prominences and negotiating a badly eroded section of pathway, some small tarns are bypassed at around the 2 000 m mark. Birdlife at these seasonal pans is transient, but blue cranes may visit them when they are full. As the path climbs beyond this level, it crests a spur called Oribi Ridge, which rises between the Two Dassies Stream and Bhicane River valleys. The path here is at its steepest, and soon you will see the bearded vulture hide just off the path to the right. Bones and meat are left here every Saturday and Sunday between May and September, and by now the

rocks in front of the hide are easily recognized by those with an interest in bird photography. The hide must be booked, preferably well in advance, for it has become a popular place to visit.

About 1,5 km from the hide the trail reaches the Contour Path, the hikers' greatest asset in the Drakensberg: it runs, more or less continuously, from Cathedral Peak all the way to Bushman's Nek, giving access to most of the range. The trail turns right here, rather than bearing left to Loteni. By now the Giant's Ridge and its crowning peak tower above the trail, with the impressive ramparts and castellations of the main Escarpment receding to the north. The path, deeply eroded in some places, dips and climbs through numerous small gullies, one having a permanent stream with a succession of very inviting pools and water slides just downstream of the crossing. The slopes and depressions around here are a favourite grazing area for eland, under the protective guard of the towering peak.

Soon the attractive stone hut appears, standing patiently in front of one of the most scenic tarns in the 'Berg. This is a grand and tranquil place, especially when oribi and rhebok arrive in file, shining in the dawn light, or waterfowl fly in at dusk to roost.

DAY 2 GIANT'S CASTLE HUT TO BANNERMAN HUT: 18 KM

This section of the hike is easy to follow: just keep the Drakensberg on your left and your feet on the well-defined Contour Path. The path here is an extenuation of the original track built in 1937 by forester J. van Heynigen, to link up the Cathedral and Cathkin Little 'Berg areas. The path runs parallel to the Escarpment wall, skirting each successive peak. The first 2 km is more or less flat, after which the path weaves out and around the myriad spurs, and in and out of stream beds. Most of these streams are intermittent but many are perennial, so water is plentiful. Looking at a topographical map of the area the path appears to stay level with the 2 000 m contour, but with a backpack the many small ups and downs can be exhausting.

After about 2,5 km the Contour Path meets the foot of Giant's Castle Pass

which, if climbed, should be done with discretion as it is steep, rocky and unstable. About 10 km from the hut the path reaches the foot of Langalibalele Pass. Having walked thus far, you might consider the names of the peaks alongside, such as Erskine and Bond, Poterill, Kambule and Katana, and why they don't conform to the typical 'Berg names. Then there are Mount Durnford and the Carbineers' Grave with its stainless steel cross catching the sunlight.

It all started in 1873 when rebellious old Langalibalele, a minor Zulu chief, refused to pay taxes to the colonial government. Some skirmishes in the lowlands drove the chief with his people and cattle onto the high ground to make a stand – and their eventual escape – up one of the traditional Bushman cattle raiding passes. A detachment of the 75th Carbineers Regiment under Major Durnford was dispatched to deal with the intransigent chief. What followed was a confrontation that Reg Pearse in his book *Barrier of Spears* calls the 'smoke on the pass'. The names of the nominally victorious major, the five Carbineers who lost their lives in the skirmish, as well as the rebellious chief, were thereafter immortalized in these mountains.

Rock martins and swifts, rock pigeons and arrow-like falcons dart among the rock bastions, while large raptors swoop across the crags. The small tarns along the way attract yellowbilled and black ducks, hamerkops, herons, egrets, storks and cranes, while you might see African marsh harriers and black harriers, maybe even the rare migrant pallid harriers, gliding sluggishly over the montane grasslands. In the grasslands three camouflaged species of francolin and the common quail rush about, darting and diving ahead of any hiker, or taking to the air with a whirr of wingbeats if surprised. Best of all are the secretary birds that strut through the rank grass, prodding and stabbing with their sturdy feet for reptiles, rodents, small birds and mammals to eat. Their name is derived from the Arabic *saqr et-tair*, meaning 'hunting bird'.

OPPOSITE Giant's Castle hut stands on the banks of an idyllic tarn, nestled below South Ridge. The ridge forms a buttress to Giant's Castle Peak.

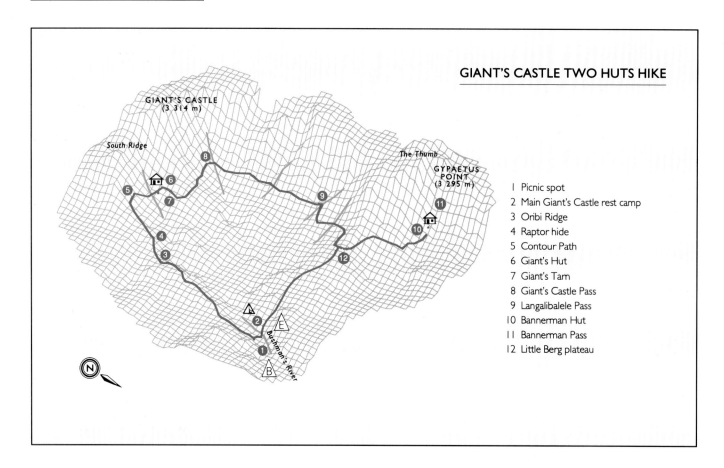

GIANT'S CASTLE TWO HUTS HIKE

GIANT'S CASTLE
(3 314 m)

South Ridge

The Thumb

GYPAETUS
POINT
(3 295 m)

Bushman's River

1 Picnic spot
2 Main Giant's Castle rest camp
3 Oribi Ridge
4 Raptor hide
5 Contour Path
6 Giant's Hut
7 Giant's Tarn
8 Giant's Castle Pass
9 Langalibalele Pass
10 Bannerman Hut
11 Bannerman Pass
12 Little Berg plateau

Looming ominously over Bannerman hut, at the head of Bannerman Pass, is Gypaetus Point. Ardent birdwatchers will know that this peak celebrates the lord of the skies, the bearded vulture (*Gypaetus barbatus*).

DAY 3 BANNERMAN HUT TO VISITORS' CAR PARK: 11 KM

From the hut the path descends quite steeply for a few hundred metres before levelling off to meander for 4 km across the Little 'Berg grasslands, crossing numerous streamlets as it goes. Here again are found some small tarns, and secretary birds are frequently seen in the area, so much so that one of the nearby streams bears that name. Higher up and to the left is Martial Eagle Stream but, although these birds are recorded in the park, the habitat is far more suited to the black eagle.

The path descends along a spur for the next 3 km, after which it slips off down the slope to the left, making for the tributary of the Bushman's River. The stream is followed for about 2 km, crossing yet another stream and negotiating some boggy stretches on the way. The final steep descent to cross the Bushman's river via the Bannerman suspension bridge is down a path that has been paved to prevent erosion. (On the way to the main caves a collection box has been fixed to a gate post, to collect funds to pave other eroded paths in the reserve.) After crossing the bridge, the trail follows the river downstream, the banks thick with sagewood bushes (*Buddleja salviifolia*). In winter the eland, whose access to the sweet Thornveld beyond has been cut off, browse these plants while the montane grasses withdraw their nutrients into their roots. A paved path eventually leads up a short, steep bank to the picnic area and car park.

LEFT Wildflowers are one of the Drakensberg's spectacular attractions. After winter grass burns, geophytic plants such as these bright pink watsonias germinate to join the regular spring display.

THE TRAIL AT A GLANCE

STARTING POINT : Giant's Castle day visitors' car park

FINISHING POINT : Giant's Castle day visitors' car park

LENGTH : 40 km

DURATION : Three days

GROUP LIMIT : 12 people

ROUTE : From the day visitors' car park the trail leads up Oribi Ridge to a stone hut, found on a plateau shelf below the Giant's Castle. The following day there is an 18 km walk along the Contour Path to Bannerman hut, at the foot of the pass of the same name. From Bannerman hut the trail leads out across the Little 'Berg, away from the main mountain range, continues along a spur and then descends a gully to cross the Bushman's River.

HOW TO GET THERE : From Estcourt, take the surfaced road west to Ntabamnhlope, which becomes gravel after a few kms. At Ntabamnhlope, turn left (south) to Rockmount, and from there follow the sign to the right (west) to the reserve. The road into the reserve is tarred.

BOOKING AUTHORITY : Natal Parks Board, P.O. Box 662, Pietermaritzburg, 3200; tel. (0331) 47-1981.

ACCOMMODATION : Two stone and thatch mountain huts, sleeping 24 people each. There are bunk beds, flush toilets, and a small kitchenette with gas stove, pots and pans, and candles. In the main rest camp there are luxury chalets that must be booked well in advance. The rest camp is otherwise not open to hikers.

CLIMATE : Summers here can be very hot, with violent thunderstorms, while in winter regular cold fronts pound the mountains and leave them dusted with snow (over the years snow has been recorded in every month). During autumn and spring mists and lingering rain are often experienced. In other words, you have to be prepared for the most extreme conditions, but in reality the weather here is just perfect most of the time.

BEST TIME TO HIKE : Spring through to autumn, but expect snow in early spring and light rain in autumn.

REFERENCES : Department of Environment Affairs (Forestry Branch) 1 : 50 000 Central Drakensberg map, compiled by Peter Slingsby; game reserve booklet sketch map. The several mountaineering and historical books by the Pearses, the Wildlife Society's field guide, as well as the hiking guide *Drakensberg Walks* can be consulted.

TERRAIN : Although the trail passes the foot of some of the highest peaks on the subcontinent, the Little 'Berg landscape through which the trail passes is relatively undemanding. The Contour Path finds its way along the minor shelf of the Little 'Berg, composed of Cave (Clarens) and Red Bed (Molteno) Sandstone deposits. The massive peaks are composed of basalt.

WHAT TO TAKE : As you can leave behind your stove and pots, take extra chocolate and 'snakebite' for emergency consumption. Seriously, you should carry water, especially on the first day's climb where none is to be found until you near the hut. Ankle-high boots for snake protection, and gaiters for grass seeds and burrs, are advisable. But the paths themselves are good and could, in fine weather, be walked in light footwear.

SPECIAL PRECAUTIONS : Three species of poisonous snake are found here, namely rinkhals (banded spitting cobra), puffadder and berg adder. But don't panic, even if bitten, as you are so close to help that there should be no need for an emergency situation to arise. Don't use a serum, especially not for a bite by a berg adder, as it does not have typical adder venom. Be sure to book in and sign the mountain register at the ranger's office, near the car park.

There are over 50 rock art sites in the reserve and with diligence you could easily locate at least one other than the Main Caves overhang. The Drakensberg harbours what has been described as the world's richest outdoor art gallery: a collection of exquisitely executed and spiritually significant images that are South Africa's greatest artistic heritage. They should be treated as rare and priceless treasures.

TRAIL OPTIONS : A third overnight hut in the Giant's Castle area is found at Meander, a mere two-hour one-way walk. There are numerous one-day walks, from the 2 km walk to the Main Caves, to the 18 km Wildebeest Plateau walk. An alternative route to the Giant's Castle hut is up the Two Dassie Stream valley (see *Drakensberg Walks*). From Bannerman hut, a two passes hike (Bannerman's and Langalibalele) could amuse hikers with time to spare although, technically, you will have to enter Lesotho on this route. The more northerly Injasuti area, recently incorporated into the reserve, is more a mountaineer's domain.

Bannerman hut is the second of the two huts on this hike. It crouches beneath the massive basalt walls of Bannerman Buttress and Gypaetus Point. These are the last two remaining mountaineers' huts in the 'Berg: all others have been demolished to remove man-made structures from wilderness areas.

CATHEDRAL PEAK
TWO PASSES HIKE

T his is, without doubt, the most awe-inspiring and demanding hike in the book. The mountains rise in 1 000 m-high flying buttresses and massive pinnacles to stab the clouds. The Cathedral range, a 6,5 km right-angled extension of the main Drakensberg Escarpment, is a jagged ridge of peaks and spires, starting with the Mitre, then the Chessmen and the two great Horns, the Bell, soaring Cathedral Peak (3 004 m) and the Puddings. Along the Escarpment wall we encounter, from the north, the Saddle, Mlambonja Buttress, the Elephant, Cleft Peak (at 3 281 m, only one metre lower than Mont-Aux-Sources and the eighth highest peak of the 'Berg), Castle Buttress, the intricately fluted basalt pillars of the Organ Pipes, and Ndumeni Dome (3 206 m). Rising in front of the Escarpment are the twin spires of the Column and Pyramid, the climbing of which are now mountaineering legends.

In 1936 Brian Godbold led five other climbers to the top of the awkward Pyramid, a climb that then announced the acme of mountaineering achievement, but is today considered a moderately inconvenient rock and grass ascent. It was with the arrival of builder George Thomson in 1940 that the more lasting climbing legend was heralded. The New Zealander had not previously done any climbing, but the 'Berg's majesty drew him forth. Within no time he was rushing around the mountains, climbing just about anything he could. The Column is not an easy peak to conquer, being the most imposing free-standing Drakensberg peak. But he did, eventually, in 1945. No-one else would go with him, so he climbed it alone, without a rope.

While the going up was hard enough (still considered a classic F3), climbing down was near impossible… and so he jumped the hardest section, just grabbing a small erica bush as he bounced off a narrow ledge to help him slide into a chimney four metres below. After that the descent was a breeze. In its time that was by far the hardest rock climb in the country. What followed was a short but incredible climbing career, during which time similarly daring escapades led to the conquering of other previously unclimbed peaks. The trail route looks out on many of these hard-won mountaineering prizes, as well as some of the tragedies.

The view northwards from Cathedral ridge: the ramparts above the Ntonjelane valley lead up to the Saddle in the centre, with the Eastern Buttress protruding into the far distance.

DAY I END OF FORESTRY ROAD TO OVERNIGHT SPOT: 8,5 KM

Whatever you do, do not try to park at the hotel or leave from their premises, as this gives hikers a bad name at what is one of the 'Berg mountaineers' best-beloved inns. Rather offload all your gear at the boom below the hotel driveway, where the hike begins, and then leave your car back at the campsite.

The first day's walk starts off up the left-hand bank of the Mlambonja River, taking a path upstream through thick riverine bush. The bush consists predominantly of the willow-like mountain sagewood (*Buddleja salviifolia*) with its lanceolate, furry, green-grey leaves, the gnarled ouhout or *itshitshi* bush (*Leucosidea sericea*) with its small, serrated leaves, and the common spike-thorn (*Maytenus heterophylla*).

The first 2,5 km is easy going, following close to the gurgling, swift flowing river. The name of the river means 'the dogs are hungry', a Zulu reference to the scarcity of game their hunters found here, as oppposed to the Injasuti River (actually eNjesuthi, or 'well fed dogs') further south. The path passes below an outcropping headland of the Little Berg, across the mouth of the Xeni River valley, and then between a second headland and the Mlambonja River. It then rears up to negotiate a steep zigzag route onto a grassy spur that bulges up between the Xeni and Mlambonja valleys.

At 2 040 m the path forks around the base of Mount Helga (2 702 m), the left prong heading towards the Xeni valley and the trail path contouring to the right. The next 2 km are far easier going than the previous two, as the path heads across the slope, above Marble Baths and back to the river, which is reached at 2 013 m. Around here you will begin to feel hemmed in by the mountains, Mlambonja Buttress crowding the sky to your left and the Inner Horn jabbing it on the right. If you have made a late start and have four days in which to do the hike, then look around you, among the boulders and *itshitshi* bushes for a place to pitch your tent on the soft river sand.

This is a fantastic area to explore. Xeni Cave, for example, is one of the largest in the 'Berg and only one of many rock shelters in the area used by San hunters until around the turn of the century.

DAY 2 OVERNIGHT SPOT TO TWINS CAVE: 4 KM

If you plan to do this hike in three days then you will have to carry on to the cave. If not, then day two offers a steep slog, but all day in which to do it; from here the path becomes steep, and then steeper still. This is the beginning of the Mlambonja Pass, a 3,5 km ascent that is one of the toughest you are ever likely to be called upon to undertake – especially if you have to carry someone else's pack too, as I did on my first ascent. Maybe that has clouded my perceptions, but most 'Berg climbers agree that this is the mother of all passes.

After about 1,5 km of muscle-bulging, step-by-step climbing, the pass crosses the river, where you should drink your fill. If your pack does not feel too heavy, consider carrying water from here for there is none at the cave. You might also want to take a quick dip to cool off. The path leaves the river valley to round a spur, above which the intricate outlines of the Chessmen rise up on the right. From this point there ensues a very steep 1,5 km climb, where you learn just how useful the coarse 'Berg grass tussocks can be to mountaineers.

This section should be taken slowly, all day if necessary, so that you might also admire the grand mountain panorama scenery opening out around you. The path slips by the Mitre and past the Twins: to find the cave veer right over the low col between the Twins and the Escarpment, where the Cathedral range forms a hinge. The cave is situated on the far north side of the Twins, looking out across the head of the Ntonjelan' ephumalanga River valley (Ntonjelane of the rising sun). A drip is found under a small overhang on the facing Escarpment crags, while a stream is reached 1 km away, directly into Lesotho. The cave is fairly roomy, sleeping about 30 people, rather than 12 as indicated on the map.

Situated at the base of the Mitre, facing the Escarpment, the cave is shaded for most of the day. But as the sun rises above the Indian Ocean, the most spectacular morning scenes unfold. When cloud covers the land below like a massive ice cap – and it often does – sunrise ignites it in salmon, pink and carmine, thrust through by the copper-tipped blades of 'Quathlamba'.

DAY 3 TWINS CAVE TO WINDY GAP: 12,5 KM

From Twins Cave it is necessary to gain the top of the pass, in order to cross over the watershed and descend into the Kwakwatsi River valley. At the top of the pass you are rewarded with a classic view of these mountains, taking in all of the Cathedral range and the Escarpment southwards to Cathkin Peak. There is a choice of routes to follow from here: for spectacular views stay close to the Escarpment edge as much as possible, or, if you prefer an easier walk, carry on up the valley, where numerous small pools are encountered. Use common sense in choosing the most suitable route to follow and, obviously, rather avoid the edge in misty conditions.

Either way, you should make for the head of Xeni pass and explore the area around the top of the Elephant, Cockade and Plume, where deep clefts and rugged slopes, rock towers, breathtaking drops and distant vistas create a dynamic interplay of images. The route crests the Elephant and then runs easily downhill to where the Tseketseke pass opens out at the top of the Escarpment. Here again you are faced with alternatives: you may tackle the uphill slog of about 250 m to climb Cleft Peak, the highest peak between Mont-Aux-Sources and Champagne Castle, or you can take the 'lower' road, behind Cleft Peak and into the upper Kakoatsan River catchment. In winter red hot poker blooms (*Kniphofia* sp.), pale yellow *Moraea* irises and tiny erica bells attract butterflies and jittery, shimmering subirds.

If you choose the former option, then you will also crest Castle Buttress, before finding your way down into Windy Gap at the head of the Organ Pipes pass. If you choose the gently sloping inland route, a path will lead over a low ridge and then down along a tributary of the Kakoatsan River. Instead of going right down into the main valley, however, the path veers off to the left to make its way towards the Escarpment into Windy Gap, a wide basin scooped out between Castle Buttress and Ndumeni Dome. There used to be a hut here, but of late one pitches tent and hopes that the Dome does not stir up one of its notorious tempests, for its Zulu name means 'the mountain of storms'.

LEFT Cycads, or bread trees, are one of the so-called 'living fossil' plants, dating back about 200 million years. They can be found in the Little 'Berg area, at the head of most wooded gorges.

BELOW Twins Cave is one of the largest and best utilized natural shelters in the Drakensberg. It is an overhang rather than a cave, but nevertheless sleeps up to 30 people.

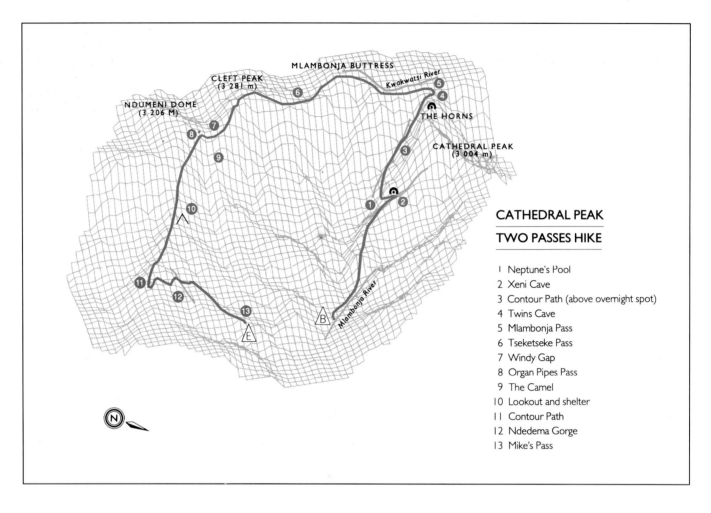

CATHEDRAL PEAK

TWO PASSES HIKE

1 Neptune's Pool
2 Xeni Cave
3 Contour Path (above overnight spot)
4 Twins Cave
5 Mlambonja Pass
6 Tseketseke Pass
7 Windy Gap
8 Organ Pipes Pass
9 The Camel
10 Lookout and shelter
11 Contour Path
12 Ndedema Gorge
13 Mike's Pass

DAY 4 *WINDY GAP TO MIKE'S PASS:* *13,5 KM*

The trip down the Organ Pipes pass is, as the name suggests, a most spiritually uplifting experience. The pass is steep in places, often wet and slippery, but inside it has the atmosphere of a cathedral nave. This pass is another of several that were earlier known as Bushman's Pass by the white settlers whose cattle disappeared over what we today realise are the easier access routes over these mountains. Strange also to consider what a task it was for commandos and later mountaineers to find and identify all the passes that today we skip up and down following well-prepared maps. In his book *Barrier of Spears* Reg Pearse, something of an expert amateur cartographer in his younger days, details much of the early work that went into the mapping and naming of these mountains.

Organ Pipes pass is certainly more confined in its upper ramparts than any other, and this makes for an intriguing journey through its corridor. Once at the foot of the main basalt crags, there is the choice of heading left to descend the Camel, or of continuing in a more or less diagonal line to the right, along a knife-edge ridge that divides the Ndumeni and Thuthumi river valleys. (There is another route that goes down the more southerly Thuthumi River pass, but starting high up on Ndumeni Dome, near the caves.)

The trail follows the middle path, but it is not always easy to keep to the path while picking one's way along the ridge, as in places it can be discerned only by the small cairns marking its route through rocky sections. When in doubt, keep to the left side of the ridge, although you should not venture too far from the crest. Follow the crest right down to the old lookout, now revamped by the Mountain Club of South Africa as an emergency shelter for mountaineers. A short cut path to the left of the lookout joins the Contour Path 4x4 track below, although the real path carries on down the crest over a steep, grassy slope.

Below you and to the right you should be able to see the lower reaches of the Thuthumi Pass path, which the trail path meets at The Nek junction, on the Contour Path. The latter is the original 4x4 track constructed by forester J. van Heynigen in 1937. The nek yields impressive views of magical Ndedema Gorge to the right, beyond Philip's Folly, and Masongwana Gorge to the the left. Turn left here to follow the 4x4 track on its meandering course for 3,5 km in and out of a tributary and the upper reaches of the main river valley, to a junction. Leave the Contour Path here by turning right along another 4x4 track that leads out across a Little 'Berg plateau, to the Mike's Pass car park. Hopefully you will have been wise enough to leave a vehicle here, because otherwise you will have to carry on for another 8 km down the long and winding pass to the Natal Parks Board campsite.

ABOVE When in flower the harebells, or dieramas, are one of the quaintest wildflowers of the Drakensberg.
LEFT From above the Umlambonja valley, Sterkhorn, Cathkin Peak, Monk's Cowl and Champagne Castle jostle for dominance on the horizon.

THE TRAIL AT A GLANCE

STARTING POINT : Cathedral Peak campsite, or the boom at the end of the forestry road, directly below the Cathedral Peak Hotel
FINISHING POINT : Top of Mike's Pass, or Cathedral Peak Natal Parks Board campsite
LENGTH : 37,5 km
DURATION : Three or four days
GROUP LIMIT : None
ROUTE : From the starting point, the trail follows the Mlambonja River's left-hand bank upstream, into the Mlambonja pass to Twins Cave. It then traces the general line of the Escarpment to Windy Gap, at the top of the Organ Pipes pass. The pass is descended, a knife-edge ridge is crossed, and the emergency shelter passed, to reach the Contour Path. This path is followed to the Mike's Pass car park, or the campsite further on down the gravel road.
HOW TO GET THERE : From Winterton take the tarred road to Cathkin and Champagne areas, cross the railway line, and shortly afterwards watch out for the turn-off right along the gravel road to Cathedral Peak. After about 9 km you have to make quick successive right-left turns past Zunckels, the Emhlawazini Store and on to the Cathedral Peak State Forest. There are two stretches of paved road, to prevent you getting stuck in deep clay after rain. You will have to pay to enter the state forest area, some distance before reaching the campsite.

BOOKING AUTHORITY : Natal Parks Board, P.O. Box 662, Pietermaritzburg, 3200; tel. (0331) 47-1981.
ACCOMMODATION : The small and often boggy campsite is situated about 4 km before the start of the hike, or you could treat yourself to a night in the hotel. On the hike one night can be spent in the very roomy Twins Cave, but otherwise a tent must be used.
CLIMATE : As with the rest of the Drakensberg, this is a summer thunderstorm and winter snowfall area, with mists and light rain in spring and autumn. Conditions are mostly pleasant, but summers can be either hot or drenched, while winters can be very cold indeed. Storms here, especially on the summit, can be frightening occurrences.
BEST TIME TO HIKE : Spring and autumn.
REFERENCES : For hiking, the Forestry/Peter Slingsby 1 : 50 000 North Drakensberg map, and *Drakensberg Walks* will suffice; for further reference the several Pearse books and the Wildlife Society field guide can be consulted.
TERRAIN : The terrain here is most dramatic, perhaps the finest in all Africa south of the equator. This is where the name *Quathlamba* – the Barrier of Spears – best describes the Drakensberg. The hike is, therefore, very demanding.
WHAT TO TAKE : You will need a good tent, and reliable rain gear (army raincoats are useless in the type of storms you are likely to encounter). Gaiters are recommended, while

proper hiking boots are essential. Avoid the less expensive, lightweight hiking boots made of synthetic fibre, as they tend to collapse if your feet pronate even slightly. Even if you leave on a sunny day, take additional warm clothing. Rather use a liquid fuel stove, as pressurized cannisters might not work at the high altitude. Between April and September, you must have thermal underwear or a warm tracksuit to sleep in, as well as a warm sleeping bag.
SPECIAL PRECAUTIONS : Do not do this as a first hike unless you feel the need to suffer unduly. Your equipment should be of sound mountaineering quality, and you must be prepared to sit out a storm for a few days if necessary. Ideally you should have two vehicles, one left at the top of Mike's Pass, if you want to make this something less than an epic. Unless you are booked into the hotel, don't go onto their property – they will be justified in being rude. With the correct attire, however, you may book for dinner, or even a weekend dinner-dance. Take your passport, as you are likely to walk for some way into Lesotho. In recent years there have been unpleasant incidents with Basotho herders or hunters, so preferably hike in a group, be courteous where possible, and carry a big stick.
TRAIL OPTIONS : This hike can be reversed, or walked in any number of alternatives, longer or shorter. From the campsite and hotel there are numerous day walks and longer hikes.

RHEBOK TRAIL

T his trail falls entirely within the Golden Gate Highlands National Park, and gets its name from the fact that rhebok were the most abundant surviving game species when the park was declared. The park incorporates an interesting part of the Drakensberg 'Little 'Berg' foot-hills, with the topography varying between 1 500 m and 2 750 m, disproving the common perception that the Orange Free State is as flat as a mealie field. This two-day trail is fairly strenuous, and the estimated times given in the trail brochure must have been calculated by timing a bounding rhebok over the distance, or at least someone without a full hiking pack.

The most imposing physical features of the park are the prominent sandstone portals that flank the Little Caledon River, the so-called Golden Gates, comprising the Brandwag (sentinel), Gladstone and Mushroom Rocks. Protruding from the incised plateau terraces on top of this sandstone base are the peaks of Wodehousekop, Generaalskop, Snow Hills and, highest of all, Ribbokskop, where the high Drakensberg basalt capping has not quite weathered away.

A bonus of hiking in this and other game reserves is that hikers have the chance of encountering game close up, on foot. It is possible, with stealth and some basic knowledge of tracking, to get very close to eland, zebra, blesbok, black wildebeest, and even mountain reedbuck, oribi and grey rhebok if you are lucky enough to surprise them on the grassy knolls where they lie up during the daytime. Alternatively, you might locate their drinking places and decide to lie up there yourself at dawn and dusk (while the others are enjoying the warm hospitality of the hut) to catch them coming down in the low light to drink. For this, your best allies are silence and dull-coloured clothing.

DAY 1 *GLEN REENEN/RUGGED GLEN CAMPS TO RHEBOK HUT: 15 KM*

Leaving Rugged Glen campsite (no. 1 on the map) the trail path crosses the Little Caledon River footbridge but, instead of taking the main path to Echo Gorge, it forks off to the left, through an ouhout (*Leucosidea sericea*) thicket where malachite sunbirds are often seen. The path continues along the base of the impressive, overhanging Red Bed and Cave Sandstone cliffs of the Brandwag buttress, where rock martins and several species of swallow swoop and wheel around their nests. In the past visitors had the privilege of seeing a bearded vultures' nest high up on the cliffs here, but about eight years ago this last pair in the Free State disappeared. This is the largest raptor in Africa and second in size only to the American condor, although the former is a more strikingly attractive creature.

The path climbs a gully on the northern side of the buttress, with a short section of chain to aid those who need it. Once

The Brandwag, one of the numerous sandstone portals that flank the Little Caledon River, and the 'golden gates' of the national park.

on top of the buttress, the physical layout of the park can be appreciated, composed as it is of one major and numerous side valleys, with the higher peaks rising from the grassy plateaux. The path continues to climb up the slopes of Wodehousekop (2 438 m), the rank grass hiding Victorin's warblers and cloud cisticolas, while black harriers hunt by gliding low over the hills. The path climbs a low barrier of cliffs, and then crosses a low col (no. 3) between two sub-peaks (both 2 427 m) before dropping down the north-western slope of the peak.

This area is a favourite grazing spot for game herds, so keep this in mind when breasting rises. Oribi, a rare and very shy species of grassland antelope, tend to hide out in the taller grass stands to the left, but you will need great skill to track them. Dropping further down to the plateau level a number of seasonal pans and salt licks attract blesbok, springbok and black wildebeest, of which the largest herd of these endemic Highveld grazers is found in the park. The path follows a stream for some distance, its banks for much of the year aglow with red hot pokers (*Kniphofia* sp.) which attract a colourful parade of birds and butterflies. It then leads to the edge of Boskloof, where the wooded ravine (no. 4) and Bridal Veil Falls can be seen below.

Further on the trail leads down into Boskloof, crisscrossing the river until reaching the Bushman Cave (no. 5), a pleasant lunch spot. The path then climbs and curves for a short way to the right, around Tweelingkop. A slippery and often indistinct path descends from the plateau level, to Wilgenhof youth camp in the main valley of the Little Caledon River, which forms the park's main axis. It then crosses the tarred road at Gladstone and follows the Ribbokspruit for about 2 km to Rhebok hut, through a dense growth of ouhout, the limbs of which suggest grotesque fairytale forms. This small tree, which the Zulus call *it-shitshi*, is the most common tree of the 'Berg foothills, growing mainly on forest margins and river banks. Spend some time exploring Cathedral Cave, found in the cliffs directly west of the hut. During the night the sonorous hooting of an eagle owl might drift down from the cliffs, a most comforting lullaby.

LEFT Hikers ford the upper reaches of the Ribbokspruit, as they approach Generaalskop. The trail is named after the grey rhebok, a species which thrives in this grassy montane habitat.
ABOVE Protea roupelliae is one of the most widespread proteas, occurring throughout the montane grasslands of southern Africa.

DAY 2 *RHEBOK HUT TO GLEN REENEN CAMP : 15 KM*

The second day involves a climb to the top of Generaalskop (2 732 m) and down again: on this section it would be wise to keep plasters and water handy. The path follows the river to its source, a boggy spring about 4 km above the hut. This section is on a gentle uphill gradient, offering a most pleasant morning stroll through the riverine bush. Along the way is the Crevasse (no. 10), where the river cuts deep into its soft sandstone bed, a bathing pool and a waterfall (no. 11), formed by a resistant dolerite shelf lying across the course of the river.

From December to March pineapple flowers (*Eucomis humilis*) bloom near the waterfall. They are easily recognized by a cylindrical yellow-green flower cluster on a stalk, topped by a knot of bunched, leaf-like bracts. Along this section I flushed quite a few mountain reedbuck from the rank grass, sometimes singly and sometimes in pairs, but they would immediately bound off up the hillslopes and vanish over the nearest horizon. If they spy you approaching you might locate these medium-size, tawny antelope by the shrill whistle they issue. But, since they rely on camouflage, you may not be able to discern their forms within the tall grass cover.

About 2 km above the waterfall a fence prevents you from falling over the sudden drop into Lesotho's Caledon River valley. This spot is the viewsite shown as no. 12 on the map. The views over the huts and fields in the valley below, and the high surrounding peaks (the three highest in the area) are splendid indeed. Follow the fence, which demarcates the borderline, steeply uphill towards the summit of Generaalskop. I had an unnerving encounter here with a large rinkhals, which probably got a far greater fright than I did: it reared up in reaction to my looming boot, then slithered away from me into the grass. The path here was overgrown so I was glad to have my stick, helpful also to sweep away dew and cobwebs, and to double up as a camera brace.

On reaching a corner of the fence you can take the lesser route, following a platform to the left around the peak, or continue up to the summit (no. 13). The braver ascent requires scrambling up a steep grassy slope and then picking your way through the basalt band to the top. One thinks of lizards as inhabiting only hot climes, but this is not so. For high up here, in an area often windswept and snowbound, geckos, skinks and small rock agamas dash about busily, in unexpected abundance. If you do make the summit, retrace your steps back down through the basalt zone, and then take the path of least resistance down to the stony terrace. The path here is most indistinct, but follow the terrace to a gully on the peak's north-western slope.

Descending the damp gully I found clumps of an attractive pink pineapple flower (*Eucomis bicolor*), as well as *Moraea* iris blooms and a tall ground orchid that I have not been able to identify. The path leads out onto a rocky mountain spine where baboons and small herds of springbok may be seen. This spur is followed all the way down to Langtoon Dam (no. 14); the dam gets its name from the Afrikaans translation of jacana, but since they do not occur here, it is more likely to refer to other resident reed skulkers such as the purple gallinule or moorhen. Continuing down the spur an artificial but pleasant willow-shaded rock pool is encountered on the Buffelspruit. Glen Reenen rest camp and Rugged Glen campsite are only a few hundred metres on from this swimming hole.

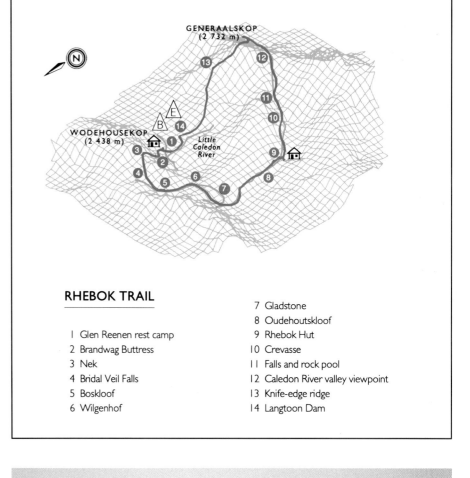

RHEBOK TRAIL

1 Glen Reenen rest camp
2 Brandwag Buttress
3 Nek
4 Bridal Veil Falls
5 Boskloof
6 Wilgenhof

7 Gladstone
8 Oudehoutskloof
9 Rhebok Hut
10 Crevasse
11 Falls and rock pool
12 Caledon River valley viewpoint
13 Knife-edge ridge
14 Langtoon Dam

OPPOSITE Holkrans Cave, less than 1 km from Brandwag rest camp, looks out over the Little Caledon River valley and the highlands of the eastern Orange Free State. *RIGHT* A female rhebok peers warily at a hiker. Although these fleet antelope are plentiful here and regularly sighted, they seldom wait to be photographed.

THE TRAIL AT A GLANCE

STARTING POINT : Glen Reenen or Rugged Glen camps

FINISHING POINT : Glen Reenen or Rugged Glen camps

LENGTH : 30 km

DURATION : Two days

GROUP LIMIT : 18 people

ROUTE : From the Golden Gate Highlands National Park campsite, the trail crosses the Little Caledon River and climbs Wodehousekop to take a circular, anti-clockwise route around the park. After recrossing the Little Caledon River the night is spent in the Rhebok hut, up a tributary of the same name. From there the path climbs Generaalskop (2 732 m) before completing the circle to Glen Reenen via a pleasant rock pool on the Buffelsspruit.

HOW TO GET THERE : From Bethlehem proceed to Clarens, where you turn left (east) up the Little Caledon River valley to the park.

BOOKING AUTHORITY : National Parks Board. Pretoria : P.O. Box 787, Pretoria,

0001; tel. (012) 343-1991.
Cape Town : P.O. Box 7400, Roggebaai, 8012; tel. (021) 22-2810.

ACCOMMODATION : A hut with bunks and mattresses, lights, cooking utensils and a gas stove, and firewood in a reed boma.

CLIMATE : The park is situated in the Drakensberg foothills, where summers are warm and regularly subjected to thunderstorms, while winters are cold to very cold, with frequent snowfalls.

BEST TIME TO HIKE : Spring and autumn, although the heaviest snowfalls also occur in spring. Towards autumn the weather becomes increasingly misty. Rain can fall at any time of year, although winter averages are low.

REFERENCES : Trail information brochure and sketch map.

TERRAIN : The trail falls entirely within the Little 'Berg foothills. In places the landscape soars above the plateaux, where basalt outliers of the high Drakensberg remain, such as Snow Hills and Ribbokskop (2 837 m). The trail is of average distance (15 km each day) but relatively demanding.

WHAT TO TAKE : Definitely rain gear and something warm to wear, except during winter and early spring when full mountaineering clothing will be needed. In summertime light boots may suffice (I fancy the range of boots made locally by the Lubbe company of Stellenbosch), though not running shoes. In winter heavier boots are recommended.

SPECIAL PRECAUTIONS : Spitting cobras (rinkhals) and puffadders are common here, so wear ankle-high boots and carry a stick to rake the grass where it overgrows the path (snake bite serum is no longer recommended by most experts, as it can complicate symptoms). Water must be carried on the first half of day one and the second half of day two.

TRAIL OPTIONS : This park was proclaimed primarily for its scenic beauty, so hiking is a major attraction. Numerous other day walks radiate out from the Rugged Glen campsite and luxury Brandwag rest camp. For further details consult *Drakensberg Walks* and the Olivier's trail guide. Horse trails are led by a ranger from the stables at Gladstone.

SUIKERBOSRAND TRAIL

Many people would argue that the Suikerbosrand Hiking Trail does not meet the requirements of one of the 'best trails in the country', but I would convince them otherwise. Its most obvious attraction is that it is so close to the PWV industrial complex, and thus provides an easy hiking opportunity for Highveld workaholics. It is also the best preserved example of the Highveld grassland habitat, and one for which I have a particular fondness. But even more important is the fact that the trail is easily accessible to the very young and old alike, as well as everyone in between.

In South Africa's very extensive hiking system, few other trails cater for the not-so-athletic outdoor enthusiasts. When I was younger, and before I had children of my own, I believed that one had to physically win one's place in the outdoors. While I still hold this to be true of wilderness areas, I now believe everyone has not just a right, but a duty to immerse themselves in nature.

The Cape Fynbos, forests and wetlands are well-known as being endangered habitats, but the open Highveld plains are fast being gobbled up by urban expansion, where they have not already been ploughed under to maize. In its natural state this veld type is as rich and attractive as any other, and perhaps more so for me as it is here that I grew up, when there were still wild tracts and even wild animals outside nature reserves.

The reserve covers 13 337 ha of hilly and, in places, craggy grassland, with some scrub and bush in the sheltered valleys and kloofs. The more hilly terrain in the east of the reserve is characterized by protea veld, the dominant species being the common sugarbush or 'suikerbossie' (*Protea caffra*), after which this range is named. As would be expected, the most common birds in the reserve are typical grassveld species such as cisticolas, larks, pipits and chats, but it is the otherwise bland widow birds and whydahs, which put on outrageous displays of breeding plumage from spring to early summer, that are the most attractive. As regards the trail, I had only two days in which to do it, so I travelled light and completed the Olivier's (see references) four-day recommended trail in two. Even this I found to be easy going with a day pack and sleeping bag. For purposes of the trail description, I will give it as two longish days' walking, skipping out two huts along the way.

Suikerbosrand preserves a part of the Highveld as it was before giving way to mines and mealies. Animals such as the black wildebeest and the bontebok were once numerous all across these grassy plains.

DAY I DIEPKLOOF TO ELAND HUT: 19 KM

Having parked in the shade at Diepkloof and reported to the visitors' centre office, take the path at the far, north-eastern corner of the car park, going eastwards (but do not follow the gravel road to Kiepersol group camp). The path leads gently over Baboon Ridge, where you will see your first 'suikerbossies' and, if these are in flower, flashy malachite sunbirds in attendance. On the north-eastern side of the ridge, above the path, you will see the largest and most concentrated specimens in the reserve of the flat-flowered aloe (*Aloe marlothii*) silhouetted against the crag.

On reaching a signposted cairn, the path turns right, up the wide and shallow grassy valley (instead of straight on to Blesbok hut). There follows an easy stroll to a low saddle, and at about the 2 km mark there is a stone wall dating back to the time of the first white settlement in the area. This wall, unlike the much older Iron Age cattle kraals found across the Highveld, was constructed to divert a subterranean reservoir into the wooded side kloof here. An old stone kraal site, one of many that are found in the western side of the reserve, can be seen at marker no. 3 of the Cheetah Interpretive Trail. Ash heaps (small knolls covered with short grass) have revealed remains of cattle, goats, river mussels, francolin, tortoises, porcupine, mongoose, jackal, wild dog, hyaena, steenbok, blesbok, eland, springbok and mountain reedbuck. A variety of clay pot shards, copper ornaments, iron rods, spears and hoes have been excavated, and millet and sorghum seeds found. These artifacts have provided anthropologists with deeper insight into the Iron Age culture.

In 1837, when the Voortrekkers first entered the Highveld, the relatively peaceful pastoralists of the region had been recently uprooted by the break-away Zulu chief Mzilikazi, during the Mfecane, the wars of forced migration. When Mzilikazi's impis encountered the vanguard trekker party under Hendrik Potgieter, near present-day Potchefstroom, they ambushed and killed them. A retaliatory commando set out to drive the renegade Zulus further into the western Transvaal. The next year, by which time white farmers had established themselves right across the southern Transvaal, a 330-strong mounted commando assembled along the northern slopes of the Suikerbosrand, and proceeded to rout Mzilikazi from his stronghold in the Marico district. He then fled across the Limpopo River to found the Matabele nation in western Zimbabwe.

Approximately 3 km from the kraal site the path levels out onto the open plateau that covers much of the reserve's eastern section. The tarred tourist route is crossed shortly afterwards at an altitude of 1 880 m. Game such as eland, Burchell's zebra, blesbok, red hartebeest, jackals, black wildebeest, mountain reedbuck and grey rhebok frequent the area, congregating in the open towards dusk. The birds of the montane grasslands include greywing and redwing francolin, whitebellied and black korhaans, ground woodpecker, anteating chat and dikkop. The four cisticolas, all of which display prominently in summer, are the fantailed, desert, cloud and Ayres' species. The longbilled lark is the most common of the larks, but spikeheeled and redcapped larks also occur. Of the pipits, the grassveld pipit frequents the short, open grasslands, the longbilled pipit the rocky areas, and the plainbacked pipit the heavily grazed or burned areas.

You should see most of these, but unless you are an experienced birder, identifying only the genus is work enough for a laden hiker. Far easier to identify, but only when displaying their mating plumage, are the widow birds. The larger and more spectacular of the two species is *iSakabuli*, the rainbird of Zulu lore, otherwise known as the longtailed widow. These birds have conspicuous long black tail plumes and red and white shoulder flashes. They forage on the ground or by clinging to a long grass stem, and display by flying between perches, the tail held to form a sickle shape. Males are polygamous, breeding during the day with whatever female takes a fancy to them, and retire to male-only roosts at night, while the females are left to rear the offspring alone. Similar, but less impressive, is the redcollared widow.

As the trail descends into Kiepersolkloof, protea veld is encountered around the rocky rim of the plateau. It then skirts another old kraal site and continues into the wooded kloof where the Springbok hut is reached at mid-altitude: this will be our lunch spot. The *kiepersol* is the mountain cabbage tree (*Cussonia paniculata*), commonly found on rocky ground in the PWV area. It is easily recognized by the rounded bunches of large, elongated, lacy palm-like leaves. This is one of about ten cabbage tree species, of which *C. spicata* is the most widespread.

The trail continues from the hut in a westerly direction, keeping for some way to the wooded kloof, where ouhout (*Leucosidea sericea*), wild olive (the 'swart olienhout') and olive sagewood ('wit olienhout) are most common. The path then regains the montane plateau, running more or less parallel to the tourist route (with pylon line in view), before reaching Blind Man's Corner. This is where the path swings sharply to the left (south), to make its way across alternately grassy and rocky, undulating terrain. The small succulent *Aloe davyana*, the pink flowers of which shimmer among winter's bleached grass cover, are found here, providing the baboons haven't ripped them all to pieces.

Descending Kareekloof (named after the karee taaibos, *Rhus lancea*), the Overvaal resort comes into view. The path continues along a grassy shoulder, and then begins the long descent of the Doringbospad, making for the mouth of Kareekloof. The Doringbospad is named after the *Acacia caffra* and *A. karroo* thorn trees that dominate the low-lying grass plains. If cheetah are to be found, and there are reportedly two left in the park, it is my guess that this is the area where they would be, since it is as close to the African Bushveld as one gets in the southern Transvaal.

In 1975 eight cheetah were caught on neighbouring farms, where they were in danger of becoming exterminated, and relocated here. So successfully did they proliferate that within several years the reserve accommodated nearly forty of these sleek predators. Most were used to restock other game reserves and only two were left here, to do their best in keeping extinction at bay. The reserve's fauna list also includes brown hyaenas and leopard. Obviously signs of both must have been found in the reserve, but I doubt its ability to sustain breeding populations of either, and presume the animals in question must be vagrants.

The thornveld and grassland mosaic

here is also the only place in the reserve where paradise whydahs, often confused with longtailed widows by novice birdwatchers, are found (pintailed whydahs are quite common in the montane grasslands). Also found in the bushveld-type habitat are black and doublecollared sunbirds, plumcoloured starlings, jacobin and redchested cuckoos (the Piet-my-vrou), honeyguides, barbets and paradise flycatchers.

The path continues down the valley, to cross the Kareekloof road, and then begins a long but undemanding ascent through the Aloe Forest (*A. marlothii* again), which in places attains a height of 6 m, although 3 m is more common.

After a 1,5 km uphill haul, the trail re-emerges on the grass plateau, contouring around the Perdekop (1 875 m), and descending once again to the acacia thornveld. On reaching the valley floor the

path turns sharp right to reach Eland hut, set among the trees in a normally dry river valley.

DAY 2 *ELAND HUT TO DIEPKLOOF: 23 KM*

If this distance seems too much to ask of a weary hiker, it is possible to take an alternative route, past Blesbok hut back to Diepkloof, of a little more than half this distance. The long route retraces the approach route to the hut for a short distance before branching off to the right, and then turns sharp right again to climb out of the valley, heading up an open grass slope. On attaining an altitude of about 1 800 m the path levels off, reaching a side junction at around the 2 km mark. If you plan to overnight at Steenbok hut, which is bypassed early on in

the day, then turn right here to take the downhill, more circuitous route. Otherwise, continue straight across the plateau to beacon no. 9.

This area is known as the Springbokvlakte, where springbok, blesbok, zebra and black wildebeest are likely to be seen. The beacon is situated at the bottom of a short downhill ramp, at a point separating two kloofs. Here the route bears right, to zigzag steeply down for about 1 km. The valley forest reaches high up the slopes, until it is checked by the prominent crags. Somewhere on a ledge up to the left breeds the resident pair of black eagles in the reserve. The

ABOVE A view over Diepkloof and the farm of the same name, now part of the rest camp. The large white building is part of the original farm built in about 1850 by Voortrekker Jan Gabriel Marais.

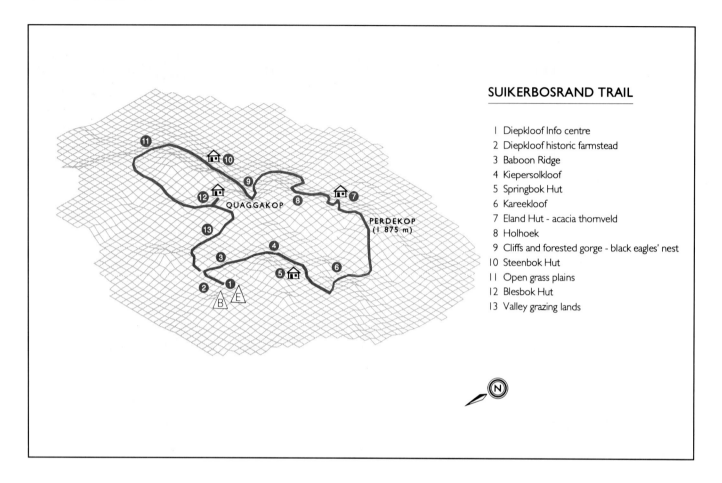

SUIKERBOSRAND TRAIL

1 Diepkloof Info centre
2 Diepkloof historic farmstead
3 Baboon Ridge
4 Kiepersolkloof
5 Springbok Hut
6 Kareekloof
7 Eland Hut - acacia thornveld
8 Holhoek
9 Cliffs and forested gorge - black eagles' nest
10 Steenbok Hut
11 Open grass plains
12 Blesbok Hut
13 Valley grazing lands

QUAGGAKOP

PERDEKOP
(1 875 m)

distribution of these magnificent birds depends almost entirely on suitable cliff nesting sites and the availability of dassies, their main prey.

Steenbok hut is found at about the 8 km mark. You should stock up with water here, but try not to intrude on other hikers who have claim to the place. (Remember that the drinking water points shown on the map apply only when the reserve's intermittent streams are flowing.) For the next 8 km the path skirts around higher ground on the left, keeping all the time to an easy contour. At first it meanders through woodland, then emerges into open grassland after about 2 km. Below and to the right the vista sweeps over the Hartebeesvlakte, where herds of red hartebeest like to gather. In places where the grass is rank shy oribi will lie up, breaking cover only at the last minute. You will then learn why the species is endangered: they will bound off for about 50 m, then stop and turn to look back at you. This behaviour makes them an easy target for even a poor shot. Reedbuck (which, together with spring-

bok are the cheetah's favourite dinner) often do the same, except they frequent a more concealing habitat.

The route continues in a northerly direction, passing side junctions at beacon nos. 14 and 15, before again crossing the tourist route road, and curving around to the west. The path heads up Hyaena Kloof, where cabbage trees, the common sugarbush and silver sugarbush grow together. Be on the lookout for eland, for they seem to favour the edge of wooded areas during the day. I flushed a black-backed jackal here, which I found to be common in the reserve. Some large old-wood trees are found where the kloof becomes densely wooded, their gnarled forms evoking nightmarish images.

Beacon no. 12 is reached at the head of the kloof, where a side path leads off to Blesbok hut. The trail route continues straight, over a rock-scattered, grassy ridge, descending into a valley with two small dams. The path approaches the reserve fence, where it joins a 4x4 track on a winding uphill course. After about 1 km it levels out on a crest, where the re-

mains of an Iron Age kraal provide an interesting diversion. The trail becomes progressively easier as it follows the 4x4 track, past grazing cows and horses. Soon beacon no. 2 is reached – the first junction encountered on the outward trip. From here the walk to Diepkloof is a mere formality.

Before you leave, however, it is worth paying a visit to the farm museum, near the information centre. The old pioneer house and outbuildings were built by Jan Gabriel Marais, who left Beaufort West with the Great Trek to settle here in about 1850. That makes the farm buildings among the oldest remaining in the Transvaal. Marais, his wife Cornelia and their eight children established a mixed farm here in Koedoekloof. The small cemetery, with its low stone wall, and the silver-gold veld beyond vividly evoke the lines of Toon van den Heever's poem *In Die Hoëveld*.

It seems almost apocryphal here, where skyscrapers from the city built on gold can be seen probing the smog-polluted sky to the north, for the poem tells of a farmer who has to pack up during the depression to get a job on the mines. While underground, dying of typhus, he dreams of his home…

'In die Hoeveld, waar dit oop is en die hemel wyd daarbo,

Waar kuddes waaigras huppel oor die veld,

Waar 'n mens nog vry kan asemhaal en aan 'n God kan glo,

Staan my huisie, wat ek moet verlaat vir geld…'

He dreams of the breeze, blowing freely across the wide-open veld, and buck playing on the fallen gravestones… In his mind he seeks out his favourite places, where as a child he made 'kleiosse'. It could have been here, at Diepkloof.

It is for good reason that the blue crane is the national bird, for it is found only in southern Africa, and is only common in the grasslands of South Africa.

THE TRAIL AT A GLANCE

STARTING POINT : Diepkloof visitors' centre
FINISHING POINT : Diepkloof visitors' centre
LENGTH : Variable, with huts being approximately 5 km to 12 km apart, but huts may be bypassed if desired.
DURATION : One to six days
GROUP LIMIT : 10 people
ROUTE : Six trail huts may be connected in any order or direction.
HOW TO GET THERE : From Johannesburg follow the N3 towards Heidelberg. Take the R550 turn-off to Nigel and Kliprivier, turning right towards the latter place. About 6 km along this road you will see the reserve signposted to the left, and it is reached 4 km further on.
BOOKING AUTHORITY : The officer-in-charge, Suikerbosrand Nature Reserve, Private Bag H616, Heidelberg, 2400; tel. (0151) 9-5060.
ACCOMMODATION : There is an Overvaal resort at Kareekloof but, for the outdoor enthusiast, the less said of this the better. There are six trail huts, with beds and mattresses, water, firewood, gas lamps and toilets. There are also 'group camps' which cater for specialist groups other than hikers, and a Meditation Hut, which accommodates only one person at a time.

CLIMATE : The Highveld has perhaps the mildest climate on earth, with an annual temperature range of not more than 30 °C. Summers are warm and winters mild, although early morning temperatures can dip just below freezing point and visitors from the coast will find the dryness irritating. Rain falls mostly in summer afternoon thunder showers, while some frost may occur in winter. Once every ten years or so, snow falls on the Highveld.
BEST TIME TO HIKE : I would avoid only the midwinter months of May to August, when it is dry and cold and the vegetation is in its least appealing state.
REFERENCES : There are various reserve brochures, such as species checklists, but otherwise literature is scant.
TERRAIN : The Suikerbosrand is a range of low hills, about 50 km south of the similar Witwatersrand range. The main difference between the two is, apart from about 4 million people and 400 million years, that the Suikerbosrand does not have any of the sparkling streams that gave their name to the more northerly ridge where gold was found. Geologically they are quite different: the Witwatersrand is a complex group of very old (600 to 700 million years old) quarzites, conglomerates, banded ironstones and shales, while the Suikerbosrand comprises

much younger (about 250 million years old) Karoo period dolerite intrusions.
WHAT TO TAKE : Unless you intentionally plan things otherwise, this is an easy hike where game- and birdwatching can be pursued at ease. For novice birdwatchers it is the trail on which to come to grips with the grassland habitat species, especially when the fantastic breeding displays of some species are apparent. Therefore, make sure you pack a bird guide and a pair of binoculars. A field guide to the lovely wildflowers of the Witwatersrand and Pretoria regions might also come in handy. The Cape cobra and rinkhals are the only potentially dangerous snakes in the reserve, but paths are good and walking easy, so footwear is up to you.
SPECIAL PRECAUTIONS : Carry enough water each day, about two litres per person depending on the weather, although you will find drinking water at the huts which the route bypasses.
TRAIL OPTIONS : As I have mentioned above, hikers may compile any route between huts in the reserve (according to availability), as long as they don't spend more than one consecutive night in each hut. The 4 km Cheetah Interpretative Trail is extremely informative, and designed to give day visitors a deeper understanding of the area's natural and human history.

RUSTENBURG TRAIL

One of the reasons for including this in my favourite hikes is that, as with the Suikerbosrand Trail, it is a relatively short and easy hike falling within the PWV area. But even if it were not so I would have chosen it. The Magaliesberg, the range within which the hike is located, is for me and all other mountaineers who know it, a very special place. It is the meeting place of two major biomes, the Highveld grasslands and Bushveld savanna, and is an interesting blend of both. To casual travellers it is merely a range of low hills, with south-facing scarps, whereas in fact it is a wonderland of montane grasslands and wooded valleys. But most impressive is the network of deeply incised, sheer-sided kloofs that dissect the range. Within these kloofs rivers plummet and waterfalls play muted liquid music. Various forest types mingle here, forming a high canopy above the labyrinthine passageways.

This is the place that I first communed with nature, among brown hyaena and leopard, Cape vultures, black and martial eagles, grey rhebok, klipspringers and mountain reedbuck, baboons and monkeys, to name a few species. Originally one circular route was designed to cover the western, more open part of the Rustenburg Nature Reserve (the Rietvallei circle which is described here), while another was to have explored the eastern part, including the Waterkloofspruit, running through one of the enticing gorges. But, for logic best known to him, the officer-in-charge has decided that 'some places are too good' to let visitors know about. Nevertheless, this hike has enough of its own charms to be highly rewarding.

The Magaliesberg has featured prominently in many vital chapters of this country's past: early hominid remains from about 2,5 million years ago have been unearthed in the nearby dolomite caves of Kromdraai and Sterkfontein, and it can therefore be assumed that the earliest *Homo sapiens* lived and hunted here too. During the time of the *Mfecane* wars local clans took refuge from Mzilikazi's marauding impis in the deep gorges of the Magaliesberg; the range is named after Mohale, the chief of one of these clans. Some of the final, decisive battles of the South African War were fought in and around the mountains near Hekpoort. During the war's guerilla phase, the maze of mountains provided a conduit by which the Boer forces moved through occupied territory. British blockhouses can still be seen guarding the approaches to some of the well-known passes.

A storm brews over the Rooihartebees hut, which will soon be subjected to a fury of rain and hail.

DAY 1 *KOEDOE HUT TO ROOIHARTEBEES HUT: 8,5 KM*

You would be wise to find parking in the shade here, for this valley simmers in the summer heat. If you have been clever and are ready to set out in the early morning, then the climb up to Sering Valley will be a most pleasant one. However, if like me you set off at midday then be sure to have a long drink and fill your water bottles from the tap at Koedoe hut. The hut, a reed and thatch boma-like structure, may be used by hikers the night before the hike commences.

Behind the hut the path zigzags up the north-facing slope of the range for about 2 km, gaining about 200 m in altitude. The slope is stony, and you can clearly see the very pure quartzite from which the Magaliesberg is composed. So glassy is the rock that one of the country's leading glass producers has a quarry east of here. Given the slope's aspect it receives a surfeit of sunshine and will, therefore, also have a high evaporation rate. The vegetation on this section thus has a close affinity with the Bushveld that stretches northwards from here: Bushveld is characterized by an evaporation rate, including transpiration by plants, that exceeds its rainfall. The dominant trees are acacia thorn trees and two species of bush-willow, the red bushwillow (*Combretum apiculatum*) and the large-fruited bush-willow (*C. zeyheri*). This latter species is said to indicate 'sour bushveld' – the veld type which Acocks designated for the area. Across the valley one can see an abundance of flat-flowered aloes (*Aloe marlothii*) growing on the hillside.

[John P.H. Acocks was employed by the Dept of Agriculture, and what turned out to be his life's work was a classification of South Africa into 'veld types' specifying the main species in each. He also identified the long- and short-term effects of man's influence on the country's natural vegetation. In the course of his work Acocks travelled hundreds of thousands of (mostly dusty) kilometres. His *Veld Types of South Africa* was first published in 1953, and since then it has become the most frequently quoted scientific text in the country.]

As one gains height, Rustenburg's suburbia comes into view, with the industry of Rustenburg Platinum Mines dominating the town. Platinum is the most important mineral extracted from the laval deposits of the Bushveld Igneous Complex geological system. These lavas were poured out onto a sandstone bed of the Transvaal Supergroup about 600 million years ago. Such was the weight of this extrusion that it compressed the sandstones, metamorphosing the contact rocks and lifting them around its perimeter. It is as if a giant foot had stepped into the middle of the Transvaal, pushing up the surrounding rocks like uptilted pavement blocks. This 'popping up' effect formed the ranges of Magaliesberg, Waterberg and the Eastern Transvaal escarpment. The kloofs within the Magaliesberg are stress fractures caused during the formation of these mountains.

Where the path levels out, the impressive crags of Kraaikrans (crow cliff) can be seen down to the right. Small sugarbushes (*Protea caffra*) grow between rocky outcrops, where they have been protected from fire, providing welcome shade on a hot day. From here the path drops down to the Seringvlakte, where path erosion has been checked with the use of sandbags. On the descent the first clear Magaliesberg vista opens out to the east. Just before crossing the tarred road to the visitors' centre, the path enters a grove of what must be the most southerly growing mountain seringas in the province. The path then rounds a rocky ridge to enter the valley of the Waterkloofspruit, known as Rietvallei.

A short way upstream there is a weir across the river, where it is advisable to fill up your water bottles; a sign warns against swimming, but you could dip your head and shoulders, and dangle your legs in the pool. Once you've cooled off, continue along the path, which skirts around fertile Rietvallei in a wide arc to the left, making its way along a rocky area towards Boekenhoutsknop. This is a most appropriate name since the rocky veld here is dominated by boekenhout trees (*Faurea saligna*). This species could be confused with the karee tree (*Rhus lancea*), but you might be surprised to find it classified as a primitive member of the very widespread protea family. It is another environmental indicator of sourveld in the Transvaal, which is confined to deficient or poorly developed soils.

A smaller, more rounded tree found in abundance in the rockier areas here is the Transvaal milkplum. The Afrikaans name of 'stamvrug' is more revealing for the sweet, apricot-like fruits are borne directly on the stems. Its botanical name *Bequaertiodendron magalismontanum* rivals the jackal-berry tree, *Diospyros mespiliformis*, as a taxonomical tongue twister. The stamvrug is confined to rocky, mountainous areas of the Transvaal and the fruits, borne in midsummer, are highly sought after and acquired by baboons and humans alike.

The path crosses numerous small, intermittent streams, shaded by tall boekenhout trees, and one perennial stream where Whitewater Pool is a welcome respite. After crossing two more, usually dry, stream beds the path meanders through open protea veld. A prominent outcrop of weathered quartzite called the Little Matopos is bypassed, and from here Rooihartebees hut is but a frisbee throw away.

The hut looks out onto a small stream, opening out beyond into a deep gorge. Stately boekenhouts shade the camp, where cooking is done in an open reed boma. Mocking chats are resident cohabitors of the camp, while redcollared widow birds flit about the rank grass and bracken-briar along the stream. Summer afternoon thunderstorms here cast gold and purple light over the western Transvaal, as great wind-formed thunder palaces rise to mask the sun.

DAY 2 *ROOIHARTEBEES HUT TO KOEDOE HUT: 12 KM*

Although most of the day's walking is downhill or on the upper plateau, there are enough ups and downs to make it more than just a stroll. The trail sets off in a westerly direction, first crossing the small stream directly opposite the hut to make a detour around the upper reaches of the gorge. The path then runs more or less parallel and fairly close to the reserve boundary, which in turn follows the line of the south-facing escarpment. For the first 2 km the path takes a slight uphill gradient towards the edge of the escarpment, where a magnificent viewsite is reached, situated among protea and stamvrug trees.

Depending on the state of the veld, various grazers might be seen along the way. After fire when the short and green

LEFT The sable, most handsome of the antelope, was first recorded in the Magaliesberg by hunter-explorer Captain William Cornwallis Harris, who shot a fine specimen and sent it to the British Museum. For a while thereafter the species was known as the 'Harris buck'. *ABOVE* Baboons, farmers and hikers in the Magaliesberg compete for the delicious fruits of the 'stamvrug' tree (*Bequaertiodendron magalismontanum*), which are borne directly on the stems in late summer.

grass is emerging, springbok, red hartebeest (after which the hut is named) and zebra are the likely species to be found here. Since entering the reserve my eyes had been scouring the tree lines for another species, one of the largest antelope species and certainly the most noble. As the path passed into a wooded depression my eye caught the graceful curve of horn and the characteristic black and white of a male sable. As we approached, it broke cover and cantered uphill, keeping to the tall grass on the edge of the tree line, its preferred habitat.

The first white person to record the species was hunter-explorer Captain William Cornwallis Harris, a year before the first party of Voortrekkers reached what

where then called the Cashan Mountains. A fine specimen he shot hereabouts was dispatched to the British Museum, and for some years afterwards the species was known as the Harris buck. Cornwallis also recorded a herd of approximately 300 elephants in the Rustenburg valley – and in true Victorian style he did his best to shoot as many as he could. The last elephant was shot here around the turn of the century by the father of a local farmer, at the Crocodile River near the Pelindaba nuclear research station.

Another animal for which I was on the lookout was the black eagle, my companion on so many Magaliesberg rock climbs when I lived near Johannesburg. And sure enough, as we reached the edge of

the escarpment I heard the familiar call; I looked up as a pair of these majestic mountain raptors soared overhead. For a few minutes they twisted and tumbled over our heads and then caught a thermal column of air. Moments later they were bound for the clouds, and soon they were virtually out of sight, all without a single flap of a wing. Then from the dense canopy of red milkwood, white stinkwood and wild fig trees on the slope below, there rose a sound conjuring dreams of lazy African days, the plaintive song of a redchested cuckoo: 'Piet-my-vrou, Piet-my-vrou'.

From the lookout, the path threads its way along the escarpment edge for a short way, before turning inland to take a

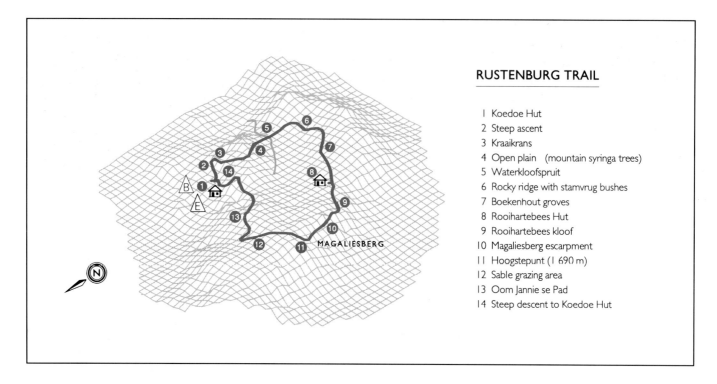

RUSTENBURG TRAIL

| 1 | Koedoe Hut
| 2 | Steep ascent
| 3 | Kraaikrans
| 4 | Open plain (mountain syringa trees)
| 5 | Waterkloofspruit
| 6 | Rocky ridge with stamvrug bushes
| 7 | Boekenhout groves
| 8 | Rooihartebees Hut
| 9 | Rooihartebees kloof
| 10 | Magaliesberg escarpment
| 11 | Hoogstepunt (1 690 m)
| 12 | Sable grazing area
| 13 | Oom Jannie se Pad
| 14 | Steep descent to Koedoe Hut

ABOVE *Aloe peglerae*, one of many plant species endemic to the Magaliesberg ecotone. *OPPOSITE* After a storm, soft evening light embraces the Magaliesberg's high plateaux, heralding a balmy Transvaal night. The climate here reflects a geographic location between the temperate Highveld and the tropical Bushveld.

slightly uphill route to Hoogstepunt (1 690 m), the highest point in the area, marked by a trig beacon. Here I saw my first eland on the hike, but as soon as it got wind of us it trotted off. For the next 10 minutes I could make out the shape of its horns just breaking the skyline as the animal kept its distance.

On an open patch of quartz gravel I spied what I think was one of the Magaliesberg's botanical rarities, *Frithia pulchra*. This minute, virtually stemless, fleshy-fingered plant resembles the stone plants of Namaqualand. Another endemic succulent, which is much easier to see, is *Aloe peglerae*, its red inflorescences lighting up the drab winter veld.

From Hoogstepunt the trail descends through grassland, crossing a boekenhout-lined stream, to make for another beacon on the Hartebeesrug ridge. Somewhere around here we lost the path in tall grass, and wandered off down a side valley. The animals weren't expecting two stupid hikers to leave the trail, and so it was with some delight (on our part) that we startled a herd of about 40 sable lying up in the shade. Near the stream (where one should carry on straight up the hill) there is one of several communities of the metre high *Protea welwitschii*. The untidy flower is small, creamy coloured and not overly impressive, but

it does have a delicious honey scent that attracts all manner of insects – which makes for good macro-photography.

Leaving Hartebeesrug the path follows the edge of a ridge, above the beckoning woods of Boskloof. Two painted feet indicate a viewsite across the gorge and Rustenburg town and not, as some unfortunate hikers presume, a route down into the kloof. It seems an obvious place to descend, but without a path it presents something of a survival course. This is an easy mistake to make as the path takes an indistinct line along the cliff edge. The head of a side gully is crossed to another high point where, surprise, the visitors' centre is virtually stumbled into.

Here the path joins Oom Jannie se Pad, a concrete service track that passes some magnificent tree aloes on its 3 km trip back to the starting point. The track ascends steeply for about 200 m, and then begins a steep, twisting descent past the culture centre and group camp. In the heat of a summer's day this northern slope bakes and the land shimmers in a heat haze. My teenage nephew longed for his skateboard, while I dreamed of iced beers to soothe my heat-blistered lips. Eventually we reached a familiar road, and once we'd negotiated what had become a river of molten tar, we arrived back at Koedoe hut.

THE TRAIL AT A GLANCE

STARTING POINT : Koedoe hut
FINISHING POINT : Koedoe hut
LENGTH : 20,6 km
DURATION : Two days
GROUP LIMIT : 10 people
ROUTE : The hike does a loop around the western half of Rustenburg Nature Reserve, with Rooihartebees hut located just short of the halfway mark, and the visitor's centre being the approximate centre of the loop.
HOW TO GET THERE : From Rustenburg there are two entrances to the reserve, the main one found along Boekenhout Road, and that to the hiking trail hut along Maroela Street. Unless you are well acquainted with the area, you will need the route map to find your way to the beginning of the trail. This will be posted to you together with your permit and map; if not, drive to the main office, collect your map and permit there, and then drive back through the town to find the other gate.
BOOKING AUTHORITY : Officer-in-charge, Rustenburg Nature Reserve, P. O. Box 511, Rustenburg, 0300; tel. (0142) 3-1050.
ACCOMMODATION : Hikers can overnight at the Koedoe hut before commencing the hike the following day. Both this and the Rooihartebees hut are pleasantly rustic, made of reed and thatch, with single beds and mattresses, firewood, and paraffin lamps (you might be lucky enough to have had the wicks replaced by the time you get there). Drinking water at Rooihartebees hut is from a nearby spring.
CLIMATE : The trail is confined to the Magaliesberg range of hills, which forms an ecotone (or meeting place) between the Highveld grasslands to the south and the Bushveld savanna to the north. It therefore represents the distributional limit of numerous species. The climate here is something between Bushveld and Highveld, being on average not quite as oppressive as the former and not quite as mild as the latter. However, summer days can be blistering, and I have experienced winter days shredded by freezing winds.
BEST TIME TO HIKE : I would avoid the months December to February inclusive, when temperatures in the valleys and on north-facing slopes can easily overcome a pack-laden hiker (especially considering the lack of water). Winter can be pleasant but, as I have suggested, cold fronts sweep the area from time to time. As with just about every other hike in the country, conditions are seldom extreme, but it is best to take your chances between March and May or August and November.
REFERENCES : Despite being told that an 'excellent' scale map of the trail was available, what I received looked as if a local kindergarten class had been given a blank piece of paper and black pens, and told to draw their own map. And for this I had to pay R3! It was possible to just make out the trail's general layout, but was quite useless as a reference. The reserve has no brochures, species checklists, or other literature, apart from that map. Vincent Carruthers' excellent book on the Magaliesberg is essential reading for all lovers of these much underestimated mountains.

TERRAIN : Hikers and mountaineers lucky enough to have access to the Magaliesberg hold it in deep regard, while the general public is sure to dismiss it as an insignificant line of hills. Nothing could be further from the truth, and this trail gives a hint (but, it is true, not the full experience) of the Magaliesberg's many attractions. Once inside the range, you will realise that it is far more rugged than one would imagine. The entire range is composed of very hard quartzite, which weathers to a rough, granular soil. Paths are good but often stony and loose, while gradients vary from easy to demanding, but never as sustained as most National Hiking Way trails.
WHAT TO TAKE : If hiking in summer, it is essential to carry at least two litres of water per person, as the natural water supplies are unreliable. Because of the lack of literature about the reserve's rich fauna and flora, you might wish to carry some kind of identification guide and binoculars.
SPECIAL PRECAUTIONS : I seem to have a habit of attracting snakes such as cobras and mambas when in the Magaliesberg, but since they have never bothered me I shouldn't bother about them. Perhaps one thing to avoid in summer is starting the trail after 10 am, when the longest ascent, up a furnace-like, north-facing slope, has to be tackled.
TRAIL OPTIONS : It was originally planned to open a second trail loop, through the more fertile eastern half of the reserve, but this option has now been shelved. The 4,5 km Peglerae Interpretative Trail can be taken from the visitors' centre.

BLYDERIVIERSPOORT TRAIL

T his trail is a good introduction to hiking for anyone who has never donned a backpack and headed into the great outdoors. Ease and shortness of daily walks, together with the trail's exquisite location, make it ideal for nature study, for swimming and for exploring the surrounding countryside. There are secret forested gorges, lofty falls and deep mountain pools, awesome mountain walls and distant views. This was the first of the National Hiking Way trails that I walked, my then purist mountaineering sentiments being wary of these manufactured intrusions. But such were the charms of this hike, that I have since become a National Hiking Way enthusiast.

The casual nature lover will find a great variety of landscapes, natural features and habitats to feast the eyes and keep the mind perpetually stimulated. For the more informed naturalist, the area is a fascinating and dynamic interface between biomes and veld types, where many endemic, rare and endangered species of fauna and flora can be observed. The trail passes through temperate Afro-montane forest on the high-lying eastern and southern slopes and ravines, sour grasslands with ribbons of riverine bush on the high plateaux, and mixed Bushveld on the north- and west-facing escarpment slopes within the Blyderivierspoort Nature Reserve. The path encounters some fynbos affinities along the canyon edge, before descending through sub-tropical gallery forest to true savanna woodland on the hot Lowveld floor.

The Blyderivierspoort is, after the Grand and Fish River canyons, the world's third-largest river-gouged canyon. From its beginnings just downstream of Bourke's Luck potholes, to its gaping mouth at the Blyderivierspoort Dam, it twists and turns through 18 km and drops some 800 m in altitude. On the fourth day, hikers follow the edge of the canyon, past sentinels such as the Three Rondavels, Swadini Peak, and massive Mariep's Kop, before heading down the Escarpment face to the Lowveld.

DAY I *GOD'S WINDOW TO WATERVALSPRUIT HUT : 5,8 KM*

The first day is a short stroll, with spectacular views along the Escarpment and over the Lowveld. From God's Window viewsite, the trail makes the short ascent of Quartzkop, through a miniature rain forest, to emerge into a delightful aloe and lichen garden, with old man's beard drooping from gnarled branches. After meandering easily through the montane grasslands away from the Escarpment edge, the path crosses the Lisbon River, where delightful Paradise Pool awaits. From the pool, fringed with tree ferns, it is a gentle uphill walk to the hut on the Watervalspruit. The hut's location is aesthetically concealed from view, having

It is really only from on high that one can appreciate the full extent of the Blyde River Canyon, the third-largest such formation on earth.

been cut into the hillside. This walk will take you less than two hours, and the rest of the day should be used for exploring upstream to the waterfalls, the riverine forest patches, and the various ruins in the area, and for admiring the views along the Escarpment.

The geology of this natural wonder is, in fact, quite simple. The great mountain wall is comprised entirely of very hard rocks known as the Black Reef quartzites. This group is the bottom-most of the Transvaal geological formation that lies underneath and encircles the more central Bushveld Igneous Complex. The great weight of this latter volcanic extrusion caused the older Transvaal rocks to sag in the middle and buckle up along the edge, like two pavement slabs being pushed down where they meet and lifting up along their outer edges. Because it is so hard, the Black Reef quartzite has successfully withstood eons of erosive forces to form the massed cliffs of the Transvaal Drakensberg.

For those more acquainted with the Cape's spartan National Hiking Way huts, the accommodation here will seem either excessive or pure luxurious bliss: showers with donkey boilers, flush toilets, and a fireplace with cast iron cooking pots provided. When I first did this trail in 1979, there was even a hut caretaker who made the fire and cleaned up, just like at the huts on Malawi's famous Mulanje mountain.

DAY 2 *WATERVALSPRUIT HUT TO CLEARSTREAM HUT: 13,5 KM*

This day's route goes from Watervalspruit to a most beautiful location at Clearstream. From Poolie Pool on the Watervalspruit, the trail winds through eroded quartzite outcrops, liberally decorated with multi-coloured lichen encrustations. After about 3 km, the path descends fairly steeply down into the Treur River valley, but it is a way yet until the river is met. Keep a lookout along here for klipspringer and grey rhebok, which inhabit these high-lying areas. It was here that I saw my first redbreasted cuckoo – which most South Africans know as the 'Piet-my-vrou' – but only after much patient observation. I also saw leopard spoor on the trail, as well as that of the Cape clawless otter.

Along this section the path is mainly downhill as it follows the edge of plantations, passes through small patches of relict forest on stream banks, and crosses slopes of sour grasslands. Some of the trees to be seen are the Transvaal milkplum or 'stamvrug', the mountain cedar, and isolated yellowwood trees.

Taking a break on a slope above the Treur River, my partner and I were suddenly enveloped in a whirling cloud of midges. While we were contemplating this phenomenon, swifts were swooping by, closer and closer, until they were darting past, just missing our ears and then peeling away. Of course, the swifts were feeding on the midges, which flocked around us for protection. The aerial combat lasted for quite a while, and I must report that, despite clever tactics, the midges lost heavily.

We descended to a patch of relict forest on the river bank, and had tea in a dappled glade, while butterflies flitted around us. There is a lot of magic to be found on this trail, if you are prepared to look for it. On the other hand, if you time yourself racing from hut to hut, the wonders of nature will simply pass you by.

The two huts at Clearstream are stone, stable-like buildings that blend in well with the surrounding rock formations. Below the hut is a delightful pool where an afternoon can be happily whiled away. If you rise early – preferably on a misty morning – and sneak quietly down to the pool, you might be lucky enough to see the resident otters at play.

The river here, which the local tribespeople called the *Setogwane*, was renamed by the Voortrekkers who had encamped here while their leader, Hendrik Potgieter, led a reconnaissance party to Mozambique. When he failed to return on the appointed day, the outspanned party named this the 'river of sorrow'.

DAY 3 *CLEARSTREAM HUT TO THE OLD MINE AT BOURKE'S LUCK : 13,6 KM*

This section begins with such promise and ends on a high note at the potholes, while the middle section I found to be a disappointment. It wanders along plantations with numerous roads and paths, past a timber yard and sawmill in sight of the main road, and past an army camp

... and all this after having been 'lost' in the wilderness for the past few days.

The path leaves Clearstream and follows the general course of the river for most of the day's walking. It passes what is thought to be the outspan place of Potgieter's Voortrekkers, and then the ruins of a gold prospector's hut, but moves away from the river where it cuts a wide loop to the north, to avoid Fann's Falls. Although about 1 km off the trail path, the high falls are well worth a visit, even if it is too cold for a dip in the deep pool. The path soon regains the river, keeping close to the bank for several kilometres. Where the river approaches the main road, the trail veers eastwards to pass behind the Crocodile Valley Estates sawmill and along the edge of the plantation for a few kilometres. About 1 km from the plantation border the path just manages to avoid what must be the most unfortunately situated army camp in the universe. But even that is soon forgotten as the path dips back down to the river and follows it to its confluence with the Blyde River at Bourke's Luck's celebrated potholes. Evidence of the old gold rush days is everywhere: rusty equipment and mine shafts, cables and pulleys litter the river above the potholes.

When I first visited the area as a young boy, only a swaying rickety wood and rope bridge offered a way across the gorge. Today the path crosses over by way of a reinforced concrete footbridge, makes its way past the nature conservation offices and information centre (an excellent display not to be missed), before moving on a short distance to the pleasant bungalows at Old Mine.

At Bourke's Luck the Treur and Blyde rivers meet on a soft shale and dolomite horizon that underlies the hard quartzites. Sediment suspended in the water, and stones carried down in flood waters, have scoured out a fantastic maze of rock caverns and cylindrical potholes, some over 6 m from the surface to water level. The entire area is fascinating, and can be explored on various long and short trails radiating out from Bourke's Luck.

In a forest patch near Bourke's Luck I

OPPOSITE The start of the Blyde River canyon, just downstream of Bourke's Luck Potholes, where the Treur and Blyde rivers meet.

RIGHT There are only a few known breeding colonies of the bald ibis, one of the country's rarest birds. The largest colony is to be found on the cliffs above the Old Mine at Bourke's Luck. *BELOW* Looking back at the Transvaal escarpment wall from near trail's end at Swadini.

also got my first tantalizing glimpse of a narina trogon, one of the most striking of all southern African forest birds. Moving from here down the escarpment into the Lowveld, one encounters the habitats of all three South African louries – namely the Knysna, purplecrested and grey, the first two inhabiting the gallery forest and the third favouring the Bushveld trees.

Perhaps the most fascinating bird found anywhere along this trail is the bald ibis. It is a turkey-sized bird with typical glossy ibis plumage and a conspicuous red head and beak. It nests communally on cliffs within the montane grassland habitat, eating a wide variety of insects, worms, small reptiles and other animals – dead or alive. A large communal ibis nest is located in the cliffs near the Old Mine at Bourke's Luck.

Plans are afoot for the Old Mine camp to be taken over for official use. The trail hut will then be moved to the more attractive house at Belvedere, the site of a failed hydro-electric power station built to supply electricity to the gold mine at Pilgrim's Rest.

DAY 4 OLD MINE TO BLYDEPOORT HUT: 18,3 KM

The path begins by dipping steeply down to the Ghost Mine, where gold was first uncovered in the 1870s and was still being recovered as recently as the 1970s. Most of the heavy machinery has been left there, creating a nostalgic atmosphere. The path then climbs steeply back up to gain the edge of the spectacular Blyderiviersport canyon. This ascent is the longest on the hike.

The trail brochure apologizes for the path following closely to the tarred road, whereas in fact it is the road planners who should apologize for routing a major road so close to this natural splendour. The trail follows the Old Coach Road for much of the way to Blydepoort, parallel to the tarred road. On the northern side of the road within the Lebowa homeland, the sprawling Hlabekisa settlement continues to spread across the veld. Rather turn your eyes always south and east, to savour the everchanging panorama of the canyon, the serpentine river far below, and its flanking bastions and turrets.

Looking down into the massive gorge,

one notices that forests spread out over the west- and south-facing slopes, where sunlight is limited and the ground is kept moist and cool throughout the year. The north- and east-facing slopes, which catch the full force of the afternoon sun, are dry and covered by hardier mixed Bushveld flora such as mountain syringa, wild pear, buffalo-thorn, bushwillow and wild olive trees, as well as aloes and other succulents.

Owing to the altitude here, some Afromontane heathland plants are also found along the canyon rim. In South Africa we call this type of vegetation 'fynbos' but, like the montane forests here, it is of tropical origin, having skipped down the East African highlands all the way to the Cape. Eight species of protea – *Protea caffra, P. gaguedi, P. laetens, P. parvula, P. rhodantha, P. roupelliae, P. rubropilosa* and *P. welwitschii* – as well as the pincushion, *Leucospermum saxosum*, erica heaths and everlastings, will be the most obvious examples of the heathland flora in this area.

The most interesting protea is perhaps the Blyderivier sugarbush, *P. laetens*. When Potgieter was finally reunited with his Trekkers in 1840, they named the river on which the party was encamped the Blyderivier, or 'river of rejoicing'. When, about 20 years ago, Mrs L. Davidson discovered an undescribed protea here, she gave it the Latin name for 'rejoicing'. Only a few hundred specimens of this attractive bush are found in the reserve, the silver, carmine and russet flower heads blooming mainly between April and May. Four cycads endemic to the Transvaal are also sheltered within the reserve.

The plateaux grasslands sweeping away to the west are virtually treeless, but some tree and bush species cling close to the canyon edge, the Highveld cabbage tree, milkplum or stamvrug, and Transvaal beech being the most common. Few people know that the beech or boekenhout tree (*Faurea saligna*) is an unusual and relatively primitive member of the protea family.

The milkplum has the daunting botanical name of *Bequaertiodendron magalismontanum*, but this does not deter the baboons and mountaineers who vie for its deliciously sweet, loquat-like fruits. All six of South Africa's primate species can be found within the reserve, some

confined to one habitat, and others more wide-ranging. Thintailed bushbabies are found only in the savanna woodlands, while their thicktailed cousins are restricted to the evergreen forests. Vervet monkeys are found mainly in the Bushveld woodlands but do range further, and the rare and shy samango monkeys are entirely confined to the evergreen forests, where their calls pierce the twilight calm. Baboons favour the rocky mountain slopes and open Bushveld. *Homo sapiens* can be found in all natural habitats, but is satisfied in none.

The path crosses the road to the Three Rondavels viewsite, a wonderland of lichens and plants, scenery and open space, best experienced at dusk. If ever a picture was worth a thousand words, then it is the panoramic view from this spot that embodies the canyon's majesty. A little further on the trail swings west to approach the new hiking hut outside the F.H. Odendaal Resort, which replaces the original one inside the resort. The hut is situated close to the Kadishi River, where one of South Africa's more interesting geological formations can be seen. The river rises near the dolomitic Sudwala Caves and flows over a quartzite base, where photosynthesizing moss extracts carbon dioxide from the water. Over the centuries the river has deposited on the bedrock a smooth, porous calcium layer, called tufa, that looks more like a liquid ooze than solid rock.

DAY 5 BLYDEPOORT HUT TO SWADINI: 13,8 KM

The road from Swadini back to Blydepoort is about 100 km, so many hikers prefer to end their hike at Blydepoort – but they are the poorer for it. If you do, then at least spend the extra day exploring the area: the viewsites, Tufa Falls and lower Kadishi River (Origstadrivier); the Guineafowl Trail and Iron Age settlements; the Leopard Trail with its grand views and great variety of vegetation.

From the Blydepoort hut the path makes its way back to the Escarpment edge and then takes a bold line downwards, just north of the Three Rondavels viewsite, towards the Blydepoort Dam. This is the most exciting section of the trail, as you move down the open rocky slopes and into the fern-green forests

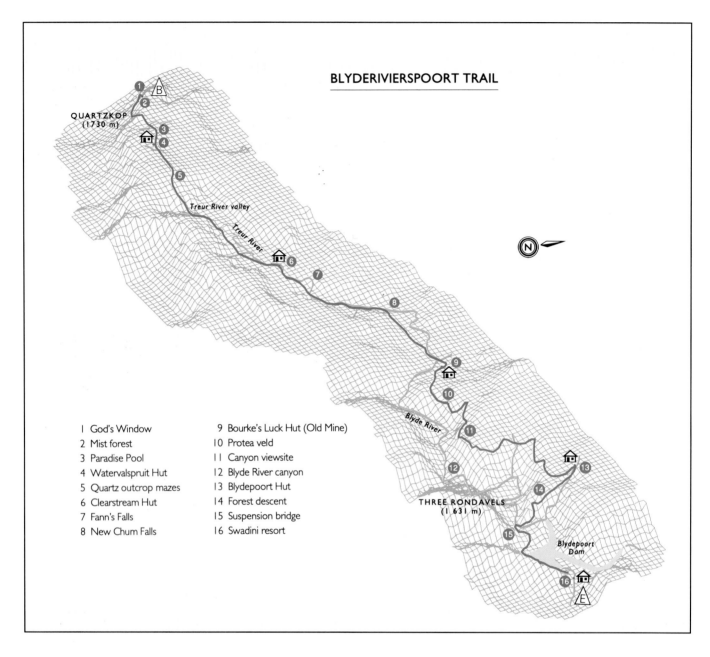

BLYDERIVIERSPOORT TRAIL

QUARTZKOP
(1730 m)

Treur River valley

Treur River

THREE RONDAVELS
(1 631 m)

Blyde River

Blydepoort
Dam

1 God's Window
2 Mist forest
3 Paradise Pool
4 Watervalspruit Hut
5 Quartz outcrop mazes
6 Clearstream Hut
7 Fann's Falls
8 New Chum Falls

9 Bourke's Luck Hut (Old Mine)
10 Protea veld
11 Canyon viewsite
12 Blyde River canyon
13 Blydepoort Hut
14 Forest descent
15 Suspension bridge
16 Swadini resort

above the Blyde River. Within the first 6 km the path loses 500 m in altitude on its steady descent, using a conveniently placed ladder to negotiate a tricky climb down at one spot. A suspension bridge crosses the river at a dramatic point above the dam, and you should heed the warning not to cross with more than three people at a time.

The trail ends at the far side of a cutting, more or less opposite the dam wall, at the reserve gate. Swadini resort is found 2 km further on, but if you plan to spend the night there it is wise to make a booking in advance.

Since, of all wild animals, crocodiles and hippos account for by far the most human deaths in Africa each year, you should also take seriously the warning to avoid them in and around the Blydepoort Dam. Both are aggressive and very swift animals, which must be given a wide berth on land and in water. From the river the path climbs fairly steeply for a short distance and then meanders through gallery forest for about 3 km. On the dam's eastern shore there is a sudden transition from cool forest to Lowveld savanna. The magnificent Bushveld scenery, defined by large leadwood,

acacia, tamboti, teak, kiaat and jackalberry trees, and the excitement of walking in the wild African veld, all create a grand ending to this superb trail.

OPPOSITE From Bourke's Luck two side trails run out across the montane grasslands to the Escarpment edge near Op De Berg. A short walk from there brings hikers to the great chasm that is the Devil's Window, where the ground drops away to the sweltering Lowveld plains 1 000 m below.

THE TRAIL AT A GLANCE

STARTING POINT : God's Window, on the edge of the Transvaal Escarpment

FINISHING POINT : Swadini Resort in the Lowveld

LENGTH : 65 km

DURATION : Five days

GROUP LIMIT : 30 people

ROUTE : The trail follows the general line of the Transvaal Drakensberg Escarpment, cuts a short way inland along the Treur River valley to Bourke's Luck, then skirts the magnificent Blyderivierspoort canyon before descending the canyon wall to the Blydepoort Dam and Swadini Resort.

HOW TO GET THERE : From Graskop take the R532 to Bourke's Luck and the Abel Erasmus Pass. A little way north of Graskop take the scenic ring route (R534) to God's Window. The National Hiking Way route begins by taking the wooden walkway through the miniature rain forest (actually a mist forest).

BOOKING AUTHORITY : Nature Conservation, Private Bag X431, Graskop, 1270; tel: (01315) 8-1216.

ACCOMMODATION : Stone huts and rondavels, with bunk beds and mattresses, flush toilets, some cooking pots and utensils, firewood and braai places.

CLIMATE : The area has an elevated Highveld climate, meaning temperate winters and warm summers, with winter nights becoming cold to very cold. Most rain falls in the summer and, because of the high-lying ground and the Escarpment wall, mists are common at this time of year.

BEST TIME TO HIKE : Spring and autumn are best, for the spring flush and the post-rainfall fullness. But summertime is also good, and seldom hot, although rainfall may be heavy.

REFERENCES : 1 : 50 000 National Hiking Way trail map (Forestry pamphlet no. 196)

TERRAIN : The terrain, although of a montane nature, is generally fairly flat and undemanding. Even where the trail follows the dramatic edge of the Blyderivierspoort canyon, the path is easy to negotiate. Only on the short Lowveld section can conditions become extreme.

WHAT TO TAKE : Since the Blyderivierspoort is subject to frequent mist and rain, pack a raincoat and warm clothing all year round.

The trail can be walked in light footwear.

SPECIAL PRECAUTIONS : None, although if you do complete the hike to Swadini, remember that the Lowveld is a malaria area and take a suitable prophylactic before entering the area. Also, make transport arrangements to get back to Bourke's Luck or God's Window.

TRAIL OPTIONS : At Bourke's Luck it is possible to do two shorter hikes, the Eerste Liefde (two days) and Op De Berg (three days) trails, which explore the montane grassland and forested area east of the Blyderivierpoort Canyon, in the Belvedere Stream valley. The former follows the old coach route between the canyon and the dramatic Escarpment wall, the latter makes its meandering way to the Op De Berg hut, spectacularly situated on a high ridge near the Devil's Window. From the F.H. Odendaal resort at Blydepoort there are several day walks and nature rambles, most interesting of which are the one to the Tufa Falls, an unusual limestone deposit formation in the bed of the Origstad River, and that to the Three Rondavels viewpoint, a truly magnificent sight.

PROSPECTOR'S TRAIL

The unique historic theme of this trail was the main factor that led me to include it. Many people would have chosen the Fanie Botha trail, the first section of the National Hiking Way System to be opened, as more representative of the Eastern Transvaal trails. However, in my opinion, the elements that constitute the Fanie Botha trail are scenic but not unique. There is also far more variety on this trail, in terms of the landscape and veld types encountered, than on most other trails. The first day of this trail coincides with the middle of the Fanie Botha trail, overnighting in an authentic miner's cottage in Pilgrim's Rest.

'On this trail you will follow in the footsteps of the early miners along routes that wind past deserted goldmines, along old coach routes and through the historic village of Pilgrim's Rest. This little town is a reminder of the heady days when gold was discovered and men ordered footbaths of champagne and lit cigars with £5 notes...' so reads the Oliviers' preface to this trail, and what better atmosphere in which to immerse oneself for the six dream-world days of the hike.

Prospecting in the Boer Zuid-Afrikaansche Republiek started in 1853 in the area around the Mac-Mac Falls, but it was only 20 years later that Alec 'Wheelbarrow' Patterson made the first significant strike at Pilgrim's Rest. This and Barberton soon became the two largest gold rush towns in the Transvaal, bustling with fortune seekers, as well as taverners, bakers, bankers and prostitutes. The mines finally ran dry in 1971, and a few years later the entire village was declared a national monument.

The Eastern Transvaal saw plenty of action in the South African War of 1899-1902; towards the end of the war the Boers established their 'state mint in the veld' near the town, and it was here that the famous gold 'veld-pond' was minted.

DAY 1 *MAC-MAC TO PILGRIM'S REST: 15,4 KM*

From the forest station the trail follows painted footprints up the gravel road next to the guesthouse. For the first 7 km the path passes through pine plantations as it gradually but steadily gains altitude. Small patches of indigenous forest that survive within the plantations are encountered along the way. The survival of these forest relics is at best precarious, besieged as they are by the monoculture of pines and the people who cultivate them. Unfortunately, once the large timber trees have been extracted, natural forest does not yield short-term economic benefits so it slowly disappears.

At the 6,7 km mark the Prospector's trail path meets and joins the Fanie Botha trail, and shortly thereafter the path crosses the old Burgers' Pass road. This area is very wet for much of the year, and mosses and ferns carpet the soggy ground beneath tall trees. After crossing

Natural aloe and lichen gardens typical of the montane grassland habitat found along the Prospector's Trail.

the pass road, the trail meets the overgrown route of the old coach road where it makes a sharp bend. Here the Fanie Botha trail branches off to the right to head for Bonnet Pass (the tarred road between Pilgrim's Rest and Graskop), while the Prospector's trail follows the coach road to the left, around the base of Stanley Bush Hill (1 807 m).

The walk along the coach road is marred by runaway infestation of pines and wattles in what should be wet montane grasslands. Where the alien invaders haven't completely displaced the natural veld, you might see silver proteas (*Protea roupelliae*) and even the Transvaal mountain protea (*P. rubropilosa*), which is confined to the Eastern Transvaal highlands. After about 11 km, where the trail begins its descent to Bonnet Pass, the Desiree Mine shaft is passed, and shortly thereafter some old ruins and graves. For about 1,5 km the trail follows a plantation road until it heads off on a contour above the main road.

The blue swallow is a natural inhabitant of the Eastern Transvaal's misty montane grasslands, where it breeds in dongas or antbear burrows, migrating to tropical Africa each winter. In 1984 the first SA Red Data Book on endangered species drew attention to the fact that this was the next bird likely to become extinct in South Africa, since its habitat has all but disappeared under pine and bluegum plantations – an industry that has proved to be very lucrative. Against the spirit of an agreement between conservationists and the timber growers, some remaining breeding areas have recently been cultivated, dashing hopes that this attractive bird, with its metallic blueblack plumage and long tail feathers, will survive into the 21st century.

Nearing Pilgrim's Rest a second abandoned mine is encountered, as well as the headgear of an old cable station which was used to convey gold-bearing ore down to the river for washing. The final 500 m entails a steep drop to the attractive miner's cottage on the outskirts of the village. The cottage is surrounded by the entangled, barbed branches of the flame acacia (*Acacia ataxacantha*) which has become a scourge of the place despite regular burning and hacking. Early photographs show that the plant was not evident here in the gold rush days, but was probably introduced later.

DAY 2 *PILGRIM'S REST TO MORGENZON HUT: 8,3 KM*

This is a short section (although 400 m altitude will be gained over the first 5 km), designed to allow hikers time to enjoy the hospitality and sights of the quaint, restored mining town. From the overnight hut the trail follows the main road through the village, past period homes and shops of the late 19th century. Tea and scones at one of the cottage tearooms, or a more substantial repast at the Royal Hotel, will fuel you up for the long climb ahead.

I first got to know the village in its declining years, just before the mine closed down. The night soil cart did its rounds early every morning, the post office telephone must have been Alexander Graham Bell's prototype, and film shows were held in the mine recreation hall. The road to Bourke's Luck was a very rough gravel one and the potholes themselves were remote, with only a swaying rope and wood bridge across them. Since then the Transvaal Provincial Administration has given the village a bright new coat of paint, the collapsing balconies have been straightened up, and the once rusty hotel has become a hub of tourist activity.

The trail crosses the Joubert Bridge, a five-arch stone structure, built in 1896 across the Blyde River. It then veers off to the left, away from the main road to Lydenburg and Bourke's Luck, making for a valley up Columbia Hill (1 509 m). As the path climbs the steep grassy hillside, one can look down on a small settlement of huts and kraals in the valley below. Unfortunately, overgrazing has resulted in severe erosion of the hillsides here. As the path climbs ever higher, the views back out over the village and across the Transvaal Drakensberg are most impressive.

Near the summit of Columbia Hill the path levels out to pass an old digging and then climbs a bit more to a large wattle thicket. Soon the path reaches an old water race that was used to channel water to the Columbia mine. The veld here is in poor condition, obviously suffering from too-frequent burnings, which have virtually eliminated the common sugarbushes (*Protea caffra*) that should otherwise be plentiful. The race is followed on the contour into a stream gully, where welcome shade is afforded

by the riverine forest. This will be the first drinking water you'll find since leaving Pilgrim's Rest. The wooden chalet is a short climb away, situated on the edge of the pine plantation.

The view from Morgenzon hut is stupendous, over the Clewer Valley, the Blyde River Valley and all the way to Graskop perched on the edge of the Escarpment. When I awoke in the morning, a low, cold coppery sun shimmered on the hazy horizon. A sea of cloud stretched from the mountain slope, about 50 m below the hut, all the way to the horizon, the sunlight flushing the puffy white swells below with a pale glow.

DAY 3 *MORGENZON HUT TO EXCELSIOR HUT: 15 KM*

After a very wet first two days, the third day dawned bright and sunny, and by the time I set off at 8 am I was already sweating. With the heat of early October and a spell of bronchitis I struggled perhaps unduly on this, the toughest section of the trail. Losing the trail near the end and walking an extra 3 km did not improve my sinking spirits. The day begins easily enough, trudging gently but persistently uphill along plantation roads for the first 6,5 km. Near the point where the path crosses the Pilgrim's Rest-Lydenburg road, a spot on the circular route back to Pilgrim's Rest commemorates the place where the last mail coach robbery in the area took place in 1912.

A water spot is marked on the map at around 6,5 km, and it is absolutely essential to drink and fill water bottles here, for this might well be the last water before reaching the hut. (It is easy to miss the little stream, concealed in a tangle of bush and canalized under the road.) From this spot the path soon leaves the road to climb steeply through plantation before emerging on a rocky slope on the side of Black Hill. For nearly 2 km the path wanders in and out of low rocky outcrops, hiding gardens of krantz aloes and small wildflowers. The final 500 m to the summit of Black Hill (2 079 m) is a gentle ramp across flat slabs of furrowed sandstone. Near the summit beacon is a small solar-powered communications mast. The panoramic view from here concentrates one's gaze on the distant blue forms of Mariepskop, the Wolkberg,

LEFT Krantz aloes *(Aloe arborescens)* flowering in early winter. The plant's Latin name means 'tree aloe', but this is a misnomer since it seldom grows taller than three metres. (The true tree aloe is *A. bainesii*, which may grow taller than 10 metres. *BELOW* The quaint village of Pilgrim's Rest, once a boom mining town, was declared a national monument in 1986, 15 years after gold was last uncovered here.

ABOVE As the dawn light breaks across the hills, a hiker at Morgenzon hut prepares for the long slog up Black Hill, the high point on the horizon.

Strydpoort and Waterberg mountains. This makes a good lunch spot but, since there is precious little shade, in summer you might choose to continue walking for a short distance.

A loose, stony descent through fynbos vegetation takes the path down from the heights into a hot valley, with small dams, patches of pine, and a cluster of holiday homes and paddocks. At about the 13 km mark the path re-enters plantation of the Morgenzon State Forest. It is easy to miss a turn-off marker in the woods and thus carry on downhill on a plantation road into the main valley. I did this and it caused me great discomfort. Excelsior hut is reached by staying on a level contour and keeping to the left, to bypass the Molototse River valley. The hut is an old holiday home built in Swiss chalet style and now crammed so tightly with bunk beds that I preferred to endure a light drizzle outside. The fireplace here (and at the other huts) is situated in a roofed shelter that becomes a smokehouse as soon as a fire is started. This is the only design fault on the trail, but a fairly annoying one.

a herd of feral horses, descendants of mounts that arrived here with the early white pioneers. The prairie steepens and the road curves to the right, climbing towards a lookout tower, where water is available from a nearby tap. Fill up with water here, for after this point drinking places are unreliable and the going gets steadily tougher.

The following few kilometres are easy going on a gentle ascent across the Oribi Flats, past Rock Heaven and Yellowwood Rock on Eldorado Ridge. During midwinter the rocky outcrops here are aflame with krantz aloe blooms. This species was ill-named *Aloe arborescens*, meaning the tree aloe. Tree it certainly is not, while the common tree aloe is named *A. bainesii* after the traveller and artist Thomas Baines. This misnaming of species is a common taxonomical phenomenon, when plants were collected by early naturalists in far-off places and sent back to Europe with incorrect information for scientific description. The laws of taxonomy state that the first name ever given to a species is the one that applies, so that any original errors remain. When a botanical species is renamed (as is often the case) it is not to correct an inappropriate name, but to apply an earlier Latin name found to have been bestowed on it, or to assign it to another genus.

After passing close to the highest point on the Oribi Flats (2 035 m) the path dips and climbs through two consecutive saddles, joining a firebreak to run across the south-western line of a ridge studded with proteas; it is obvious that, the need for firebreaks notwithstanding, the proteas and the grass would be in better condition but for the many burns inflicted on the veld. Two species evident are the large common sugarbush (*P. caffra*), the most widespread protea in South Africa, and the African sugarbush (*P. gaguedi*). The latter species has a distribution extending from Natal right up into Ethiopia. The species name is that used to describe the plant by native Ethiopians.

Francolin are often flushed from the area where the grass is rank, especially near clumps of bush that signal surface water. At about the 9 km mark there is a seepage with a trickle of water in all but the driest times, but do not rely on it for drinking. Another few hundred metres further on a vague path leads off to the right, to a viewsite on the edge of ridge

looking down the Sacramento Creek valley, across the Blyderivierspoort and right down to the Lowveld. A plaque here marks the 1 000th kilometre reached on the National Hiking Way System. Shade is afforded by smallish coral trees and large specimens of the broad-leaved waxberry (*Myrica pilulifera*), while the ground is adorned with a number of flowering plants (including, I think, a type of bulbine lily).

The main path turns tightly around the farthest end of the narrow ridge, passing the dark shaft of an old mine, which on close inspection turns out to be only about 10 m deep. From the mine the path quickly loses about 100 m in altitude as it makes its way below the line of kranzes, and then another 100 m as it descends diagonally for just over 1 km through rocky *Protea roupelliae* veld, dotted with occasional *Cussonia* cabbage trees. Baboons are frequent visitors to this ridge so a chorus of their sharp barks is most likely to accompany your walk. As you will probably hike this last section in mid- to late afternoon, the dry, north-east facing slope will bake in the summer sun. At the 13 km mark the path begins its very steep, 200 m descent of the Enkelbreek (ankle-break) spur. The vegetation here is thorny and scratchy, adding to one's discomfort.

Sacramento hut is finally reached across the boulder-strewn bed of an intermittent stream. The larger trees surrounding the hut are knob thorns (*Acacia nigrescens*), whose delicate white flower spikes are most conspicuous in low altitude woodlands; they are an indication of good ranching country. In a crumbling cutaway next to the hut a mine shaft has been blocked off with an iron gate, barbed wire and logs, but determined adventurers have forced a way in.

DAY 4 EXCELSIOR HUT TO SACRAMENTO HUT: 15 KM

This, in my memory, is another section that starts out easily in the morning coolness and ends in blazing heat, with very little water available *en route*. After weaving through the semi-natural aloe and protea rock garden behind the Excelsior hut, the path crosses a boggy area to emerge on The Prairie. Nearing the 1 km mark the path joins a 4x4 track, and along this open grass plain you might see

DAY 5 SACRAMENTO HUT TO BOURKE'S LUCK: 15,5 KM

From the hut the path climbs over three grassy spurs between stream courses, and then over another spur to emerge on the top of a cliffline above the Droë-Olienkloof valley, 200 m above the hut. The path traces the edge of the cliffs to reach the head of the valley, where it descends steeply through wild pear trees (*Dombeya rotundifolia*) which make

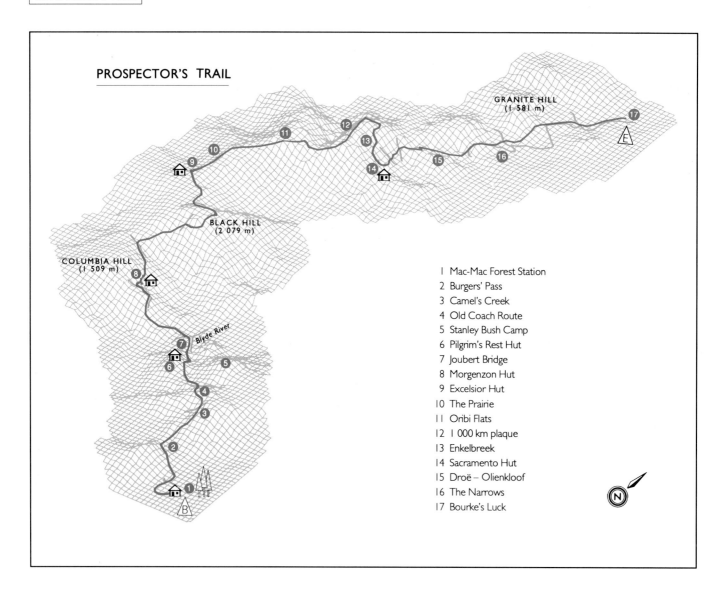

PROSPECTOR'S TRAIL

GRANITE HILL
(1 581 m)

BLACK HILL
(2 079 m)

COLUMBIA HILL
(1 509 m)

Blyde River

1 Mac-Mac Forest Station
2 Burgers' Pass
3 Camel's Creek
4 Old Coach Route
5 Stanley Bush Camp
6 Pilgrim's Rest Hut
7 Joubert Bridge
8 Morgenzon Hut
9 Excelsior Hut
10 The Prairie
11 Oribi Flats
12 1 000 km plaque
13 Enkelbreek
14 Sacramento Hut
15 Droë – Olienkloof
16 The Narrows
17 Bourke's Luck

handsome, frost-resistant garden subjects. The valley floor, as its name suggests, is dry and well-grown with tall wild olive trees (*Olea europaea*).

Approaching a loop in the Blyde River, the path reaches a flat gravel road at The Narrows, a strip of land squeezed between the river and a line of cliffs on the left. While the river is good for a dip on a hot day, remember that its water is not fit for drinking untreated. The Narrows forms part of the Kaspersnek Road, the route used by Voortrekker leader Hendrik Potgieter to descend the Escarpment near Graskop. It is named after Kasper Kruger, father of the famous Boer leader Paul Kruger, who was an important member of Potgieter's group.

After 2 km the path leaves the road, passes through a farm gate and crosses the Mapalageli River, rounds Granite Hill (1 581 m) and then skirts irrigated fields along the bottom of the Bramble Cliffs. This is an uncomfortable section, as the path either attempts to break through the dense riverine thicket or grovels higher up among the brambles and loose scree. At the far end of the cliffs the tarred road to Bourke's Luck and the army camp aerials come into view, and then you know you are a few kilometres from the end of the trail.

First, however, you must pass through a fast expanding settlement of Lebowa, complete with speeding taxis, chicken farm, and laundry activities in the river. The potholes at Bourke's Luck were once one of my favourite spots, until the area was developed into a tourist centre, together with army camp and sewage works alongside. In time to come, when our children look back and judge our efforts, I do not think they will condone this 'improvement' of one of the province's best beauty spots. After all, the thing that was originally attractive – namely the spectacular natural environment – has now been lost.

About a decade ago, while hiking in the area, I stopped off at the potholes. A combi with foreign licence plates pulled up with a squeal and out jumped an elderly but spritely, post-hippy American tourist. He rushed off down the path to the famous potholes, but within a few minutes he was back, grumbling loudly: 'Ah've driven theeousands of keelometrrs to see these derned paatholes end ah don't hev no feelm in ma cemerah!' And off he zoomed.

On the outskirts of Pilgrim's Rest the Joubert Bridge, built in 1896, crosses the Blyde River.

THE TRAIL AT A GLANCE

STARTING POINT : Mac-Mac forest station

FINISHING POINT : Bourke's Luck potholes and visitors' centre

LENGTH : 69 km

DURATION : Five days

GROUP LIMIT : 30 people

ROUTE : This is a linear trail through the Eastern Transvaal highlands. It begins at the forest station near Mac-Mac Falls, passes through Pilgrim's Rest, climbs to Morgenzon, then wanders past Excelsior and Sacramento Creek huts before ending at the Bourke's Luck tourist centre.

HOW TO GET THERE : From Johannesburg or Pretoria, take the N4 past Middelberg. Just before reaching Nelspruit take the R539 past the Sudwala Caves and on to Sabie. After passing a level crossing and the Mac-Mac Falls, about 10 km short of the Graskop- Pilgrim's Rest T-junction, the forest station is found just off the road on the left.

BOOKING AUTHORITY : National Hiking Way office, Eastern Transvaal Forest Region, Private Bag X503, Sabie, 1260; tel. (01315) 4-1058.

ACCOMMODATION : Consecutive nights are spent in a converted miner's cottage, a wooden mountain hut, a Swiss chalet style ex-holiday home and a stone hut. All have bunk beds and mattresses, flush toilets, firewood and some pots. It is also possible to book sleeping accommodation at the beginning of the hike, at Mac-Mac forest station.

CLIMATE : Climate along the trail varies considerably, from mist-shrouded peaks near Pilgrim's Rest to the hot thornbush at Sacramento Creek. It can be said to have a mild montane climate in the summer rainfall area. The average summer maximum temperature in Pilgrim's Rest is 26 °C, the minimum around 20 °C. The highest average rainfall falls in January (about 350 mm) and the lowest between June and July (about 15 mm). Hail and lightning are common from October to April, with frost and snow likely between June and September. Mist from Mac-Mac to Morgenzon is prevalent in all but the midwinter months.

BEST TIME TO HIKE : Since winters here can be uncomfortably cold, with little drinking water available on the trail, spring through to autumn is the best time to hike. Keep in mind, however, that the actual daily maximum temperature reaches into the mid-30s in summertime, while the midwinter daily minimum dips to about -5 °C.

REFERENCES : National Hiking Way Board 1 : 50 000 trail map. While the front side of the map has the usual topographical information, the reverse side has traded natural history information for that of the area's economic activities.

TERRAIN : The terrain here is best described as broken, the trail encountering forested peaks, montane grasslands, rocky crests and protea veld slopes. The vegetation of the Eastern Transvaal highlands, originally almost exclusively montane grasslands and protea veld, is now largely given over to pine plantations. The trail does pass through some plantation, but not nearly as much as in the case of the Fanie Botha trail. Between Mac-Mac and Pilgrim's Rest some indigenous forest, growing within the plantations, is passed through.

WHAT TO TAKE : Only the first day of the trail is wooded, and often very wet as well, while otherwise it mostly crosses open veld.

Protection from both sun and rain will be needed throughout the year, but especially in winter when the air is brittle, cold and dry. On this and all other trails where firewood is provided, it is useful to carry firelighters as kindling wood is usually hard to find. In wet conditions the first day should be walked in boots; otherwise one can alternate between running shoes and light boots, although boots will be appreciated on some steep sections (particularly the descent of Black Hill). Gaiters will protect your legs from tick bites and grass seed prickles.

SPECIAL PRECAUTIONS : With the exception of a few permanent streams, this is a dry trail between huts so hikers will have to carry their own water.

TRAIL OPTIONS : From Excelsior hut it is possible to hike back to Morgenzon forest station, to complete a 4-day hike, or you can take a daypack and do the Morgenzon loop trail and then spend an extra night at Excelsior hut before completing the trail. The 17 km loop explores wet vlei areas, eroded rock gardens festooned with aloes and lichens, miniature forests and montane grasslands.

The Prospector's Hiking Trail begins in the vicinity of the strenuous Fanie Botha Trail, and ends midway along the easier, scenically spectacular Blyderivierspoort trail at Bourke's Luck. From the potholes there are two overnight trails (Op-De-Berg and Eerste Liefde) that are highly recommended (see Blyderivierspoort trail). There are also numerous day walks laid out in the Blyderivierspoort Nature Reserve, while it is possible to do a circular two-night hike in the Pilgrim's Rest Nature Reserve, starting and ending in the village and overnighting at Morgenzon hut.

MAGOEBASKLOOF TRAIL

The Magoebaskloof Hiking Trail consists of two separate circular routes, namely the Dokolewa and Grootbosch sections. They are laid out as an elongated figure eight with the first 10 km of each taking the same route from the De Hoek forest station near Tzaneen. I have chosen the Grootbosch section largely because it is one of only two trails in the country that do not provide overnight huts (the other being Ciskei's Shipwreck Trail). This is a tough trail, with daily distances averaging 17 km and very few level sections on the way.

The other major attraction of this hike is that it is situated almost entirely within the Grootbosch forest, one of the largest indigenous forests in the country, and by far the most impressive montane forest in the Transvaal. For three days the trail weaves between massive tree trunks and through dense undergrowth: a completely green, penumbral world. At only two points does the forest open out to allow views of the landscape beyond, although these are likely to be obscured by mist in summer and by the haze of veld fire smoke in winter.

The area is named after the Sotho chief Magoeba, who tried in vain to stem the invasion of fortune seekers, hunters, woodsmen and farmers that followed the discovery of gold here in the early 1870s. The tribesmen harassed the miners and burned farmhouses; in retaliation the Boer government sent a force of nearly 900 mounted commandos and artillery, plus a few hundred Swazi and Shangaan mercenary troops, to deal with Magoeba. He retreated with his warriors into the Grootbosch, and for a year defied attempts to dislodge him. The commandos were so hampered by the hellish terrain, dense forest, rains and mist that they called it 'Helsche Bosch'. Eventually, in June 1895, the forest was extensively shelled, Magoeba's kraal captured and razed, and the chief (so the story goes) beheaded by Swazi mercenaries.

DAY I *GROOTBOSCH HUT TO GROOTBOSCH LAPA: 18 KM*

There are few places in southern Africa where one can walk for three long, consecutive days in dense primeval forest: this is one. So unusual is the experience for a person more familiar with fynbos scrub and barren Karoo landscapes, that towards the end of the hike I suspected that claustrophobia was setting in. This displaced feeling is compounded by the fact that there are few landmarks by which one can orientate oneself.

The trail sets off easily enough, descending a forestry road for a few kilometres to cross the gurgling Debengeni River. Some trees alongside the road have been marked with their national tree list numbers for easy identification from the species list provided. It is worthwhile using this opportunity to recognize the marked species, for once in

For three days the Magoebaskloof Trail weaves its way through Grootbosch, the largest Afro-montane forest remnant in the Transvaal.

the high forest this is a most difficult and frustrating pastime. (You can also pursue this game at the delightful Debengeni Falls picnic area.)

The path takes a sharp upward turn once within a patch of mature pine plantation, starting at about the 4 km mark. The very steep section continues for about 1 km, during which time you enter the realm of mythical beings – the real indigenous woods. This section is possibly the wettest part of Grootbosch, where ferns and mosses grow in thick coatings on every tree trunk and branch, on every stone and drooping vine, and forest flowers bedeck the ground. The path crosses a few small streams which, despite the damp microclimate, carry very little water. But, since the going is tough, you should drink wherever you can.

You will see few large yellowwoods or stinkwoods here, for they were the first trees to be felled by woodcutters who supplied timber for the mines in the province. At around the 5 km mark their impact is preserved in saw pits that were used to cut the enormous trunks into rough beams. A felled tree would be laid lengthwise across a pit and two men, one in the pit and one standing on the trunk, would cut the beams with large push-pull saws.

At the top of the steepest section the path levels out at a lookout post, having gained a staggering 600 m in altitude. From here, for the next 3,5 km, the path keeps more or less to the contour, and occasional breaks in the forest canopy afford glimpses of the far-off Lowveld.

As the path finds its way over to the western slope of the main mountain ridge, you will notice that the forest is becoming drier, the floor being made up of decaying leaf litter rather than a spongy moss carpet. For a short way the path crosses a scrubby clearing (presumably where pines have previously been felled), before entering a plantation. At the 10 km mark it emerges on a gravel road, and this is where the Dokolewa and Grootbosch paths diverge. This is as good a lunch spot as any, and perhaps a good place to contemplate.

Lying in the shade of those aromatic pines and fanned by a mountain breeze, I reflected upon the path my life has taken. But I eventually had to raise my body and my burdensome pack and head off up the road to the right. The trail follows this 4x4 track first through plantation and then back into the Grootbosch. From a vantage point outside the forest it is possible to see how the plantations have intruded into the forest, usually in those areas that were previously grassy glades.

A short detour leads to a rock formation known as the 'Huilklip' which, when struck with a hard object, makes a ringing noise: but as for crying, that must be someone's distinctly romantic illusion. It is rather odd to see this lone boulder here, which appears to be a remnant ironstone or doleritic rock from an eroded surface. Although the mountains here are geographically classified as being part of the Transvaal Drakensberg, they are geologically quite distinct from the more prominent escarpment that stretches southwards from here. The trail is set on granites and gneisses of the Old Granite system, which is at least twice as old as the Transvaal Supergroup rocks (themselves between about 600 to 700 million years old) that form the impressive mountain wall between Graskop and the Strydpoort Mountains near Haenertsburg.

Compared to the previous section the rest of the day's hiking is much easier, although the distance does begin to take its toll and there are still a few short and steep ups and downs to negotiate. About 1,5 km before reaching the lapa the first of three crossings of the Kudu River is encountered. This small tributary of the Mosukodutsi and Little Letaba rivers is never deep enough to swim in – or even to take a dip – but it provides the only water for the lapa. The final climb up to the lapa is a 300 m haul, and not one that you would care to repeat too often. Around the lapa are some small yellowwoods and Transvaal bottlebrushes (*Greyia radlkoferi*), with flowers even more showy than those of the better known Natal bottlebrush.

DAY 2 *GROOTBOSCH LAPA TO BERG-EN-DAL LAPA : 18 KM*

Hikers can expect at any time to become suddenly embraced by cold mist and drizzle on this trail. This was my experience on the second day, although the first and third days were hot and humid. The sensation of walking in the forest in such conditions is eerie and exciting: mist vapours waft through the woods, concealing and revealing like the cloak of an omnipresent sourcerer. Conversations tend to be minimal, only the occasional observation being uttered between companions, each person drifting dreamily.

After about 3 km the path steepens to reach the day's highest point at Vaalkrans (1 600 m), marked by an open glade where fynbos species are evident, and a trigonometrical beacon. When our party reached the spot the cloud momentarily lifted, revealing the upper catchment of the Little Letaba River. Soon after this the path re-enters the forest and begins a series of descents, losing some 500 m in altitude. As all experienced hikers know, what goes down must come up: the path dips and rises a few times before reaching the second lapa, although two reasonably long level sections are also (thankfully) encountered.

Within the very much consistent scene under the forest's high umbrella canopy, one of the sights that stands out is the huge wild figs that have thrown out stout side roots, forming natural archways about 10 m high. Some African tribes regard these trees with deep reverence, ascribing to them magical properties. Individual trees may be worshipped as shrines to Earth and Forest spirits, both powerful symbols of fertility.

After turning sharply back on itself, the trail once more finds its way into the very moist eastern aspect of the forest. Here clivias grow thickly on the ground, and epiphytically in the clefts of branches, along with a flush of crocuses and various epiphytic forest orchids (epiphytic means that they use a host plant as a growing platform, but do not live off it as do parasites). There are four species of clivia found in South Africa, all endemic, which makes them something of a special attraction. *Clivia miniata* grows in the forests of Natal, from where it has been cultivated as a longtime garden favourite. In the Transvaal we find the bush lily, *C. caulescens*, with its clusters of drooping flowers. From late spring the blooms emerge to set the otherwise monotonous greenery alive with bursts of bright orange flares.

Forests do not harbour high numbers of large animals, being essentially systems of decay, rather than of growth, that favour invertebrates. Those vertebrates that do occur here are mostly shy and

LEFT Part roots, part trunk of a wild strangler fig tree form a natural archway near the 'Huilklip': the left-hand arch originally strangled a host tree, which has since died and rotted away. *ABOVE* From spring through early summer clivias bloom in fiery displays on the ground and in the clefts of tree boughs, where the plants grow as epiphytes.

elusive, and often nocturnal. Most likely to be seen are samango monkeys, Knysna louries and, if you are lucky, bushpigs. These stout animals (similar to the kind that Obelix likes to eat) are relatives of the Bushveld's warthog, but are larger and lack the warthog's impressive tusks. Their essential habitat requirements are water and deep cover, and in areas such as this they extend their foraging into daylight hours – although they remain elusive. They are omnivorous and mainly root for rhizomes and roots on the forest floor, while frequently following troops of monkeys to pick up any fruit that is accidentally dropped from the tree canopy.

Berg-en-Dal lapa is, I thought, a fairly untidy corrugated iron and wood struc-ture where litter has been allowed to become an eyesore. Studies into moutain-eering and mountain ecology have shown that providing rubbish bins on trails (as is done here) does not help the litter problem, and also often exacerbates it. One of the main offenders are plastic colddrink bottles that have been used to carry water to the lapa, only to be dis-carded after use. I personally curse the people who do this, and I'm sure the authorities do too. It should be the re-sponsibilty of all hikers to pick up and carry out any litter they find on the trail.

The streams that one crosses on the long descent to the lapa all flow down into the fertile valley of the Big Letaba River. After good rains many of them form small but attractive waterfalls.

DAY 3 *BERG-EN-DAL LAPA TO GROOTBOSCH HUT: 15 KM*

From the hut the path drops down for about 500 m to reach a captivating pool, fringed with ferns and fed by a low waterfall. The path crosses a log bridge at the lower end of the pool, and then climbs alongside the enchanting river to two more waterfalls. Swim here and drink your fill, for more ups and downs await you, but with less and less water along the way.

The path climbs for 3 km, gaining over 400 m in altitude, before reaching the only long level stretch on day three. What is alarming (and should give a hint as to what lies in store), is that in the trail brochure this relatively short section is

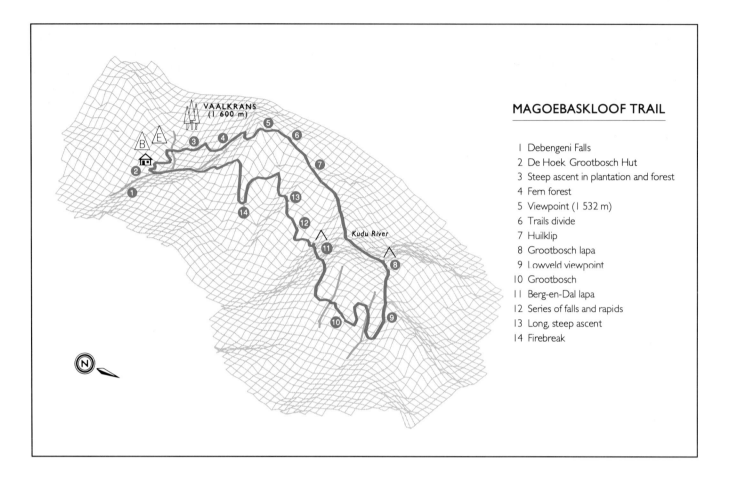

MAGOEBASKLOOF TRAIL

1 Debengeni Falls
2 De Hoek Grootbosch Hut
3 Steep ascent in plantation and forest
4 Fern forest
5 Viewpoint (1 532 m)
6 Trails divide
7 Huilklip
8 Grootbosch lapa
9 Lowveld viewpoint
10 Grootbosch
11 Berg-en-Dal lapa
12 Series of falls and rapids
13 Long, steep ascent
14 Firebreak

given a walking time equal to that of the two longer ones. I know that daily conditions can greatly affect one's personal experiences on a hike, but in the heat and dryness that characterized most of the day, I found this stretch to be one of the most dispiriting that I have yet encountered. That is not to say that it is not in places extremely beautiful and captivating, for it is, but some parts are less so than the rest of the trail. Whenever I felt particularly weary I would seek out the smooth cool trunk of a Transvaal (some say Cape) plane tree (*Ochna arborea*), to lean my tired body up against. I have no idea why these trees are always so refreshingly cool, but this phenomenon is a sure way of identifying the species.

During the flattish run from about the 3 km to the 5 km mark, especially where the forest canopy was broken or where one could look down onto the lower tree tops, I saw several louries and two troops of samango monkeys, both species being otherwise elusive. The official route description maintains that there are waterfalls and streams around just about every

corner. Don't bet on finding water, although the path can become fairly dangerous where it crosses the damp and slippery water courses.

At about the halfway mark the path leaves the forest and joins a firebreak that runs like a roller coaster over two ridges. Between the two a stream has been dammed, forming a marshy reservoir within a sylvan screen just below the path. You might not find the water here drinkable, but it is a good spot to take a break. In summer this stretch, the up slopes facing directly into the sun, seems oppressively hot after the cool embrace of the forest, so be sure to carry plenty of water.

The path continues due west for nearly 2 km, directly into the sun, and then turns sharply around to the right and back into cool forest. This provides a respite from the heat, but soon the sloping, crumbling gradient makes walking in a straight line far from a straightforward matter. After climbing for about 250 m the path reaches its highest point of the day, and from here one can see the far-off

De Hoek forest station. The final 4 km are almost entirely downhill, weaving back and forth in plantation and areas where the pines have recently been felled. The last short section to reach the hut is uphill, but after this trying trail each 100 m feels like a kilometre. I felt it a pity that the suspended reality of the forest interior could not have been sustained right to the end, for the last section is a comparatively bland slog.

OPPOSITE After leaving the Berg-en-Dal lapa, water bottles are filled for the muscle-straining, 3 km climb ahead.

THE TRAIL AT A GLANCE

STARTING POINT : Grootbosch hut, De Hoek forest station

FINISHING POINT : Grootbosch hut

LENGTH : 50 km

DURATION : Three days

GROUP LIMIT : 12 people

ROUTE : This elongated, circular trail cuts a tortuous – and torturous – path through the Magoebaskloof mountains. The first day is spent cresting a series of high ridges, to reach Grootbosch lapa on one such ridge. From there the path rises and falls periodically, turning a tight corner and dropping down to Berg-en-Dal lapa. The final leg begins with a long climb followed by a heartbreaking number of steep ups and downs to finish at the Grootbosch hut.

HOW TO GET THERE : The turn-off to De Hoek is found at the bottom of Magoebaskloof pass, between Haenertsburg and Tzaneen, at the upper end of Magoebaskloof dam. A signpost directs one along the gravel Forest Drive to the Debengeni Falls. De Hoek forest station and Grootbosch hut are found 7 km up Forest Drive.

BOOKING AUTHORITY : National Hiking Way Office, Northern Transvaal Forest Region, Private Bag X2413, Louis Trichardt, 0920; tel. (01551) 5-1152.

ACCOMMODATION : Grootbosch hut, sited just below the foresty offices at De Hoek, has hot and cold running water, electric lights, gas stove, pots, pans, flush toilet and showers. It may be used by both Grootbosch and Dokolewa trailists the night before starting the trail. The Grootbosch lapa is a very basic structure sleeping six, and at a squeeze, eight. Since 12 people are allowed on the trail at once, some might have to carry tents or bivouac bags. Berg-en-Dal lapa sleeps 12 people. Only firewood (if you're lucky) and chemical toilets are provided. This is the first National Hiking Way trail where overnight huts are not provided. There is no water at either lapa, so you must carry some from the last stream before reaching the overnight spots (the streams are marked 'last water').

CLIMATE : The climate here is similar to that experienced on the other Transvaal Escarpment trails (Prospector's and Blyderivierspoort), with high summer rainfall reaching a maximum average of about 250 mm in December and January. Summer temperatures hover between 12 and 23 °C, dropping to between 3 and 17 °C in winter. In summer mist and drizzle is the order of the day, while the forest interior becomes very humid.

BEST TIME TO HIKE : Since sunlight is a rare commodity on this trail, hiking here in winter is not recommended. This is also the dry period when most forest streams all but dry up. In summer the steep paths become muddy and slippery, but at least then there is plenty of water to drink. The best times to hike are from September to November and March to April inclusive.

REFERENCES : There is currently only a fairly poor, photocopied map available that shows little more than the trail shape and location of the overnight spots. (A standard, high-quality National Hiking Way map is in production.) Hikers are given a comprehensive tree list with Latin and common names and species list numbers, a typed route description, information about procedures and booking, general rules and hiking hints.

TERRAIN : Although one seldom gets the chance to visually appreciate the rugged mountainous landscape through which the trail passes, your legs and feet will pass the message up. The trail is situated in the northernmost extension of the Transvaal Drakensberg mountainland, between Magoebaskloof and Duiwelskloof. The entire trail, except for a few short stretches, is confined to the Grootbosch Forest.

WHAT TO TAKE : Depending on the size and composition of your group, you may need to carry a tent or, if you so choose, a ground sheet or 'bivvy' bag. There are long stretches where little or no drinking water is available, so you should carry sufficient. Also, take containers to store water at the lapas, where no water is available. A raincoat is essential, as well as candles and firelighters. Type of footwear is optional, although the path may become very muddy and slippery at times, and there are also some steep and loose sections to negotiate.

SPECIAL PRECAUTIONS : Because of the sensitivity of the forest environment, extra care must be taken here not to upset the natural balance. Use only biodegradable soaps and shampoo, and wash yourself and your utensils well away from any stream. This is a demanding trail, not open to anyone under 12 years of age. Vehicles left anywhere but at the Grootbosch hut will be towed away.

TRAIL OPTIONS : The Dokolewa 3-day trail also begins at De Hoek (Grootbosch hut). Anyone visiting the Grootbosch should plan to spend some time at the magnificent Debengeni Falls, found about 2 km below De Hoek on Forest Drive. Perhaps picnic here before or after your hike, and swim in the pools. However, take care, for the rapids and potholes below the main falls are extremely dangerous.

KLIPSPRINGER TRAIL

Many people may find this trail an unexpected choice, but there are two reasons for including it: firstly, because of the spectacular falls and gorge formed by the Orange River at Augrabies, and secondly because it is the only trail in the country occurring in a true desert environment. Its greatest appeal lies in the bold contrast between this stark landscape and the splendour of the country's largest river.

The Khoi people (either Bushmen or Hottentots, who can be distinguished only by differing lifestyles rather than genetically) lived here for tens of thousands of years before white men arrived, and named the Orange River the *Garieb* or 'great river'. Early explorers noted how the region's indigenous people were fearful of the falls they called the 'place of great noise'. While they roamed the river's upper and lower reaches, they seldom cared to approach the Augrabies Falls close enough for even a peek.

The Augrabies Falls National Park extends across to the northern side of the river, where large game species such as eland and black rhino have been introduced, but this area is not yet open to the public. The geomorphological history of the river is interesting, in that its course has wandered up and down the west coast, at various times finding its way to the sea at the Olifants River mouth, Doringbaai, Hondeklipbaai, Groenrivier, Kleinsee, its present mouth at Alexander Bay, and even northwards at Elizabeth and Luderitz bays – in fact all the existing bays along the coast. Geologists believe that this is how the rich diamond deposits came to be spread so widely along the west coast of southern Africa.

DAY I *PARK REST CAMP TO FISH EAGLE HUT: 14 KM*

Unless you have already spent some time in the park, you should really begin your hike by exploring the area around the spectacular falls. There are many viewpoints, situated on precarious exfoliating granite shields, but take care. Since the park opened to tourists in 1966 at least 16 people have lost their lives to the terrifying 'water monkey' spirit of Khoi mythology by falling into the churning chasm 90 m below. From the main falls, the Orange River races and cascades down its 18 km-long gorge before emerging to wander aimlessly across the Bushmanland plains.

The two large pools at the base of the thunderous falls are thought to be at least 130 m deep and are believed to contain a great wealth in diamonds that have been washed over the falls, carried from diamondiferous deposits near Kimberley. But such is the force of the water falling into the pools that no-one has been able to verify either fact. During the terrible drought in 1934 the main falls dried up completely, but no-one thought then to scour the pools below for diamonds. Then, in 1974 and again in 1988, the river came down in such spate that it overflowed the huge gorge.

Once you've explored the falls, begin the trail at the far corner of the campsite.

The Augrabies Falls plunge 90 m into the gorge below, which encloses the river for 18 km before it emerges on the Bushmanland plains.

The path follows the painted klip-springer signs for 2 km, close to the gorge lip, making its way to the tip of Arrow Point, which is possibly the most impressive viewsite in the park. From here a wide backtrack is necessary to negotiate a side gorge and regain the main gorge at Mist Falls, 5 km further on. Rock pigeons roost on the cliff walls, while rock martins wheel about in the misty air, catching their insect prey and revelling in their aerobatic skills. The path along this stony and sandy section is often vague, but it is hard to get lost. A little further on the path swings around yet again to make a long backtrack, to reach the Potholes. Take some time to explore them, for they are more extensive than at first seems apparent.

Next the path traverses a 4 km section across possibly the rockiest part of the trail, with alternating sandy areas, to reach the dry river bed of Kukurasiep. Quarrelsome baboons and dainty klipspringers are fairly common in this area, with an occasional steenbok, and I flushed a startled, chubby scrub hare where I lost the path. Rather than big game, though, it is the reptiles of the area that are especially interesting. Most conspicuous here are the three species of colourful rock agamas, or *koggelmanders*, found in the reserve. Other lizards include geckos, skinks, sand lizards, flat and plated lizards and, most striking of all, the Karoo girdled lizard. Of the nineteen snake species living here, four can be said to be potentially dangerous (Cape and black-necked spitting cobra, coral snake and puffadder) and another two poisonous, although all I saw was a fleeing sand snake. The only tortoise found here is the small Kalahari tent tortoise *(Psammobates oculifer)*, with its geometrically patterned and knobbed yellow and brown carapace.

Another few barren kilometres lead to Ararat, a massive granite formation on the edge of the gorge, from where a fish eagle's nest can be spotted in a tree on the far bank. The path then continues between the river and Swart Rante hills to Oranjekom, a viewsite and picnic area. The dominant plants in this area are the hotnotsriem *(Ceraria namaquensis)* and the kersbos *(Sarcocaulon marlothii)*, the hollow branches of which were once used as candle moulds. From Oranjekom the trail follows a service track for a kilometre to the hut.

DAY 2 FISH EAGLE HUT TO BERG HUT: 13 KM

The second section begins by threading a way through a hilly area of the Swart Rante; the booklet tells hikers to look out for diamond diggings here, but since my eyes were mostly focussed on the ground at my feet I saw none. The path descends into a gully which leads to the river's southern bank, at a point where the Augrabies gorge peters out. The first section of river bank is rocky, after which it becomes sandy for 3,5 km. Hikers should be on the lookout here for animal spoor, especially that of baboon, Cape clawless otter, small antelope and large wading birds. An unexpected sight is that of the black storks that nest on the tiny ledges of the gorge's vertical sides. African fish eagles are commonly seen along this stretch of river. If you wish to bathe, keep to the shallows as the river currents are strong and treacherous.

Along the sandy bank, past Echo Corner and on to Witkruiskrans, the walking is easiest on the harder sand close to the river, but it is often obstructed by dense reed and bush. The slog on higher ground is unpleasant, but not as bad as trying to hack through the thickets. At Witkruiskrans the path takes a sharp left turn up the wide, dry river bed at Diepkloof. There are interesting rock formations in the lower kloof, and seepage areas are evidence of the underground stream. Black eagles nest in the cliffs near the junction, and from here hunt for dassies, the most abundant mammals in the park and their favourite prey.

For the next 6,5 km the trail keeps to the sandy river bed, which is like walking on soft beach sand. Shade is provided by river bushwillows, wild olive, sweet thorn, jacket plum and boer-bean trees. Where the river forks, the trail path takes the left-bearing valley for about 1,5 km to the hut, perched on the left-hand bank. Evening and morning light paints the surrounding hills in exquisite tones of gold, silver, copper and black.

OPPOSITE The Swart Rante and Bushmanland plains burnish in the sunset, while hikers prepare for dinner at the Berg hut. ABOVE The dainty antelope after which the trail is named. Its hooves are well-adapted for bounding over rocky terrain, being pointed downward and tipped with rubbery cushion pads.

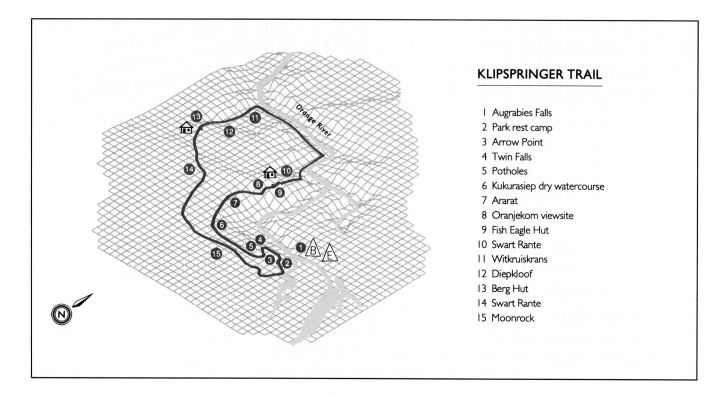

KLIPSPRINGER TRAIL

DAY 3 BERG HUT TO THE PARK REST CAMP: 12,3 KM

The last day's hike leads off down the 4x4 track, through a gate and past a ranger's hut to the right, before veering left to approach the main ridge of the Swart Rante, a prominence of weathered black dolerite that protrudes above its older and paler granite base. As the path winds up the ridge, past the jagged forms of quiver trees, or kokerbooms (*Aloe dichotoma*), you might disturb dassies sunning themselves on the rocks. Birds likely to be seen here are cisticolas in the low scrub, small, darting flocks of waxbills, as well as palewing starlings, dusky sunbirds and bokmakieries that issue their distinctive call from a conspicuous perch.

However strange as it seems today, rounded pebbles found along the crest of the Swart Rante suggest that it must have been part of a river bed at some time in the distant past. Descending the Swart Rante the path crosses a dry river course, where herds of springbok like to browse the sweet thorn (*Acacia karroo*) and buffalo thorn (*Ziziphus* sp.) shrubs.

A little further on the path passes close by two large quiver trees, in which sociable weavers have made their massive nests. These small, sparrow-like birds are the real estate developers of what Acocks* calls the Orange River Broken Veld region, their communal nests being the favoured homes of a host of other squatters such as rosyfaced lovebirds, goshawks and kestrels, as well as snakes who might have the added bonus of finding a ready meal there in the form of eggs or nestlings. (*See explanatory notes on Acocks in the Rustenburg Trail description on page 110.)

Here the trail joins a gravel road, taking the turn-off to the Moonrock, a granite batholith whose imposing parabolic sides have been created by exfoliation, or heat weathering. The effect, exclusive to granitic rock, is that the exposed surface seems to peel away like consecutive layers of an onion, leaving typically dome-like hills. Although you are most likely to reach here by late morning, the best time to visit the Moonrock is at dusk, just as the setting sun casts long shadows across the desert plain and colours this and other emergent features a deep crimson. From here the rest camp is a mere 3 km away, first along parallel rock pavements laced with Namaqua fig trees (*Ficus cordata*), then along a sandy wash plain, and finally along a gravel road into the rest camp area.

OPPOSITE From Fish Eagle hut the path descends a side gorge to reach the southern bank of the Orange River. For about 4 km the river bank is followed, first over great granite slabs, and later across deep, soft river sand where the walking becomes most taxing.

THE TRAIL AT A GLANCE

STARTING POINT : Augrabies Falls National Park rest camp, starting in the far (north-western) corner of the campsite

FINISHING POINT : Augrabies Falls National Park rest camp

LENGTH : 40 km

DURATION : Three days

GROUP LIMIT : 12 people

ROUTE : From the campsite, the trail follows close to the edge of the Orange River gorge, making a wide detour to bypass the deep cleft formed by the Arrow, to the Fish Eagle hut at the foot of the Swart Rante. The next day the path descends to the river, following the bank for several kilometres, before taking the dry bed up Diepkloof to the Berg hut. From here the path crosses the Swart Rante and passes the batholithic Moonrock before returning to the rest camp.

HOW TO GET THERE : Three roads lead to Augrabies, namely the R64 from Springbok, the R27 via Kenhardt, Keimoes and Kakamas, and the R64 from Upington. From the R64 at Alheit there is a turn-off to Augrabies,

20 km away (if you arrive after dark when the park gates are closed, consider staying at the Augrabies Falls Hotel, 5 km from the park).

BOOKING AUTHORITY : National Parks Board. Pretoria : P.O. Box 787, Pretoria, 0001; tel. (012) 343-1991.
Cape Town : P.O. Box 7400, Roggebaai, 8012; tel. (021) 47-1981.

ACCOMMODATION : Stone huts with bunks and mattresses, gas stove and pots, and chemical toilets.

CLIMATE : Being a true desert environment, receiving less than 200 mm of precipitation a year, the chances of being rained on here are very slim indeed. Winter days are usually warm to cool but can become chilly, while the nights are distinctly cold; summer is hot to very hot, with very little shade en route. Summer daytime temperatures range between 25 and 40 °C, and those in winter 10 to 25 °C.

BEST TIME TO HIKE : The trail is closed during the hottest months, from the beginning of November to the end of February. Since the trail is not strenuous, any time during the rest of the year is good.

REFERENCES : A National Parks trail booklet, with notes and a sketch map. There are also brochures on the park fauna.

TERRAIN : The area is mostly flat, stony and barren, with the exception of the river gorge. There are a few descents and ascents through side gullies, but they are never sustained. The vegetation is at best sparse, consisting mainly of short grass and small succulent plants, with bushy trees in the dry river beds. The most conspicuous plants are the quiver trees or kokerbooms.

WHAT TO TAKE : Suncream and a hat are essential all year round. Since much of trail is along 4x4 tracks or sandy river beds, light boots or running shoes should suffice.

SPECIAL PRECAUTIONS : There is no water to be found between huts, except on day two where the trail follows the river. Hikers should therefore carry enough water to cope in the desert climate: in winter at least one litre per person per day, and double this in summer. Report to the park office before setting out.

TRAIL OPTIONS : None, although one is free to go walkabout from the rest camp.

FURTHER READING

ACOCKS, J.P.H. (1975) 'Veld Types of South Africa.' *Memoirs of the Botanical Survey of South Africa*, No. 40, Botanical Research Institute and Dept. of Agricultural Technical Services, Pretoria.

BRISTOW, D. & WARD, C. (1985) *Mountains of Southern Africa.* Struik Publishers, Cape Town.

BRISTOW, D. (1987) *Drakensberg Walks.* Struik Publishers, Cape Town.

BRISTOW, D. (1990) *Western Cape Walks.* Struik Publishers, Cape Town.

BURMAN, L. & BEAN, A. (1985) *Wildflower Guide: Hottentots Holland to Hermanus.* Botanical Society of South Africa, Cape Town.

CAMERON, T. (ed.) (1986) *An Illustrated History of South Africa.* Southern Book Publishers, Johannesburg and Human & Rousseau, Cape Town.

IRWIN, P., ACKHURST, J. & IRWIN, D. (1980) *A Field Guide to the Natal Drakensberg.* Natal Branch of the Wildlife Society of Southern Africa, Durban.

LEDGER, J. (1990) *Southern Africa's Threatened Wildlife.* Endangered Wildlife Trust, Johannesburg.

LEVY, J. (1987) *The Complete Guide to Walks and Trails of Southern Africa.* Struik Publishers, Cape Town.

MACLEAN, G.L. (1985) *Roberts' Birds of Southern Africa.* The John Voelcker Bird Book Trust, Cape Town.

MEADOWS, M. (1985) *Biogeography and Ecosystems of South Africa.* SA Geography and Environmental Series, Juta, Cape Town.

MIGDOLL, I. (1987) *Field Guide to the Butterflies of Southern Africa.* Struik Publishers, Cape Town.

MOLL, E. & SCOTT, L. (1981) *Trees and Shrubs of the Cape Peninsula.* University of Cape Town, Eco-lab Trust Fund, Cape Town.

MORIARTY, A. (1982) *Wildflower Guide: Outeniqua, Tsitsikamma to the Eastern Little Karoo.* Botanical Society of South Africa, Cape Town.

OLIVIER, S. & OLIVIER, W. (1989) *The Guide to Backpacking and Wilderness Areas.* Southern Book Publishers, Johannesburg.

OLIVIER, S. & OLIVIER, W. (1991) *The Guide to Hiking Trails.* Southern Book Publishers, Johannesburg.

PALGRAVE, K.C. (1983) (2nd edition) *Trees of Southern Africa.* Struik Publishers, Cape Town.

PEARSE, R.O. (1973) *Barrier of Spears: Drama of the Drakensberg.* Howard Timmins, Cape Town.

SMITHERS, R.H.N. (1982) *The Mammals of the Southern African Subregion.* Mammal Research Institute, University of Pretoria, Pretoria.

VOGTS, M. (1982) *Proteaceae: know them and grow them.* Struik Publishers, Cape Town.

WAGNER, P. (1988) *The Otter Trail and the Tsitsikamma Coastal National Park.* Struik Publishers, Cape Town.

INDEX

Entries in **bold** type refer to photographs

Acocks, J.P.H. 110, 140
Aloe arborescens **125**, 127
  A. dichotoma 140
  A. peglerae **112**
Anvil **13**
Assegaaiboskloof **19**

Bakenkop 44
Bald ibis **118**, 119
Bannerman Buttress **89**
Bay
  Banana 63
  Catalina 76, 77
  Coffee 61, 64, 65
  Mpande 62
  Prelies 63
  Silaka 61, 65
  Strachan's 63
Beaufort Group rocks 47, 59
Bequaertiodendron magalismontanum 110, **111**, 119
Berghofkloof 44
Bitis gabonica 74

Black Hill 124, **126**
Bloukrans River gorge 31, **35**
Blue crane **107**
Blue swallow 124
Blyde River Canyon 8, **114/115**, 115, 117, 119, 121
Blyderivier sugarbush 119
Boegoekloof 18
Boekenhoutsknop 110
Boesmanskloof **16/17**, 18
Boscia albitrunca 70
Boskloof **22/23**, 24, 98, 112
Bourke's Luck **117**, 118, 120, 124, 128, 129
Brandwag **96/97**, 97
Brazen Head 62
Buffelskloof 24
Buffelspruit 100
Bushmanland plains 137, **140**
Bushman paintings 80, **81**, 83, 89
Bushman's Castle 18
Bushman's Nek 79, 82, 83, 86
Bushpig 133

Bushveld Igneous Complex 116
Buys se Pad 17

Camel 94
Camelpile 29
Carbineers' Grave 86
Castle Buttress 91, 92
Cathedral Peak Two Passes Hike 91-95
Cats Pad 20
Cave
  Bathplug 80
  Bushman 98
  Cathedral 98
  Guano 38
  Holkrans **100**
  Langalibalele 82
  Strandloper 41
  Sudwala 119
  Twins 92, **93**, 95
  Welbedacht 12, 14, 15
Cedarberg Wilderness Area 8, 11-15

Champagne Castle 92, **95**
Chessmen 91, 92
Chisel **13**
Chrysospalax trevelyani 50
Clanwilliam cedar 11, **13**, 15
Clearstream 116
Clivias 132, **133**
Cockade 92
Columbia Hill 124
Column 91
Cycads **93**
Cyclone Demoina 67

Dam
  Blydepoort **114/115**, 115, 119, 120, 121
  Doornhoek 46
  Langtoon 100
  Maden 49, 59
  Navarone 80
Dengezi 70
Desiree Mine 124
Devil's Window **121**